Defending the American Presidency

Also by Robert Busby

REAGAN AND THE IRAN–CONTRA AFFAIR: The Politics of Presidential Recovery

Defending the American Presidency

Clinton and the Lewinsky Scandal

Robert Busby
Lecturer in American Studies
Liverpool Hope University College

First published 2001 by
PALGRAVE
Houndmills, Basingstoke, Hampshire RG21 6XS and
175 Fifth Avenue, New York, N. Y. 10010
Companies and representatives throughout the world

PALGRAVE is the new global academic imprint of
St. Martin's Press LLC Scholarly and Reference Division and
Palgrave Publishers Ltd (formerly Macmillan Press Ltd).

ISBN 0–333–91250–0

This book is printed on paper suitable for recycling and made from fully managed and sustained forest sources.

A catalogue record for this book is available from the British Library.

Library of Congress Cataloging-in-Publication Data
Busby, Robert.
    Defending the American presidency : Clinton and the Lewinsky scandal / Robert Busby.
        p. cm.
    Includes bibliographical references and index.
    ISBN 0–333–91250–0
        1. Clinton, Bill, 1946—Impeachment. 2. Clinton, Bill, 1946—
    –Public opinion. 3. Clinton, Bill, 1946—Sexual behavior.
    4. Lewinsky, Monica S. (Monica Samille), 1973– 5. United States–
    –Politics and government—1993–2001. 6. Scandals—United
    States—History—20th century. 7. Public relations and politics–
    –United States—History—20th century. 8. Public opinion–
    –United States—History—20th century. 9. Crisis management in
    government—United States—History—20th century. 10. Mass
    media—Political aspects—United States—History—20th century.
    I. Title.

E886.2 .B87 2001
973.929′092—dc21

2001031546

10 9 8 7 6 5 4 3 2 1
10 09 08 07 06 05 04 03 02 01

Printed in Great Britain by Antony Rowe Ltd, Chippenham, Wiltshire

Contents

List of Tables and Exhibits

Tables

Exhibit

Acknowledgements

I'm most grateful to Louise Atkinson for her encouragement and understanding during the creation of this work and for tolerating my preoccupation with the Clinton scandals over many months. Thanks to my parents and sister for their support during the development of this work. Several friends and colleagues offered helpful and constructive advice in the creation of this text and their input proved invaluable, particularly Mike O'Grady, Kevin Felstead and Steve Perrin. I am particularly grateful to Palgrave and its editorial staff, in particular Alison Howson.

I'd also like to express my appreciation to Tim Grace, Dan Needs, Rob Martell, Steve Martell, Barry Jervis and all those who took an interest in the progress of the research into the Clinton scandals.

ROBERT BUSBY

To Louise

Introduction

The presidency of William Jefferson Clinton was blighted by accusation of scandal, personal indiscretion, and inappropriate private conduct. For all the President's public achievements, it appears likely that Clinton's presidential legacy will be forever tarnished by scandal. Whether Clinton deserves a place in infamy alongside Andrew Johnson and Richard Nixon as only the third President to face impeachment proceedings is debatable, each episode set against different contextual circumstances. Nevertheless, the mere fact that Clinton faced proceedings testifies to contemporaneous perceptions of high crimes and misdemeanors during his time in office. The fallout from scandal has left an indelible mark upon his personal legacy, and also influenced the wider development of the presidency as an institution. Clinton's experiences in dealing with the Monica Lewinsky scandal were, however, far from exceptional or unique. Several Presidents had previously faced muted allegations of sexual indiscretion or had been subjected to subtle insinuations about their private lives. Similarly, Presidents in the late twentieth century have faced allegation of political scandal, all, barring Richard Nixon, having survived the experience. That said, the Lewinsky affair, as much as it reflected past episodes, was very much a Clinton scandal. It involved sexual matters, contained intrigue and allegations of conspiracy, and, when concluded, left President Clinton's job approval figures virtually untouched. On the surface, at least, it appeared that Clinton had assumed the Teflon reputation of Ronald Reagan.

Bill Clinton won two presidential elections, in 1992 and 1996. He was the first Democrat to successfully compete in a re-election campaign since Franklin D. Roosevelt in 1944, and in 1992, campaigning on a pledge of reform he convincingly fended off a third party candidate.

Alongside the legacy of scandal and allegations of sleaze lay an array of policies and attempted social reforms which showed the Clinton presidency to be one of ambition and foresight. Economically, the United States prospered during the Clinton years, partly the product of luck and partly the product of tough decision-making aimed at balancing the budget and reducing the deficit. Ultimately, the economic fortunes of the country would inadvertently benefit Clinton during his elongated struggle with allegations of scandalous behavior. By no means all aspects of Clinton's public programs were successful. Health care, the flagship of the first term reforms, suffered an ignominious defeat under the stewardship of the First Lady, Hillary Clinton. Thought unsuitable and too far-reaching by both Democrats and Republicans in the Congress, it struggled onwards for almost two years, satisfied no core constituency, and eventually fragmented once the Republican party won the 1994 mid-term elections. In the areas of deficit reduction, civil rights, and gun control, Clinton advocated a multitude of policies which resonated with key Democratic constituencies, whilst also attracting disaffected Republicans and Independents to the 'New' Democrat message. As testament to his appeal, he won re-election in 1996 after heavy Democratic congressional losses in 1994, strongly reinforcing his reputation as the 'Comeback Kid'. Selling an image of a prosperous, positive, and buoyant America, ready to confront the new millennium, he repelled the challenge of Republican candidate Bob Dole with ease, capturing 379 electoral college votes to 159, and taking 31 states.[1] On the face of it, in conventional political life, Bill Clinton was a winner, at both state and national level.

Yet for all the gloss, the superficial images and the sound-bytes, there existed a darker side to the Clinton presidency which would ultimately undermine the reputation of the President, particularly in his second term. Political and personal scandal enveloped Clinton to a degree experienced by few other politicians of modern times. From his time as Governor of Arkansas, through the presidential campaign of 1992, to the pitfalls of the second term, Clinton was beset by allegation of sexual philandering. While not all of the allegations were proven to be true or could be substantiated, and hence were of marginal significance, several refused to go away or resurfaced at politically inconvenient times. Allegations of sexual harassment by Paula Jones and Kathleen Willey, and affairs with Gennifer Flowers and Monica Lewinsky, proved at best inconvenient and, at worst, impeachable. It also placed untold pressure upon Clinton and as yet undisclosed stress on his marriage and family life. The sexual revelations begged several questions of the occupant of the Oval Office, and impacted upon the presidential office. Was adultery by the President acceptable to the nation? To what extent could a President's private activities be examined by the Office of Independent Counsel? Was the Monica Lewinsky scandal about sexual matters or did it entail a purposeful deception by the President to conceal sexual activity? At the heart of the debate lies the question of how and why Clinton survived the Lewinsky episode. This text addresses this primary concern. In 1987, Democratic presidential contender Gary Hart's campaign was derailed by a discreet sexual liaison with a model. Yet in 1998, a President widely despised by the Republican right, facing a Republican Congress, and having openly admitted to having 'sinned', sustained high levels of public support. Was it possible that no one, aside from politically motivated Republicans and a dogged Independent Counsel, really cared? After all, what the President did, as long as it was consensual, was theoretically no one's business but his own. The Republican party, particularly within the House of Representatives, entertained an alternative interpretation. Clinton had, it contended, lied under oath, encouraged others to do so, and had purposefully obstructed justice. The President's detractors argued that this was not a sex scandal, but rather constituted a violation of law. Attention should not therefore be directed at moral concerns, but at legal issues and whether the President considered himself to be above the law. Conflicting interpretations about the actions and words of the President when attempting to prevent disclosure of his relationship with Lewinsky underpinned the Lewinsky scandal of 1998–9.

Clinton was not the first President to endure an investigation of his private and political conduct, nor was he the first to be besieged by scandal and assailed by members of an opposing political party. For several decades one President after another had succumbed to the allure of politics by unconventional means and, as a consequence, had fallen into disrepute and been pilloried by the media and political adversaries.[2] Lyndon Johnson had endured the long arduous Vietnam conflict, and seeking to make the war palatable for the American public, had been drawn into making statements that did not always correspond with reality. The 'credibility gap' was born. Thereafter, the plight of his successor, Richard Nixon, is well documented. Elected President for a second term by a landslide in 1972, he was to resign from the presidential office in disgrace less than two years later. Nixon's efforts to acquire political intelligence were motivated, in part, by personal aspirations and, more importantly, constituted an abuse of the powers granted him by the presidential office. Despite the trauma caused by Watergate, there existed hope that the political system had been cleansed, that Constitutional law had prevailed, and that the guilty officials had been subjected to appropriate punishment. Yet few were imprisoned, with Nixon being granted a presidential pardon by his successor Gerald Ford for all crimes committed during Watergate.

A congressional resurgence prompted by Watergate seemed to give the Legislative branch renewed vigor, and there appeared to be structural changes as constraints, particularly in the realm of foreign affairs, were imposed upon the Executive branch of government. Additionally, the role of the Independent Prosecutor was re-examined in an effort to enhance its ability to conduct a non-partisan and impartial investigation of alleged presidential wrongdoing. Indeed, the frequent re-evaluation of the function of the Independent Prosecutor, renamed the Independent Counsel, became a characteristic of presidential investigation following Watergate. Independent Counsel Kenneth Starr courted controversy throughout the Clinton years, and did little to bolster confidence in an oft-criticized position at the heart of the American political system.

President Reagan's problems with scandal were memorable and substantial. In keeping with the experiences of Nixon and Clinton, they occurred in the second term of his presidency, and followed a landslide victory. Unsurprisingly, an Independent Counsel, Lawrence Walsh, played a leading role in scandal investigations. The President faced lingering questions about the legality of arms deals with the Iranian government and the diversion of profits to the Nicaraguan Contra forces. This was exposed to the American public in 1986, and was entitled the Iran-Contra scandal. Reagan's direct involvement remains a matter of speculation. Moreover, Reagan's experience suggested that the Watergate episode might not be a unique event, that the problems created and endured by the presidency were perhaps deeper and more widespread. There were however many differences between Watergate and Iran-Contra. Reagan retained the affinity he had built up with the American people. As much as his competency was in doubt, and his lackluster management of the presidency openly criticized, he retained high approval ratings as a person throughout his second term. Lessons had been learned from Watergate, and Iran-Contra, for all its complexity, failed to oust Reagan from office or prove injurious in the longer term. As much as the investigative machinery involved in scandal politics had improved across time, and mechanisms were in place to conduct thorough probes of presidential activity, presidential defense against charges of wrongdoing had likewise improved and Reagan avoided the initiation of impeachment with some ease. This occurred as a result of the willingness of others to assume blame, alongside a lack of incriminating evidence. This, as much as anything, allowed Reagan to personally exculpate himself from charges of wrongdoing.

George Bush, who managed to avoid, to a great extent, charges of personal impropriety or involvement in scandal politics when President, received no substantive reward for this accomplishment. His re-election campaign in 1992 ended with a loss to a presidential candidate, Bill Clinton, who had been charged with conducting an extramarital affair, alongside several other indiscretions, including a claim that he had inhaled marijuana. Scandal politics failed to resonate as an election issue. The American people were ostensibly more interested in the state of the nation's economy and the attention paid to them by the President, there being an underlying feeling that George Bush was overly preoccupied with foreign affairs and less so with the domestic prosperity of the United States. Bush, a president who had avoided scandal, was voted out of office in favor of a presidential candidate who, even before he had embarked on the campaign trail, was embroiled in controversy. Clinton, Governor of Arkansas, an already experienced practitioner of scandal politics, was elected to the White House by an American public ready to give an opportunity to a 'New' Democrat.

When Clinton entered office, much had changed in Washington since the days of Richard Nixon. While an Independent Counsel could investigate presidential wrongdoing, and an inquisitive Congress might call witnesses in televised hearings, the modern prosecution of scandal politics had changed significantly. No longer were news anchormen the principal source of information. Rather, cable television with live feeds brought the developmental aspects of scandal politics into the home as they happened. Analysis had become a secondary feature of news reporting. This had occurred to some degree during Watergate. However, the instantaneous delivery of the message and primary news material made for a revolutionary portrayal of scandal politics in the 1990s. A key feature of the Clinton scandals, particularly in 1998 and 1999, was the use of the Internet to relay information and documents to the American people. Documents and source materials were often released firstly on this medium and thereafter in paper form. The immediate global dissemination of material generally harmful to the President's position put information into the public realm before the President's advisers had had sufficient time to review it and craft a coherent riposte. This resulted in a frantic effort, by both the President and his detractors, to advance lines of argument to court American public opinion. Cyber-culture had invaded the industry of scandal politics. For example, in August 1998, following a dramatic Clinton speech, the website for Cable News Network (CNN) attracted 20.4 million visitors on a single day. This number was almost a third more than the previous record number of visits, although it should be noted that the visitors were not necessarily American.[3]

The Lewinsky scandal witnessed further innovations in the presentation of scandal politics. Clinton was filmed testifying to a Grand Jury, and the recording was later released into the public domain, giving a dramatic portrayal of the severity of his predicament and the nature of his defense in attempting to counter allegations of perjury. The fact that the material was recorded gives the scholar and the public alike a frank and stark portrayal of a President entwined in a quagmire of scandal politics. The visual image and the Internet, in partnership with traditional print outlets, had a distinctive role to play in shaping the Lewinsky scandal, and cast the President's predicament in several forms, from the comic, to that of a Constitutional crisis. The American people had more information at their disposal than ever about the alleged wrongdoings of the Chief Executive. Moreover, it was accessible at the touch of a computer button, as well as on television and in the newspapers. Yet, the increased availability of information did not appear, at first sight, to enhance popular understanding of the political process or of the severity of the scandal faced by Clinton. The President's dramatic 17 August 1998 speech aside, popular interest generally remained low, as did viewing figures for Clinton's impeachment hearings, a marked contrast to the congressional hearings which investigated Watergate in 1973–4.

At an elite level the Lewinsky scandal impacted upon the presidency as an institution, as well as on Clinton as an individual. Given that impeachment proceedings are such a rare occurrence, and Clinton was impeached by the House and faced a trial in the Senate, there is much to be drawn from the Clinton experience in understanding why he was subject to such exceptional prosecution. Occupants of the presidential office are of course unique. The characteristics they possess, the men and women they appoint, the problems they face at home and abroad; all tend to be different and bring out individual strengths and weaknesses. Clinton was no different. His vision of an inclusive America stimulated social change and promised a more equitable society. However, his constant struggle with scandal ensured that his character and personal attributes are linked with that subject as much as any other. It was notable that during the Lewinsky episode the scandal was portrayed primarily as an outcome of Clinton's personal excesses and misdemeanors, rather than one founded, like Watergate, upon a crime of institutional abuse. A charge of that nature surfaced briefly in a failed effort to get an article of impeachment to reflect a charge of abuse of power by Clinton. The President's legal team and partisan supporters dismissed it quite readily. During the congressional impeachment process several pertinent questions asked whether the President was above the law, and what precedent would be set if Clinton's alleged wrongdoings were left unpunished, or alternatively, if he were removed from office by the Senate. Alongside these questions lay others about an ill-defined area between the President's private life and his public duties and responsibilities. When did private behavior become a public concern, and more significantly, an impeachable issue? Or was the Lewinsky matter a weighty legal quandary about whether the President had acted in an unlawful way and had violated the 'high crimes and misdemeanors' statute of the Constitution? The various partisan coalitions in the American government, and particularly in the Congress, assumed several different standpoints on the key issues, positions central to an interpretation of the presidency as an institution, and as an equal partner in the American government.

The Lewinsky scandal entailed more than politics and the venerable clauses of the Constitution. It broadened interest in the presidential office because it dealt with salacious aspects of the President's private conduct. This scandal was a soap opera with identifiable characters and, at times, an absurd plot. From the infamous stained blue dress held by Monica Lewinsky, to the outpouring of humor on Clinton's predicament, certain aspects of the scandal contributed to a vast array of material tangentially related to politics. Whether an individual wished to study the historical and legal details of impeachment, or desired Clinton jokes on the Internet, the Lewinsky scandal delivered the goods. Bumper stickers proclaimed 'Jail to the Chief' and 'It Takes a Village Idiot to Believe Clinton'.[4] But the aggregate effect of the detrimental comments also, as many of the President's detractors claimed, appeared to demean the presidential office. The President, according to those prosecuting Clinton, was another politician who lacked credibility and, in this case, a total absence of moral leadership. A majority of the public appeared to agree, but did not believe the President should be impeached. Indeed, a key feature of this Clinton scandal was a cleavage between elite and popular opinion about Clinton's actions and the meting out of an appropriate punishment. A relationship with a young intern might be inadvisable, but a consistent and sizeable majority in the polls in 1998–9, did not deem to it be an impeachable offence. This, however, obscured the main charges advanced by Independent Counsel Starr, which hinged not upon moral transgression, but rather upon the more serious problems of lying under oath and obstruction of justice. Those prosecuting Clinton struggled to get the legal charges to outweigh comment and discussion about sexual matters, and this only served to complicate the debate, reduce the clarity of the charges, and facilitate Clinton's retention of the presidential office.

This text considers the Clinton administration's damage limitation strategies enacted during the Lewinsky scandal of 1998–9. It deals with the subject in a thematic manner, addressing several factors which contributed to Clinton's ability to accommodate charges of wrongdoing. It reviews Clinton's encounters with scandal in the prelude to the Lewinsky scandal and considers his experience of the Lewinsky scandal. His personal leadership and attempts to contain the political and legal damage resulting from the Lewinsky revelations are then examined. Thereafter, the efforts of his administration and the reaction of members of the Congress in the prelude to the impeachment proceedings are discussed. Underpinning the analysis is an identification and evaluation of the tactics adopted by Clinton to suppress speculation about Lewinsky and minimize the impact of scandal upon his presidency. The impact of the *Starr Report* is then reviewed. It served to shape elite interpretation of the scandal. Moreover, it encouraged members of the Congress to initiate impeachment hearings and debate the future of the Clinton presidency. Once again the Clinton White House was forced to implement damage limitation strategies to counter a potentially fatal political threat. Finally, two aspects of the scandal which affected Clinton's fortunes are examined. The media held a pivotal role in portraying the drama to the American people. While Clinton could only have a limited influence upon media interpretation of the scandal, internal debate and division within its ranks served to bolster his chances of survival and inadvertently contributed to his damage limitation offensive. Accordingly, the role of the media in this scandal is of note. Public opinion, the target of media presentation, constitutes the final theme of this text. It appeared unconvinced that Clinton, for all his misleading words and controversial actions, deserved removal from office, and clashed markedly with elite opinion. This text explains why the public failed to endorse Clinton's impeachment and remained unpersuaded by media demands for presidential resignation. It evaluates why Clinton's damage limitation strategies, while moderately successful at the elite level, worked more effectively in the nation at large.

Chapter 1 addresses the Clinton scandal epidemic, considering a host of allegations leveled at the President during his time in office. Of all the problems faced by Clinton, the Lewinsky case was, of course, by far the most serious, leading to the impeachment proceedings of 1998–9. However, it developed as a result of other allegations of wrongdoing by Clinton. Several episodes originated in Arkansas. They concerned both public and private duties, but in the main blew over within a short period of time. More serious however were allegations about activity undertaken by Hillary Clinton in Arkansas before the President had assumed office. Land deals involving the Whitewater Development Corporation led to financial irregularities and pointed questions about the legal standing of the Clintons' investments. An Independent Counsel was appointed to investigate the Clintons' activity. To complicate matters, in 1993, a close Clinton aide involved in Whitewater matters was found dead in a park in Washington. This stimulated conspiracy theories and fueled speculation about a cover-up of Whitewater dealings. Chapter 1 considers the Clinton experience with scandal in the prelude to the Lewinsky crisis, and pinpoints the damage limitation strategies employed to deal with charges of wrongdoing.

Following hard on the heels of Whitewater came several allegations of sexual malpractice by the President. The most prominent and visible of these involved a charge of sexual harassment by Paula Jones, a case which served as a prelude to the Lewinsky matter and precipitated that event. Clinton, fending off charges of harassment, took his case all the way to the Supreme Court. It ruled that he had to contest the suit while in office. This led ultimately to a request that Monica Lewinsky, a former White House intern, submit material to Jones's lawyers about her sexual contacts with the President. Chapter 2 accordingly examines the President's conduct during the Jones case and identifies how and why it gave rise to the President's involvement in the Lewinsky crisis.

With a central focus on the Lewinsky scandal, Chapter 3 examines the damage limitation efforts initiated by the Clinton administration in its efforts to minimize focus on scandal and protect the President politically and legally. This chapter considers three key aspects of damage limitation: firstly, the role of the President in conducting a response to the allegations of an illicit affair; secondly, the more expansive response of the administration in presenting a united front and endorsing the message advanced by Clinton; and, thirdly, the sparring between the Congress and the White House as evidence accumulated to suggest that Clinton's version of events might prove unsustainable. The chapter considers the period from the public exposure of the scandal in January 1998 through to the prelude to the impeachment hearings in October 1998. Clinton had a central role to play in orchestrating a response to charges of lying under oath about his involvement with Lewinsky, and encouraging others to do likewise. His personal statements, public appearances, and combative approach to the media and the investigation of Kenneth Starr testified to a resolute but ultimately misplaced effort to counter the claims of opponents that he had conducted an affair and had lied about it. Chapter 3 considers Clinton's role and strategy in the emergent damage control measures during this critical period. The response of Clinton's aides and advisers proved to be important as the scandal unfolded. Coordinating a balanced response between the legal and political demands imposed upon the administration was no easy task, and the stress of commonplace politics, when placed alongside the Starr investigation, put undue pressure on aides to uphold the President's tenuous claims and appear united at a troubled time. The First Lady and key legal advisers played particularly prominent roles as the scandal developed, and suffered visibly when Clinton altered his versions of events in August 1998. Clinton's ability to marshal his aides to his cause, even when it was clear they had been misled, proved pivotal and necessary in the midst of the crisis. This chapter therefore evaluates how Clinton's aides defended the administration and the President and how damage limitation was advanced across a broad front to defend the President. Chapter 3 lastly considers the relationship between the White House and the Congress. A trickle of criticism grew into a flood as members of Congress, of both parties, became aware of the President's verbal doublespeak and of his misleading comments about Lewinsky. It was important that the White House address congressional opinion, for it would decide the President's fate following the submission of Starr's report recommending the impeachment of the President. Complicating the matter, at the outset, was the fact that Republicans held both chambers of the Congress. Clinton's battle was additionally taxing as a result. Chapter 3 considers the attempt by the White House to placate congressional opinion and offset the likelihood of impeachment.

Chapter 4 addresses the Starr inquiry and, in particular, the White House response to the investigation and the report which recommended impeachment. Starr and the President had an adversarial relationship throughout Starr's tenure as Independent Counsel. The White House took exception to many of Starr's investigative techniques during the Lewinsky scandal, and similarly, Starr accused the White House of stonewalling and of preventing an efficient probe of presidential activity. Starr's report to the Congress accomplished its goal as impeachment articles were drawn up against the President. However, he faced significant challenges in selling his message to the American people, and suffered as the sexual detail contained within the report appeared to stimulate more interest than the detail of legal transgression. The White House exacerbated this perception and to some extent succeeded in portraying this as a sex scandal as opposed to one founded upon perjury and obstruction of justice. Chapter 4 evaluates the White House strategy which promoted an alternative interpretation of the *Starr Report* and the Independent Counsel investigation.

Chapter 5 examines the approach of the Congress to the Lewinsky affair, and its subsequent conduct of the impeachment proceedings. From the House Judiciary Committee through to the Senate trial, the Congress was pivotal in determining the fate of Bill Clinton. The initial decision to advance impeachment resolutions came about as a consequence of a referral from Independent Counsel Kenneth Starr, in September 1998. Republicans, both at committee level and in the House as a whole, embraced many of Starr's charges and initiated a partisan struggle to get the resolutions through the chamber and onwards to a Senate trial. In the Senate too, the overriding atmosphere was one of partisanship and of two political parties arguing over legal technicalities and vastly different interpretations of the President's actions. The President played a minor role in the proceedings, commenting upon their development only sporadically, while discreetly attempting to solidify a Democratic base of support and safeguard his own future. Clinton's legal aides conducted his defense on the floor of the House and Senate. This chapter reviews Clinton's strategy at this critical time, and identifies how traditional partisan division, not of the President's own making, played a significant role in salvaging his presidency.

The role of the media and its interaction with the White House is the focus of Chapter 6. Although the President rarely talked voluntarily about the Lewinsky matter once it had become public knowledge, the few statements he made to media sources as it broke shaped perceptions of his innocence. They would later allow comparative analysis of the President's changed interpretation of his role in this scandal. Initial acceptance of media reporting of this story was later replaced by a more hesitant strategy, one which saw the President use selective occasions to advance a defensive message. Internal debate within the media was a significant factor in shaping the portrayal and evolution of the scandal. There also existed the problem of maintaining a focus on legal issues, and avoiding overly lurid concentration on the sexual elements of the matter, a difficult task given their frequent centrality to the case mounted by the prosecution. Clinton faced significant opposition from media sources and endured repeated calls for his resignation from media outlets of repute. Moreover, he had to confront the new technology of the Internet, and encompass its impact upon the presentation of scandal politics. However, to Clinton's benefit, its presence proved as much a distraction for the traditional media as it did for the White House.

The final theme addressed by this text is public opinion. The American people had twice elected Clinton to the White House, and had tolerated the countless allegations of scandal leveled against him. His job approval ratings in the second term had, moreover, been consistently high and stable. The onset of the Lewinsky scandal threatened to undermine the President's position and cause the onset of a credibility gap. Clinton, however, did not suffer unduly as a result of the information released during the Lewinsky scandal. Indeed, his job approval ratings rose as details of the President's actions were released into the public domain. Chapter 7 evaluates why potentially damaging information about the President failed to have a negative political impact, and why impeachment failed to capture the attention of the nation. Elite opinion and popular opinion were at odds during this scandal, and while public opinion had only an indirect role to play in its development, it placed pressure upon those in Washington to act in accordance with the messages advanced by opinion polls. Clinton played heavily to public sentiment during the scandal. He stressed the need to consider non-scandal issues and to press on with a legislative agenda. His message appeared to have greater resonance than the scandal agenda offered by Starr and the Republican members of the Congress.

In the true tradition of scandal politics there has been an abundance of government documents released into the public realm at an early stage. Not only have these been printed by the United States Government Printing Office, but also, in many instances, they have been released onto the Internet and published by the Congress in an electronic format. Likewise, given the prominence of the Lewinsky story, many media outlets, the heavyweight *New York Times* and *Washington Post* among them, devoted space in electronic format to the scandal and its socio-political impact. Transcripts of political pro-ceedings form a great part of the primary sources available for the Lewinsky scandal. The impeachment hearings are an obvious source of primary documentation about the scandal and how it affected the pres-idency, and they provide a reservoir of information from politicians, academics, and lawyers about interpretations of Clinton's deeds and how they impacted upon the institutions of government. Transcripts emanated from the House, the committees involved in the impeach-ment process, and the Senate trial. The investigation by Kenneth Starr and the Office of Independent Counsel (OIC) advanced, in a stark form, the case against Clinton. The *Starr Report*, in particular, high-lighted the reasons for the initiation of impeachment proceedings, and became a key document during the fall of 1998, bluntly laying out the alleged crimes committed by Clinton. Also accessible in transcript form are the testimonies of many of the participants in the Lewinsky matter, from Monica Lewinsky to the testimony given by the President before a Grand Jury in August 1998. There are even the surreptitious record-ings made by Linda Tripp of conversations between her and Monica Lewinsky, recordings containing revealing material about the covert relationship between Lewinsky and Clinton. For all the discussions during the scandal about a right to privacy, it did not take long for publishers and websites to reproduce the private conversations of Lewinsky. Scandal politics appears to respect few boundaries and, in this instance, the fact that the conversations represented incriminating evidence in the case against Clinton made it all the easier to justify their publication. Beyond the legal documentation and transcripts are, of course, the numerous comments and statements made by govern-ment officials, President Clinton among them. There have been few issues in modern American politics that have received such heavy polling, and public opinion is appropriately chronicled in a host of sources. The Lewinsky scandal lends itself, as with no other issue during the Clinton presidency, to evaluation and review, and the documentation available, as well as the wider attention the issue amassed, makes this both a defining moment in, and the most accessible topic of, the Clinton era.

The fact that Clinton faced impeachment proceedings makes the Lewinsky scandal important to the history of the American presidency. Whether it was, as Senator Tom Harkin (D-Iowa) believed, 'a sanc-tioned witchhunt into the president's personal life', or an episode, as House Majority Leader Dick Armey (R-Tx) contended, that 'has brought shame to the presidency', lies at the core of an interpretation of this political scandal.[5] Whatever the explanations for the Clinton debacle, it is clear that scandal retains a prominent position at the fore-front of the debate on the fortunes of the modern presidency. Clinton's damage limitation techniques failed to prevent impeachment and were problematic in many respects, particularly as he made several statements which he claimed were truthful, but turned out to be mis-leading. This only served, on numerous occasions, to exacerbate his political concerns. The Constitution of the United States confers upon the Congress the power to remove a President for treason, bribery, and high crimes and misdemeanors. The failure to convict Clinton in the Senate, after he had been successfully impeached by the House, leaves the door open for lasting debate into how he altered the face of the presidency, and whether his two terms in office and pervasive involve-ment in scandal changed the institution for the better or for the worse.

1
The Clinton Scandal Epidemic

The Lewinsky scandal, exposed to the American public in January 1998, was by no means the first scandal to be faced by President Clinton or his administration. Time and again, when a Governor and when President of the United States, Clinton had faced investigation into his public and private behavior. Many scandal allegations centered on a narrow framework of issues: a number of questionable investments in a land development corporation and, thereafter, a plethora of sexual allegations from a variety of women across several years. Clinton's experience of having to face accusations of wrongdoing, and of waging politics by other means, both reflected and enhanced the prominence of the scandal industry in modern American politics. A combination of institutional factors, partisanship, media interest and the desire of some individuals to gain publicity helped to promote scandal as a mainstay of American political life. During the 1990s, the President had no choice but to deal with an onslaught of allegations about his activity, and spin control was, as such, a necessary and familiar part of the presidential public relations machine.

There was more to Clinton's experience of scandal than commonplace accusations of presidential wrongdoing. This President, like no other, faced a constant barrage of questions about his past, his personal life, his relationships and his private dealings. Some, such as Richard Nixon, had faced inquiries about personal financial matters, and others, like Kennedy, had endured whispered suggestions about illicit affairs. However, no President had openly faced hostile and publicized allegations of wrongdoing to such a marked degree about activity that was not a central part of their political mandate. Clinton's personal and private affairs seemed to dominate the political forum as much as his political activity and his legislative program. The Lewinsky affair, for instance, overshadowed the President's 1998 State of the Union address and drew public attention away from conventional politics and towards salacious gossip.[1] Scandal, or the mere suggestions of it, therefore sidetracked the focus of the public policy debate. As much as scandal themes contributed markedly to Clinton's problems in 1998 and induced a trench warfare mentality in the White House, the President's private conduct, for which he was forced to openly apologize, fueled and stimulated investigation and reporting of his activity. In this sense, as much as the scandal machinery was already in place in an institutional form, Clinton, in no small way, created an environment conducive for scandal, one where he was considered a legitimate target for the media, Independent Counsel investigation, and partisan opponents alike.

This chapter considers several allegations of scandal directed at Clinton, and addresses the centrality of scandal to this particular President and the institution of the presidency. Clinton's contact with the scandal industry was frequent and pervasive. Although there were few occasions during his first or second term when he was not under investigation for activity undertaken as Governor of Arkansas or President of the United States, there was more to the Clinton experience than accusation of individual excess. More irritating to the President perhaps was that his wife, Hillary Clinton, was frequently under legal investigation for business dealings whilst in Arkansas. A public relations war was initiated to defend presidential credibility, one complicated both by political opposition and legal investigation, based in both Washington and Little Rock Arkansas, and with no determinable end, a common feature of scandal politics.

It appeared to those besieged in the White House that as one scandal accusation was contained, another would materialize. The list of prominent Clinton scandals seemed endless: Whitewater, Filegate, Troopergate and Zippergate among them. This, at face value, did little more than create a conspiratorial atmosphere, one identified by the First Lady once the Lewinsky scandal broke. Hillary Clinton, dismayed by the constant focus on the personal life of the President and the ongoing Independent Counsel investigations, alleged that 'a vast right-wing conspiracy' was persecuting her husband.[2] A permanent focus on scandal politics, combined with a need to conduct and finance a defense, made for an arduous damage limitation strategy, one not helped by a Supreme Court decision exposing the President to law suits while he was still in office. This changed the institutional balance significantly against the presidential office at a most crucial moment.

Clinton found it difficult to escape scandal, whether it originated in Washington or elsewhere, and found his past activity in Arkansas to be a constant irritant. A sexual harassment case filed against him by Paula Jones, coming into conflict with a discreet affair with Monica Lewinsky, proved to be unduly problematic for his presidency.

Theoretical underpinnings

Scandal has played an important role in the history of the American presidency and, in no small way, has defined, mythologized, or tarnished many presidential legacies. Clinton followed a long line of Presidents who confronted scandal while in the Oval Office. Several of those who experienced scandal politics endured allegations of wrongdoing yet avoided elongated debates about presidential malfeasance. In the early 1960s Eisenhower and Kennedy, on vastly different issues, seemed to brush off potentially scandalous events with ease. Others, however, such as President Nixon, faced impeachment proceedings in the Congress, invoked to curtail perceptions of an imperial presidency and redress institutional imbalance. Whilst the experiences of Nixon are the most instructive in understanding Clinton's impeachment problems in the Congress, the fact that other Presidents engaged in discreet and adulterous sexual liaisons, while making the Clinton activity no more excusable begs the question as to why Clinton was pursued with such vigor by the Independent Counsel and the Republican-controlled Congress, and why the Lewinsky scandal entertained such media prominence.

Several key themes and questions have periodically come to the fore when scandal has afflicted the modern presidency. They include:

- What did a President do?
- How did the President deal with allegations of wrongdoing?
- Did the matter in question involve public or private activity?
- How was scandal exposed to the public?
- Did the President break any laws?
- What action was taken, legally and politically, in seeking to rectify perceived wrongdoing?

There is no rigid format for the evolution and resolution of presidential scandals, this being one of the reasons why so many Presidents have had such great difficulty in dealing with them. Nevertheless, the questions listed above are broadly pertinent to scandals of an institutional nature or, as faced by Clinton, those emanating from essentially private conduct.

Existing theory on scandals differentiates between contrasting phases of scandal politics.[3] Often it is not a questionable action which causes problems and induces scandal politics, but rather the means employed to deal with its effects. For example, Nixon suffered during Watergate as a consequence of his efforts to cover up his involvement in the aftermath of the burglary. The initial action did not have critical significance, and would hardly have resulted in a Constitutional crisis if openly confronted by the President when he appreciated the true nature of the intelligence gathering operations. Hindsight is however beneficial in this instance, and fails to compensate for the paranoid political climate of the time and the pressures facing the Nixon White House. Clinton too, it should be noted, suffered from similarly mis-placed decisions. His impeachment problems came not because he had an affair with a 21 year-old intern in the White House, but rather he was attacked on a legal front because many, particularly the Office of Independent Counsel (OIC) and members of the Republican party, believed that he had lied under oath and obstructed justice in trying to deny that an affair had ever taken place. The initial action in a scandal scenario is termed the substantive action, normally a precipitous event which encourages participants to adopt unorthodox measures to limit the political damage which might be inflicted upon them. The second stage of the scandal process is termed the procedural stage. This has often proved to be the decisive and damaging stage, where cover-ups and spin control are employed to gloss over a presidential blunder or potentially illegal action. Clinton's affair with Monica Lewinsky might have caused him only moderate political damage if it had been uncov-ered as a singular episode of adultery while Clinton was resident in the White House. After all, as a consequence of the Gennifer Flowers affair, exposed when Clinton was a candidate for the presidency in 1992, the American public was already well-versed about his marital problems. There were no legal penalties for marital infidelity, but there were pit-falls for the President if he denied, under oath, that he had had an affair with a White House intern. Scandal theory, whether it is applied to institutional scandals or sexual scandals, employs the substantive and procedural stages as a framework, with an erroneous or question-able presidential action, followed thereafter by activity to conceal or deal with the initial violation of law or contemporaneous moral values. How this has manifested itself with regard to the modern presidency is summarized in Table 1.1.

Table 1.1 Modern presidential scandal: a summary

Presidential scandal	Substantive scandal elements	Procedural aspects
Nixon: Watergate	• Watergate burglary. • Acquisition of political intelligence	• Cover-up • Bribery • Abuse of power
Reagan: Iran-Contra	• Arms sales to Iran • Diversion of profits to Contra guerilla forces	• Cover-up • Plausible deniability • Scapegoating of aides
Clinton: Lewinsky	• Affair with Monica Lewinsky • Sexual harassment allegations	• Cover-up • Allegedly lying under oath • Misleading disclaimers • Alleged obstruction of justice • Alleged subornation of perjury

Modern scandals and modern Presidents

There is a crucial distinction to be made between several of the major scandals of modern times, such as Watergate and Iran-Contra, and the Lewinsky scandal. Both Watergate and Iran-Contra involved the *institutional* abuse of power by the Executive branch of government, and demonstrated that Presidents had a capacity to use and abuse powers at the disposal of the Chief Executive. The Lewinsky scandal, by contrast, involved misleading comments by the President and did not entail the inappropriate employment of units of the Executive branch in its substantive or procedural periods.

Watergate witnessed the abuse of presidential power to institute a cover-up, endorse bribery and acquire political intelligence by unorthodox means. It resulted in a battle between the branches of the federal government, a battle, in essence, for information about what the President did, and what he ordered others to do in an attempt to cover up questionable political activity. Richard Nixon was at the heart of the scandalous activity, denying access to recorded tapes which clearly showed that he had illegally sought to bribe defendants and buy their silence. He invoked executive privilege, temporarily depriving the Legislative branch access to the private material which in Nixon's opinion was owned, and should be retained, by the Chief Executive.

This proved to be little more than an effort to deny incriminating material to a Special Prosecutor, appointed to investigate possible illegality by the President. Thereafter, once the tapes had become public, and congressional impeachment proceedings were under way, the President had few choices available to him. During Watergate the President abused the power of his office. This spurred bipartisan action against Nixon in the House Judiciary Committee. His actions violated the public trust and he failed to ensure, as demanded of him by the Constitution, that the laws were faithfully executed. As stated by the House Judiciary Committee in solemn tones: 'In all of this, Richard M. Nixon has acted in a manner contrary to his trust as President and subversive of constitutional government, to the great prejudice of the cause of law and justice and to the manifest injury of the people of the United States.'[4] By August 1974, Nixon, having betrayed the trust of the American people, had little option but to resign.

The Iran-Contra scandal of 1986–7 also involved the use of presidential power and covert Executive activity, most of which was purposefully shielded from the eyes of the Congress. This too was an institutional scandal. The National Security Council, Central Intelligence Agency and a variety of private sources were employed to circumvent conventional policy process, sell arms to Iran, and fund the Contra guerilla movement in Central America. This violated several laws, such as the Boland Amendments, and created short-term resentment in the Congress. If some laws were vague and difficult to interpret, there at least existed the feeling that their intention, and a spirit of cooperation and partnership between the branches of government, had been undermined. The central focus of investigation, when the matter became public, was whether President Reagan knew of the covert activity originating in the Executive branch. Investigations during Watergate had focused on the question of 'What did the President know and when did he know it?' Iran-Contra, by contrast, focused on a more simple issue, 'What did the President know?' Reagan's detached management style and a purposeful decision on the part of several of his aides, such as National Security Adviser John Poindexter, to shield him from the detail of policy implementation made it plausible to contend that Reagan was an innocent player in the whole process. The scandal was portrayed by the White House as not so much a purposeful deception on the part of the President, but rather a betrayal of his trust, and product of lax presidential oversight. Nevertheless, this episode was a prominent reminder of the gravity of scandal politics, pitting the public relations mechanisms at the disposal of the Executive branch against the investigative power of the Congress. It resurrected questions of an 'imperial presidency', one which had haunted the Nixon administration and encapsulated its appetite for additional political power.

There were significant differences between Iran-Contra and Watergate. In Watergate there was a 'smoking gun', hard evidence which proved direct presidential involvement in the bribery of the burglary suspects, among other things. This set the scene for the ensuing battle for the incriminating tapes, and left few in any doubt that the President had lied about his involvement in the matter and had played an instrumental role in this episode. In Iran-Contra, by contrast, there existed a lack of hard evidence to support accusations that Reagan had masterminded the covert operations. There were also scapegoats, like Oliver North and Poindexter, who were initially willing to assume liability for the operations, and thereby shielded the President, at least in the short term, from singular blame. The Iran-Contra episode had also drawn lessons from the Watergate experience. Scandal politics was not a new phenomenon, and many of Nixon's aides such as Pat Buchanan and George Shultz, experienced observers of scandal, were able to advise Reagan on how to extricate himself from Iran-Contra. Clinton too would later accommodate the lessons of scandals of the 1970s and 1980s, and calculate the most profitable strategy to avoid a Nixonian fate.

The role and impact of public opinion was a further difference between Reagan and Nixon in the field of scandal. Nixon's levels of support plummeted in 1973–4 when incriminating evidence and televised congressional hearings undermined his credibility. This declining support caused a political loss of confidence in Washington, congressional members wanting little association with a man widely thought to be a lame-duck and a liability. Consider the contrast with Reagan. He retained high levels of personal approval during Iran-Contra and suffered only in the realm of his job approval. He may have been perceived as incompetent, but he was not viewed as crooked. This aided in his fight with the Congress, members of that institution being somewhat reluctant to attack a personally admired politician for fear of public disapproval.

The lessons derived from the Nixon and Reagan experiences were instrumental to the Clinton administration in its battle to fend off impeachment in 1998–9. But, as mentioned previously, there were significant differences between the Lewinsky scandal and Iran-Contra and Watergate. They were institutional scandals, rooted in the abuse of presidential power. Clinton's scandal experience developed through his personal activity, with little evidence of abuse of office and scant evidence that he manipulated the instruments of government to conduct his illicit affairs. Clinton acted for his own personal benefit and enjoyment, not to enhance the powers of the Executive branch of government, or to violate the rights and privileges of the other branches. His initial problems were less institutional and more personal. The difficulty for Clinton was that his private and consensual actions mutated and evolved into a public issue following the OIC investigation, and the Congress thereafter became involved. The President had to defend himself against charges of a cover-up and lying under oath. This episode provides an example where the substantive scandal issues were rooted in private individual action, whereas the procedural phase was very much a public concern. Moreover, the Clinton experience with Lewinsky accommodates existing theoretical models of scandal, with the procedural phase causing more political damage for the President than the substantive phase.

There has been an abundance of sexual scandals involving previous Presidents of the United States which are instructive in understanding Clinton's predicament. A decisive factor is that most have been exposed, or at the least debated, after the fact. Clinton stands alone in having his extraneous marital affairs discussed while he was still a sitting President, and having them investigated by the OIC and the Congress. Fourteen Presidents have been confronted with allegations of improper personal relationships. Chester Arthur, when confronted with rumor about his private life commented, 'Why, this is worse than assassination!'[5] Key leaders and icons of the twentieth century have been involved in such activity, it not being reserved for leaders from bygone eras of differing moral standards. Franklin D. Roosevelt, President from 1933 to 1945, had an affair with his wife's social secretary, Lucy Page Mercer.[6] This lasted for some time, yet never made public headlines or caused a moral outcry to the detriment of FDR's political career. In particular, John F. Kennedy, President from 1960 to 1963, gained a reputation for infidelity. Speculation abounds about a string of actresses and prominent public women, Marilyn Monroe and Jayne Mansfield among them, with whom Kennedy may have had affairs. And yet, for all the glamour and the publicity an affair between a President and movie icon would generate, open discussion about Kennedy's private life never really occurred until some time after his death. The President's private life remained beyond the bounds of journalistic or political investigation in the pre-Watergate period. As James W. Davis, author of *The American Presidency*, has asserted: 'The press in those days honored the privacy of the White House. It was a different era.'[7] Watergate was, as much as it was an institutional scandal, a threshold whereby Presidents were thereafter fair game for investigation, a fact not lost on those wishing to emulate the investigative exploits of journalists Woodward and Bernstein during that particular scandal.

Clinton's experience broadly reflected that of his predecessors. If the substantive action, in this case sexual activity undertaken by the President, had not changed much across time, Clinton could readily be perceived as a victim of the passing of time, a victim of the institutions of scandal politics which were now in place to exploit his lack of self-discipline. But other factors must also be accommodated. Morality changes according to the prevailing social attitudes at any given time. It would be erroneous to directly compare Clinton with Presidents of the nineteenth century, as different social mores were in place. Also, the Republican prosecutors in the Lewinsky matter claimed that the Clinton scandal was not about sex, and that the sexual liaison was not the focus of their investigation or of the charges laid against Clinton. Rather, it was the fact that the President lied under oath about his sexual relations that prompted the initiation of impeachment proceedings.

In reviewing the Clinton scandals other factors require consideration. Public opinion, and its faith in the institutions of government, had declined across time. Clinton faced a different scenario from that encountered by Nixon, one where less was expected of politicians, and where the President was not seen to be untouchable or beyond temptation. Politically, this made for a general apathy towards politics. Rumor of Kennedy's affairs and extra-marital activity was in the public domain well in advance of Clinton entering office. This did not make for a lessening of an aura of respect, nor indeed did it tarnish Kennedy's legacy. When Clinton entered office the notion that Presidents might not always be faithful to their wives, yet could still be perceived as good politicians, was one that could readily be recognized. Similarly, popular attitudes to morality had changed across time. Tolerance of alternative sexual practices, recognition of the issue of infidelity, and an acceptance that there were many unhappy marriages and extra-marital affairs within America created a backdrop to the Clinton–Lewinsky scandal which was different from the personal scandals faced by Clinton's predecessors. This explains, in part, why the Republican party was at pains to stress that the scandal faced by Clinton was not one that revolved around the issue of sex, for that, as shown in the polls and discussed further in Chapter 7 of this text, was not a politically pertinent theme. It was an issue of fascination and one of great embarrassment to Clinton as an individual, but certainly not one where the Republicans could press home a case that an affair warranted the Constitutional definition of a high crime and misdemeanor. The Lewinsky scandal was one rooted in 1990s morality, and one where, with previous scandals as a backdrop, the American people accepted that political leaders were subject to temptation, and that lustful exuberance, while it might not be an admirable quality, was something which could ultimately be tolerated.

While the differences between the institutional scandals and personal sex scandals are many, all the Presidents involved in scandal politics in contemporary America have endured common experiences which make the genre of scandal broad but nevertheless quite inclusive.

Clinton, Reagan and Nixon all faced their most testing experience of scandal politics during their second terms. All had been re-elected by comfortable margins and appeared to harbor the trust of the American people. Interestingly, the key scandals faced by Clinton and Nixon began whilst they were serving their first term, and were only exposed once the election season was over. Part of the reason for this was that during the election campaigns, saturation coverage of a number of issues overshadowed any one particular matter, potentially scandalous events included. This only served to dilute public attention on a single issue. Moreover, public policy concerns and the state of the national economy were considered more important than unsubstantiated scandalous accusations, especially when the issue of scandal often appeared to be inspired by partisan hatred, as opposed to an objective search for truth and justice. It seems too simple to suggest that Presidents become overconfident in their own ability, or that there is an institutional drive or structural fault which promotes scandal in the second term. That the onset of the three major scandals of modern times occurred in the second term of three popular Presidents can be attributed to little more than chance in terms of timing and their appearance. After all, in the Clinton case, the Independent Counsel had been pursuing the President for some time on several issues, unable, until the acquisition of incriminating evidence in the Lewinsky matter, to make substantiated claims of presidential wrongdoing.

A more likely catalyst for the onset of scandal is partisanship, primarily in the Congress, but also now a relevant subject regarding Independent Counsel. The separation of powers in the American system of government invites partisan struggle at the heart of the American government. During Watergate, the Republican party controlled the Executive, while the Democrats were in control of Congress.

This gave the Democrats control of the key investigating committees and suggested partisan motivation. This was fragmented however by the support of several Republicans for impeachment when the House Judiciary Committee debated articles in 1974. That said, many Republicans, including 1992 presidential campaigner Patrick Buchanan, believed that partisan vindictiveness lay at the core of the movement to oust President Nixon. Similarly, partisan division was visible during Iran-Contra. The Congressional Report on Iran-Contra, produced at the end of the congressional hearings in 1987, reflected well-defined interpretations of the meaning and severity of the scandal. These interpretations mirrored, in an overwhelming majority of cases, the partisan standings of the members of the investigating committees. It was relatively easy to argue that Reagan had been a victim of partisan politics, rather than a perpetrator of scandal. This was illustrated by opinion poll statistics, which showed that a significantly higher number of Democrats frowned upon Reagan's actions than did Republican voters. One of the main indicators of tolerance or disapproval of Reagan's actions was, therefore, pre-existing partisan allegiance.

The Clinton experience of scandal, when viewed in a broad context, highlights similar experiences to those faced by his predecessors. Initially, his fortunes looked as though they might follow a different path, that the separation of powers might in fact look favorably upon this particular President. From 1992 to 1994, Clinton, a Democrat in the White House, enjoyed the rare occurrence of a Legislative branch controlled by the same party. This did not make for a sweeping bout of social legislation and public policy, for as much as anything else, the times did not demand radicalism of this President. Indeed, the failure of health care reform highlighted that partisan bonding between the White House and the Congress was not a foregone conclusion. The scenario changed dramatically when the Republican party captured both chambers in the 1994 mid-term elections. Now, with Republican control of pivotal committees in Congress, and with additional opportunity to investigate the President, there was an added impetus to the investigation of the President's private activities. In the long term this had important political consequences, as the House Judiciary Committee, among others, played a crucial role once the Independent Counsel had filed a referral outlining grounds for impeachment proceedings against the President in 1998. Previous investigations into Whitewater, led principally by New York Senator Al D'Amato, had failed to charge the President or the First Lady with any specific impropriety. However, partisanship, aligned with the extraneous efforts of the Independent Counsel to investigate the President, ensured that by 1998 the fact that the Congress had been lost by the Democrats in 1994, and had not been regained in 1996, was to have important ramifications for Clinton and his engagement with scandal politics.

The onset of scandal at these times of partisan division, at the least, supports an interpretation of scandal politics as a product of party politics. This is substantiated by the acceleration of the investigation into Bill Clinton, and a severe downturn in his fortunes, once the Republican party had gained control of the Congress in 1994. This, in many respects, is commonplace, and Clinton could have expected nothing less than vociferous attacks upon his credibility, moreover because the Republican platform advanced in 1994 was based on the mandate of the Republican right, a wing of the party strongly opposed to Clinton as a man and a politician. Clinton also threatened to assume the role of a lame-duck President as a result of the scandal he faced, in conjunction with the partisan divisions within Congress. This too underlined the importance of party politics, and left the White House with problems in advancing a credible legislative agenda, one which bore the hallmark of the President and had any realistic chance of succeeding. As a consequence, the Lewinsky scandal had a substantial bearing on Clinton's political fortunes and legacy.

The Clinton scandal epidemic

Clinton, by the time he faced the Lewinsky matter, was an experienced practitioner in both the creation and the resolution of scandal politics. In Arkansas and Washington, he left a trail of scandals in his wake. As a prelude to the Lewinsky case, the other scandals faced by this President certainly suggested that he had a penchant for associating with individuals who would later feel betrayed by him, or would seek to expose his activities in a public forum. As much as this text evaluates the manner in which the Clinton administration sought to limit the damage inflicted by the Lewinsky scandal, his previous experiences with scandal are instructive in gauging Clinton's attitude to a habitual problem. Moreover, the plethora of scandals he faced desensitized the American people to some degree. Another charge of scandal against President Clinton was no surprise; it had been advanced before and would no doubt be heard again. The fact that Clinton was involved in so many scandalous episodes lessened, in public eyes at least, the gravity of any one single charge.

Clinton was assailed by numerous minor allegations of inappropriate presidential behavior. While these did not constitute illegal actions, they, as an aggregate mass, created an atmosphere of suspicion and a lack of trust in the President's word. The nickname of 'Slick Willie', suggesting evasiveness, alongside that of 'Comeback Kid', testament to Clinton's reputation for bouncing back from adversity, were well deserved. He had, for example, allowed individuals who had made donations to the Democratic party to stay in the White House overnight. They were accommodated in the Lincoln bedroom and had granted the Democrats at least 250,000 dollars. This was not illegal, but seemed to transform the White House into an expensive bed and breakfast, and grant political favors in return for money. Further financial controversy centered upon fund-raising at a Buddhist Temple in California. This problem was principally a concern for Vice-President Gore, but was time-consuming for the President and created further diversions from the policy agenda. Fund-raising had been a problem for other Presidents, particularly Nixon. After his departure several laws were passed to ensure that donations would be recorded and limited in scope from any one individual. The perception that the Clinton administration was playing fast and loose in this realm alienated Republicans in particular, but as with so many Clinton issues, they were unable to substantiate allegations or transform them into a major political liability for the President.

Among the other episodes which negatively colored Clinton's rule were Nannygate and his infamous 200-dollar haircut on an airport runway.[8] Nannygate centered on the nomination of Zoe Baird for the position of Attorney General at the start of his first term in 1993. Baird, however, was exposed by the media as having employed illegal immigrants in the position of Nanny and Chauffeur, and of having profited financially as a result.[9] Coming at a time when Clinton wanted to appoint a number of women to his new cabinet, this came as a blow, and raised questions about his judgement and also of how well he knew his appointees' credentials.[10] Baird's nomination proved to be unsuccessful and, as well as raising doubts in the Congress about Clinton's appointees, it underscored division within the administration about who to select for pivotal Executive jobs. Clinton believed that things could have been handled differently, particularly if more time had been taken to consider the issues: 'In retrospect what I should have done is to basically delay the whole thing for a few days and look into it in greater depth.'[11] This might have also been pertinent advice in advance of his statements on Monica Lewinsky in January 1998 when he denied a sexual relationship with his former intern. The President also raised questions of his own judgement and his private perceptions of the authority of the Oval Office when he received a haircut on a plane stationed on a runway at Los Angeles International Airport.[12] This delayed aircraft and seemed to place the President above and beyond Middle America, a constituency he was eager to identify with. The haircut also cost two hundred dollars, considered by many as an excessive price, again placing him in a category of the elite and stimulating criticism by the press.

An allegation of scandal suggests a violation of contemporaneous moral standards alongside a potential violation of existing law. In all these aforementioned issues, alongside several policy problems about gays in the military, and health care, there was little more than clumsiness and poor political decision-making. Clinton and Gore were not charged with any specific wrongdoing on the fund-raising concerns, and the haircut issue and Baird nomination were little more than ill-advised and ill-considered political errors, wholly unwanted, but dealt with via conventional spin control and public relations mechanisms.

Whitewater

Clinton's greatest pre-Lewinsky problems came not because of his sexual antics, as much as they would consume his presidency at a later stage, but rather because of business investments made in Little Rock Arkansas, well before he became President. In 1978 the Arkansas Attorney General, namely Bill Clinton, alongside his wife Hillary, in partnership with James and Susan McDougal, agreed to purchase 220 acres of land in the Ozark mountains with the Whitewater Development Corporation. In 1979 Clinton, now Governor of Arkansas, took a minor interest in Whitewater and how it performed, claiming to be a passive investor.[13] Hillary Clinton was perhaps the more involved of the two, as she, as a member of the Rose Law firm, had interests and employment associated with James McDougal's business investments, commencing in 1985.[14] Whitewater was not deemed to be a sensitive political issue or a potentially scandalous event. On a business front it failed to realize a profit and collapsed in 1992. The Clintons lost a considerable amount of money, approximately 70,000 dollars, according to one account, later revised to about 40,000 dollars.[15] The American taxpayer, as part of the broader Savings and Loan banking fiasco, had to bail out the Whitewater investments.

However, this was not uncommon at this time, and the Clintons were only two of many speculators who had reasons to feel disillusioned about the unprofitability of their investments.

Little was made of the investment portfolio until, in 1992, media investigation of Clinton during his election campaign suggested that McDougal might not have acted ethically while investing Whitewater funds. Given that the Clintons were participants in this venture, and were at the time a potential President and First Lady, they were subject to attention. A feature of Whitewater was its intricacy. The private financial dealings of two individuals, alongside the complexities of an investment corporation linked to a defunct Savings and Loan scheme did not make for a simplistic summation, and trying to uncover wrongdoing or questionable action by the President would take time. Moreover, during the campaign no political opponent tried to exploit any emergent questions about Whitewater, as much because of a lack of hard evidence as anything else.

In keeping with the post-election development of scandal politics, where additional time and the ability to focus on a particular issue allows deeper and more thorough investigation, Whitewater emerged as a potentially scandalous issue in 1993. Questions about the Clintons' involvement were received by the Justice Department, with the Federal Resolution Trust Corporation alleging that they might have been 'potential beneficiaries' of illegal monies from the Madison Saving and Loan company. In early 1993 Whitewater was a mere sideshow, with little to suggest that it warranted extensive investigation. Scandal theory suggests that presidential scandals frequently contain events which cannot be explained and leave lingering doubt in the public and political mind, that they cannot be proved to the benefit of the President, nor indeed to the benefit of his accusers. Whitewater fits the bill perfectly. In July 1993, Deputy White House Counsel Vincent Foster, a friend and long-time legal associate of Hillary Clinton, and an individual integrally involved in the White House defense against charges of wrongdoing in the Whitewater affair, was found dead in a Washington park, killed by a single gunshot to the head.[16] The reasons for Foster's untimely death have been a matter for speculation, giving substantial fuel to conspiracy theorists. Likewise, the contents of Foster's office, and access to it, became a source of political concern, as White House officials proceeded to search it, even though it was a potential crime scene containing evidence pertaining to Foster's suicide.[17] It was relatively easy for conspiracy theorists to conclude that Foster died because he had something to hide about the

Whitewater affair. Investigations by two Independent Counsels suggested otherwise.

A report by Independent Counsel Robert B. Fiske Jr., compiled in 1994 by a large team of medical aides and government employees, and incorporating 125 witnesses, concluded that Foster killed himself because of mounting pressure, stress, and depressive illness.[18] This was tangentially related to political issues, mainly a minor scandal called Travelgate, which involved the sacking of several members of the White House Travel Office and an FBI investigation. The impact of scandal politics played its part, Foster commenting to a participant in the Whitewater matter: 'in Washington you are assumed to have done something wrong even if you have not . . .'.[19] A further investigation and report by Kenneth Starr, successor to Fiske, reaffirmed that there were no suspicious circumstances in this tragic episode. It stated: 'to a 100 per cent degree of medical certainty, the death of Vincent Foster was a suicide'.[20] However, Starr suggested links to the Whitewater case, citing it as a contributory factor in the death of Foster, and concluding that Whitewater was a 'can of worms'.[21] In response, the White House contended that Starr's report contained nothing that was out of the ordinary. White House spokesman Michael McCurry stated: 'We certainly hope and pray that it [Starr's report] brings a very sad chapter in the history of this White House to a conclusion, as it should, and as it should have long ago.'[22] The Foster incident was in keeping with the genre of scandal politics. His death was surrounded by mystery and, initially at least, produced more questions than answers. Furthermore, it had a direct linkage to the Clintons and, to add insult to injury, a superficial connection to a series of events already embraced by scandal politics. As much as the White House wanted discussion of this tragic incident to subside, it simply would not, resulting in conspiratorial claims and comprehensive investigations by two Independent Counsels, at considerable cost to the taxpayer. The conclusions: Foster suffered from depression and took his own life when faced by stressful circumstances.

Whitewater was a scandal which assailed the White House on two main fronts, politically through congressional hearings, and legally, via elongated and pervasive investigations by two Independent Counsels. Janet Reno, the Attorney General, appointed the first Independent Counsel, Robert Fiske, on 20 January 1994.[23] His mandate was to investigate Clinton's involvement in Whitewater and that organization's relationship to the failed Arkansas Savings and Loan institution, Madison Guaranty.[24] He was permitted, amongst other things, to investigate the financial transactions of the Clintons, the death of

Vincent Foster, and the legal work undertaken by Hillary Clinton for Whitewater compatriot James McDougal. The scope for his investigation was wide and elastic, as he conceded: 'I have been told time and again by the top officials of the Justice Department, including the Attorney General, that there are no limits on what I can do.'[25] Fiske's investigation was not wholly to the liking of several members of the Republican party who deemed it, and his techniques, to be lackluster and without the cutting edge needed to combat the Clinton White House. Nevertheless, even when Fiske was appointed, Clinton complained: 'we've got a lifelong Republican that is the Special [Independent] Counsel'.[26] Partisanship appeared to be a contributory factor, influencing the Clintons' fortunes and, in the longer term, impacting upon the evolution of the Whitewater case and the scandal accusations faced by the Clintons.

In August 1994, Kenneth Starr, a Republican who had previously served the Reagan administration and had been Solicitor General to President Bush, replaced Fiske.[27] Although the position of the Independent Counsel is theoretically impartial, Starr's background lent credence to allegations that he entertained a partisan bias against the President. He claimed he would 'build on' Fiske's work, and his mandate was initially limited to investigating criminal activity involving Whitewater. The details of Starr's investigations are exhaustive and expansive. Several key points nevertheless come to the fore. Starr conducted interviews with both the President and the First Lady in early 1995, although no evidence was immediately forthcoming to substantiate wrongdoing by either party.[28] He successfully indicted several individuals involved in Arkansas financial dealings, including James McDougal, Susan McDougal and Arkansas Governor Jim Guy Tucker.[29] This occurred in August 1995. In May 1996, both the McDougals and Tucker were convicted on several charges of fraud, receiving prison sentences and hefty fines as punishment. This was one of the few successes for Starr during his extensive inquisition.

The legal maze of investigations, charges, suppositions and conspiracies failed to resolve Whitewater. Two major trials and several indictments did not suppress speculation about the Clintons' involvement. No charges were leveled directly at the Clintons for their activity in Arkansas, yet their actions while in Washington in dealing with the Whitewater matter raised several questions. Records of legal work undertaken by Hillary Clinton went missing after Foster's death, only to reappear on a table in the White House in January 1996, having been packed away by an aide, in a box of 'knick-knacks'.[30] This prompted

Table 1.2 The Whitewater investigation: the key events

Date	Event
1994	
20 January	Robert B. Fiske appointed Independent Counsel
30 June	Fiske issues statement on Foster's death
5 August	Kenneth Starr replaces Fiske
1995	
22 April	Clintons interviewed by Starr
17 August	Grand Jury charges James and Susan McDougal and Arkansas Governor Tucker with fraud and conspiracy
1996	
5 January	Rose Law Firm billing records are found in the White House
22 January	Hillary Clinton subpoenaed by Starr
26 January	Hillary Clinton testifies before a Grand Jury
4 March	Whitewater trial of the McDougals and Tucker begins
26 May	Tucker and the McDougals are convicted
19 August	Tucker receives a four-year suspended sentence
20 August	Susan McDougal sentenced to two years
1997	
17 February	Starr announces he will leave his post, but changes his mind four days later
14 April	James McDougal sentenced to three years
22 April	Grand Jury term extended by six months
25 June	Whitewater prosecutors start to investigate Clinton's extramarital affairs
15 July	Starr reports on Vincent Foster's death
1998	
8 March	James McDougal dies in prison
25 April	Hillary Clinton interviewed on videotape for five hours about Whitewater by Office of Independent Counsel

questions of a cover-up involving the First Lady and undermined her statements about the extent of her legal work on the Whitewater issue.[31] Indeed, Bill Safire, the *New York Times* columnist, called Hillary Clinton 'a congenital liar'.[32] President Clinton, in response, was said to have wanted to 'punch William Safire in the nose' for his remarks.[33] She had claimed that all documents in the hands of the White House relating to Whitewater had been advanced voluntarily. In an interview in January 1996 she asserted that on a previous occasion, in 1992, she had turned over all pertinent information: 'We took every document we had, which again I have to say were not many. We laid them all out ...'.[34] She then declared: 'I was delighted when these documents showed up. I want everybody to know everything because frankly there's a lot about this I don't remember', and thereafter in a different interview announced: 'There would be no reason for anyone I know, including myself, not to have wanted them to come out years ago.'[35] Members of the Congress were unimpressed. D'Amato (R-NY), Chairman of the Senate committee investigating Whitewater, believed that the billing records 'may have been taken from Vincent Foster's office'.[36] Hillary Clinton was subpoenaed to testify before the Whitewater Grand Jury about the records, bringing unwanted attention to the White House, her own personal role in events and, moreover, to the Whitewater episode as a lingering political sore. Hillary Clinton was again questioned by the OIC in 1998 as part of the four-year-long investigation into Whitewater, the sixth time she had been questioned, although she only once testified before a Grand Jury.[37] What this demonstrated was that the Independent Counsel was prepared to habitually investigate the Clintons to look for illegality and any linkage to the fraud perpetrated by others in Arkansas.

Whitewater was classic scandal politics. No evidence has, as yet, emerged of criminality by the Clintons. But in seeking to extricate themselves from allegations of wrongdoing, more problems were created than were resolved. The untimely death of Foster and the questionable removal of files from his office, the disappearance and reappearance of documents sought by the Independent Counsel, the high-profile testimony of the First Lady before the Grand Jury, and the failure of the White House to repeatedly stem allegations about Whitewater, all elevated an Arkansas investment opportunity to a long-running political scandal of seemingly endless intricacy.

Congress was involved in Whitewater when it investigated the role of Bill and Hillary Clinton in the unfolding financial controversy. There were logistical problems, as congressional investigation proved problematic for the Independent Counsel and impacted upon attempts to call witnesses who had not already given evidence, and might be offered immunity in exchange for testimony. This was a problem familiar to Counsels of the past.[38] Lawrence Walsh, Independent Counsel during the Iran-Contra fiasco, encountered difficulty in obtaining testimony and offering immunity because of highly publicized congressional hearings. Republican demands for hearings into the Clintons' involvement in Whitewater were commonplace, but initially warranted little attention given that the Democrats held the Congress, and evidence of wrongdoing in Whitewater was limited in scope. In early 1994 proceedings commenced to allow the Congress to investigate Whitewater, although progress was slow. Banking committees conducted the initial probes,

but there was little in the way of new evidence, and partisan wrangling alongside the reluctance of the Democrats to investigate on a
broad front effectively nullified the power of the Congress to investigate the Clintons. Votes to establish the investigative mandate of the
committees went along partisan lines, underscoring impressions that
Whitewater was being exploited by Republicans to undermine
Clinton's political authority. In the Democrat-controlled House, questioning was limited to five minutes per member, and interrogation of
witnesses was restricted. At the close of the initial hearings in August
1994, 35 witnesses had appeared in the Congress with 114 hours of
testimony taking place.[39] Little political benefit was forthcoming for
either side, but the scenario changed significantly once the
Republican party assumed control of the Congress following historic
gains in the 1994 mid-term elections.

A Republican with a key interest in Whitewater, Senator Alfonse
D'Amato (R-NY), hoped to initiate hearings once the new Congress
assembled, but initially agreed to a delay to avoid overlap or conflict with
Independent Counsel Kenneth Starr.[40] In May 1995 the pace of congres-

Table 1.3 Congressional investigation of Whitewater: the key events

Date	Event
1994	
26 July	House Banking Committee begins hearings
28 July	Ten White House officials testify to the House Banking Committee
29 July	Senate Banking Committee begins hearings
5 August	Hearings are completed
1995	
3 January	Senate Banking Committee issues its report on its Whitewater investigation
February	White House appoints a team of lawyers to deal with congressional inquiries
17 May	Senate approves a resolution (96–3) to schedule Whitewater hearings
18 July	Senate Special Committee on Whitewater Development Corporation and Related Matters begins hearings
7 August	House Banking Committee, now in Republican hands, continues investigation of Whitewater
1996	
29 February	Senate Whitewater Committee mandate expires
18 June	Senate Whitewater Committee releases a 650-page report critical of the Clintons

sional investigation accelerated with Republicans now at the helm. A 'Special Committee on Whitewater Development Corporation and Related Matters' was established in the Senate, while in the House, the House Banking Committee, now in Republican hands, refined its investigative mandate. The Senate Committee examined the following issues:

- The removal of documents from Vincent Foster's office following his death
- Preparation of White House witnesses before the 1994 Banking Committee hearings
- Inconsistent testimony at Banking Committee hearings
- Any possible cover-up
- Arkansas financial matters relating to the President

The House examined the financial irregularities which took place between Madison Savings and Loan and the Whitewater corporation. The individuals summoned by the Senate discussed a host of details relating to the Whitewater episode in both Washington and Arkansas. They included White House aides and individuals involved with Whitewater. Calls were made for Hillary Clinton to testify, but this was not pursued and, although she frequently appeared before the OIC, she avoided an appearance before the Congress.

In the House, Republican Chairman Jim Leach (R-Iowa) understood his committee's investigation to be a part of the wider industry of scandal politics and was critical of the Democrats' conduct during this episode. He stated:

> From a public perspective, Whitewater is a case model in how not to handle scandal. At every step in the road the White House and Congressional leadership moved in lock-step to avoid full disclosure and a hearing on the failure of Madison Guaranty and its ties to Whitewater.[41]

The congressional committees charged with investigating Whitewater sparred with the White House over the release of information to assist their investigations, and attempted to court favor with media elements and public opinion. Both the House and the Senate covered familiar ground: the death of Vincent Foster, the availability and location of records pertaining to Whitewater, and the role of the Clintons in the episode. The hearings created considerable paperwork, but little else. There were few strong leads and little in the way of substantive evidence to firmly pin blame on the Clintons for any wrongdoing. As the editorial from *US News and World Report* stated:

> So when you cut through all the smoke from D'Amato's committee and almost hysterical press reports such as those emanating from the editorial page of the *Wall Street Journal*, what you have is smoke and no fire. No Whitewater wrongdoing to cover up, no incriminating documents to be stolen, no connection between the Clintons and any illegal activities from the real-estate business failure and the web of political and legal ties known as Whitewater.[42]

The report issued by D'Amato's committee, released on 18 June 1996, charged the Clinton administration with concealing evidence and the improper removal of evidence from Vince Foster's office. The investigation had been extensive: 60 sessions of hearings, 300 hours of testimony, almost 11,000 pages of testimony and 35,000 pages of depositions.[43] The Republican members of the committee issued a majority report. It was critical of the testimony of White House officials who, in its opinion, had stonewalled and had been less than helpful in assisting in the investigation.[44] For example, during the hearings, Deputy White House Counsel Bruce Lindsey testified that he could not read his own handwriting from a memo pertaining to a Whitewater-related phone call.[45] Yet Republicans could not get charges to stick to the Clintons. A minority report, issued by Democrats, exonerated the Clintons and defended the sporadic release of documentary evidence. Moreover, it contended that ill-considered investments did not equate with conspiracy or wrongdoing and, unsurprisingly, found no reason to criticize the President or First Lady, or to continue with any further investigation of Whitewater. Democrats contended that the Republican counsel, Michael Chertoff, had been trying to 'hammer evidence – no matter how ill-fitting – into the precast mold of its [the report] conclusions'.[46] The investigation by the Congress into a potentially scandalous event involving the President and First Lady found little to substantiate allegations of wrongdoing. As a consequence, Whitewater degenerated into a partisan fight to uphold or disprove the validity of a long-running, expensive, and ultimately fruitless investigation of the Clintons' Arkansas past.

Whitewater: damage limitation

It is important to recognize that the congressional investigation and the inquiry by the Independent Counsel were only two parts of a bigger political picture. Clinton's defense against allegations of wrong-doing was of considerable importance in determining the outcome of this political matter. If too much attention were given to Whitewater it might prove to be a distraction to his presidency. If no attention were paid to it there was the chance, albeit a remote one, that it might undermine his presidential authority and even threaten chances of re-election in 1996.

The Clintons' damage limitation effort initially rested upon claims of openness, but only to the extent that the administration would coop-erate with congressional and Independent Counsel investigations. There was also the added complication that the matter involved the personal material of the President and First Lady, as opposed to official documents produced while in public service. Hillary Clinton told reporters in 1993: 'I am bewildered that a losing investment ... is still a topic of inquiry ... I think we've done what we should have done and don't feel the need to do any more than we've done.'[47] Evidence was surrendered to investigatory bodies, albeit slowly and not always on schedule. The White House also assembled a team of advisers to coor-dinate a defense against Whitewater allegations and schedule the release of selected documents. This team consisted of senior members of the administration and indicated, if any evidence was needed, that Whitewater was being addressed with the utmost seriousness. The team consisted of Ickes, Stephanopolous, Gergen, Gearan, Lindsey, and two other external advisers, Carville and Begala. Dick Morris, a strategic adviser to the President, offered advice about how to contend with the Whitewater matter. This advice appears to have underpinned the general strategy of the White House in its approach to Whitewater, and its broad thrust is identifiable in the damage limitation strategies adopted to combat the Lewinsky scandal. Morris urged the President to 'increase his public focus on the values issue' and emphasize the 'parti-san' disposition of those trying to discredit the President. A third piece of advice advanced by Morris is particularly applicable to both Whitewater and the Lewinsky scandal:

> I urged the President himself never to mention Whitewater or any of the other supposed scandals and to leave the rebuttals to his lawyers, staff and spokespeople. By talking about these scandals, he would have identified himself with them. Otherwise, the public would feel they concerned only his staff at most or his wife at worst.[48]

The President's detachment from scandal was to be a feature of damage limitation during the numerous scandal allegations which followed Whitewater. That the President was already well-versed in damage limitation strategies in advance of the Lewinsky matter was a contributory factor in his ability to survive that particular scandal.

The President agreed to the appointment of an Independent Counsel to investigate Whitewater. While this superficially enhanced his declarations of openness and compliance, in reality he had little choice. Failure to act would only have intensified perceptions of White House evasiveness. Defending himself against Whitewater questions from the media on 7 March 1994, Clinton asserted that the administration was one where openness prevailed, and where comparisons between Watergate and Whitewater were groundless. He condemned Republicans for their 'partisan clamor and careless use of language and careless use of the facts[.]'[49] Reiterating his open strategy, Clinton refuted charges of a 'bunker mentality' in the White House. He had to walk a fine line. Absolute openness would not be advantageous to the Clintons. Their personal materials were under legal review, yet they held the same privacy rights as ordinary Americans. However, suggestions that not all documents were being submitted, when requested, predictably evoked claims of a cover-up.

On 24 March 1994, when attention on Whitewater was at its height, President Clinton conducted a news conference. Besieged by questions on this single issue, he affirmed his support for an investigation, and emphasized that it was he, an individual under investigation, who had agreed to the appointment of an Independent Counsel in the first instance, even though he was under considerable pressure at the time to do so.[50] He also believed that the legacy of scandal had influenced perceptions of his involvement in Whitewater: 'because of the experiences of the last several decades, of which I was not a part in this city, I think there is a level of suspicion here that is greater than that which I have been used to in the past – and I don't complain about it'.[51] Drawing the attention of the American people to the extensive attention paid to Whitewater by the Republican party and the media, Clinton repeatedly stressed that the matter was irksome and distracted the administration from its conventional political duties. He stated: 'I know that many people around America must believe that Washington is overwhelmingly preoccupied with the Whitewater matter. But our administration is preoccupied with the business we were sent here to do for the American people.'[52] He also claimed: 'When I read in the *New York Times* that there had been 3 times as much coverage of Whitewater as there had been of health care, I'm amazed that there hasn't been more change in the polls. I think what the American people are really upset about is the thought that this investment that we made 16 years ago that lost money ... might somehow divert any of us from doing the work of the country ...'.[53] This strategy would continue during the Lewinsky scandal and became a familiar component in the damage limitation armory of the Clinton administration. Attempts to set the agenda, however, were generally unsuccessful at this time, particularly after the Republican party won a convincing victory in November 1994 and was able, thereafter, to establish a Special Senate Committee to investigate the Whitewater matter. Scrutiny of this particular issue continued, irrespective of administration claims that it was of marginal importance to the governance of the nation. Even in advance of the Republican victory, Clinton pressed home his message, that the 'American people are going to wonder why the Congress is spending so much time and money on something that has already been looked into in great detail.'[54]

The administration was also eager to assert that it was conducting its defense in an ethical manner, and while privacy was a valid consideration with regard to the Clintons' personal affairs, secrecy was not. Clinton referred to Watergate, and remarks made by Sam Dash, a Special Counsel during that presidential scandal. Clinton cited Dash, who had asserted that Clinton's administration was 'not like previous administrations; they haven't stonewalled; they've given up all the information. Every time there's a subpoena they quickly comply.'[55] When scandal allegation would not subside, Clinton became ever more forceful in his admonitions: 'All I can tell you is that I said we would cooperate fully, and we have. I have said repeatedly that I did nothing wrong, and I didn't.'[56] In 1994 Clinton also identified that he faced a problem which was new to the modern presidential office: 'has any other previous President ever had to say, "Here's what we did 16, 17 years ago"?'[57] This concern was to grow ever greater as, at a later stage, the courts deemed it permissible for lawyers in the Jones sexual harassment case to probe Clinton's personal history, and question women with whom he had allegedly had relationships. The Clinton presidency concerned more than his time in the Oval Office; it was as much about Clinton the man as it was about Clinton the President, and in early 1994, soon after coming to office, the President appeared to recognize that this transformation in the perceptions of the presidency had taken place, and was to be an unwelcome distraction.

The White House reaction to the decision to hold Senate hearings on Whitewater was one of dismay and frustration, particularly because, following the probes by the Independent Counsels, there were still many in the Congress who wished to continue with an investigation. A White House press release issued on the day the Senate voted to hold hearings captured the dejected mood:

> The Senate Resolution is a continuation of the Whitewater-related hearings that Congress began last summer. We are certain that the facts, presented in fair hearings, will continue to show that the amorphous and ever-shifting Whitewater charges are without merit.[58]

The hearings conflicted with administration hopes that a meaningful legislative agenda could be enacted, and underscored the partisan division between the White House and the resurgent right wing of the Republican party. Through 1995 and into 1996 Clinton viewed Whitewater as a saga with no determinable end, constantly being resurrected by opponents in the vague hope that evidence of an incriminating nature would be uncovered. As he stated of Whitewater in August 1995: 'There is nothing else for me to do.'[59] Hillary Clinton was in an entirely different position, facing calls for testimony before the Senate Whitewater Committee once the billing records were discovered in the White House in January 1996. Although the administration had endeavoured to present itself as open and having nothing to hide, events such as this created impressions of a cover-up and compromised the Clintons' attempts to appear helpful to investigations. The President, for his part, seemed to merely want events to run their course. Responding to calls for his wife to testify he stated: 'she has said that she will do whatever is necessary to answer all the appropriate questions, and I think that she should do that . . . She has begun to answer those questions.'[60] He also dismissed questions that she was too controversial and that the 'two for the price of one' slogan, championed during the 1992 presidential campaign, was not something, given Hillary Clinton's experiences in politics, that was likely to be advanced in the 1996 platform. Nevertheless, she reduced her visibility as the first term progressed. Her periodic appearances before Starr, like those of her husband, were an unwanted reminder that Whitewater was an ongoing irritant, unlikely to be resolved in the short term.

Clinton's reaction to Whitewater received a mixed response from the American public. Poll samples highlighted a duality that reappeared when the Lewinsky scandal erupted, indicating that popular tolerance of Clinton's wrongdoing, or at the least the perception of wrongdoing, was identifiable in advance of the most critical of the Clinton scandals. In May 1996, perceptions of a presidential cover-up, perhaps the most serious of all scandal allegations, were evident in poll samples. A question asked: 'Is Bill Clinton hiding something regarding his role in these matters?' Sixty per cent believed that he was, while only 30 per cent believed that he was not.[61] This hardly sanctioned Clinton's claims of innocence, nor endorsed his damage limitation strategy. The figure of 60 per cent marked an increase of nine since a similar poll had been taken in July 1995. This occurred as a consequence of lost billing records suddenly reappearing in the White House. It seemed that the longer the scandal was in view, and the longer the Republican party could keep it alive as a political issue, then the more American citizens would view it as a political concern. Clinton was not viewed as believable either. His Slick Willie reputation, alongside the Whitewater matter, impacted upon his credibility. When asked 'Do you think that what Bill Clinton has said in public about the Whitewater matter has been completely true?' only 4 per cent responded in the affirmative.[62] Forty-seven per cent thought that his comments were 'mostly true', but just below 30 per cent believed his statements to be 'mostly false'. The statistics did not adversely affect his job approval ratings, which changed in insignificant amounts as a result of Whitewater revelations. One reason was that the congressional hearings were not held in high esteem and were widely deemed to be unnecessary. In August 1995, for example, only 30 per cent of respondents thought hearings necessary to investigate the Clintons while 63 per cent considered them unnecessary.[63] Enthusiasm for investigation was limited, and helps explain why, although many thought Clinton guilty of an unnamed offense, he survived Whitewater allegations and retained respectable levels of public approval. Moreover, political scientist Matthew Kerbel contends that media portrayal of Whitewater influenced its resonance with the American people. It focused, in part, upon the partisan battle between the White House and the Republican Congress, emphasizing White House intransigence and the Republican enthusiasm for Whitewater investigations. What Whitewater was all about, and what it meant to the Clinton presidency and the nation as a whole, was generally overlooked and underplayed. This affected public understanding of the issue, as Kerbel makes clear:

> Deprived of a framework for understanding Whitewater as a well-developed, internally consistent series of meaningful events, people related to it in the context provided by strategic news – as scan-

dalous and problematic but lacking a substantive core and therefore overblown by the media.[64]

A combination of factors brought Whitewater to the fore as a political issue which warranted the appointment of an Independent Counsel, and investigation by several congressional committees. The prosecutors, however, failed to bring the Clintons to account, despite the elongated nature of the proceedings and both political and legal investigations. Thereafter, the ramifications in the public forum were limited as media presentation of the institutional conflict failed to make clear or applicable the nature of the charges leveled at the President. Whitewater, therefore, was a scandal with limited impact. It contained the ingredients for scandal politics, had an extensive cast of characters, and a plot replete with intrigue and mystery. Yet, it was complicated and ridden with partisan grievance. What was new about a Republican assault upon a Democratic President? It was predictable, and with the 1994 mid-term election failure and a sizeable popular defection to the Republican camp, Clinton could readily paint the matter as little more than partisan vindictiveness and, moreover, cast subtle aspersions upon the impartiality of an Independent Counsel who was a life-long Republican. Whitewater was intriguing, offered an insight into modern scandal politics, and suggested that Republicans would engage the Clinton White House until they managed to pin something on this scandal-ridden, but ultimately elusive, President.

Sexual scandal

The issue which undermined the Clinton presidency, and in 1998–9 dominated discussion of scandal politics, was sex. As much as there was enough fodder in other areas to give the Republican party ammunition, and allow it to attack Clinton on familiar political territory, sex was the theme which came to the fore and swept conventional political matter aside. Gennifer Flowers alleged that she had had an affair of twelve years with Clinton during the election campaign of 1992. This came at a key moment on the campaign trail, during the New Hampshire primary, where political careers are made and lost. Clinton, although forced to admit this indiscretion, had the crucial backing of his wife, whose decision to stand by him both enhanced his prospects and cast her as a strong individual of admirable character. The Flowers exposé was viewed as opportunistic. Flowers decided to publicize her affair when it would gain maximum publicity and, thereafter, attempted to capitalize by appearing on talk shows and releasing a book about her experience. Her memoirs were entitled *Sleeping with the President*, hardly an inspiring title, but one which certainly got straight to the point. This exploitation of Clinton's action by an individual seeking financial gain was a factor that reappeared during the Lewinsky matter. Linda Tripp attempted to expose Clinton's affair to the Independent Counsel, having had extensive negotiations with a literary agent. In some senses therefore, the scandal industry has profit as a motive, and maximum publicity, and exploitation of that publicity, is clearly an advantageous route to selling a major story. The Flowers case did not have an adverse impact upon the Clinton campaign in 1992. There were, alongside this particular revelation, several other stories of similar magnitude, such as the smoking of marijuana and the avoidance of the draft, which offered hope to Clinton's opponents. That said, both Bush and Perot avoided attacking Clinton on personal grounds, for fear of reducing the election to a mud-slinging contest. There was, additionally, little need for either to assail Clinton for his scandal-ridden private life, as the media and those involved in the scandals themselves made capital out of the events with little need for further political interference. The Flowers scandal was short-term and superficial in nature. It alerted the American public to the fact that if they selected Bill Clinton as their President then they would be electing a man with a troubled personal life and one with a penchant for straying from his marriage. Despite the problems, Clinton was elected convincingly in 1992.

Troopergate

Clinton faced allegations of sexual indiscretion in 1993 when three Arkansas State Troopers claimed to have been offered employment in return for remaining silent about extra-marital activity by Clinton. Labeled Troopergate, the issue was potentially serious for Clinton. If it were proven that he had made offers of employment and bought the Troopers' silence, then prosecution could follow. The story was recounted in the media in December 1993, but received only limited coverage from mainstream elements. It was exposed in the *American Spectator* magazine by journalist David Brock, and was entitled 'Life With the Clintons'.[65] The Troopers advanced their accounts of Clinton's meetings with women, with some evidence that they wished to profit financially as a consequence.[66] One of the alleged liaisons took place between Bill Clinton and Paula Corbin Jones in 1991; a meeting which was to have important repercussions for Clinton's presidency. However, the allegations made by the Troopers lacked real credibility, as it was later reported that two had previously been involved in a fraudulent effort to claim money in an insurance scam.[67]

The Clinton White House launched a limited damage control war against the Troopers, but the rapid disappearance of the story only demanded a short-term campaign. The allegations failed to hold sway with the media or directly damage the President for several reasons.[68] Conflict existed between the account of the Troopers and the word of the President. It had few obvious offshoots and seemed to offer little political capital. Likewise sexual allegations involving the President required a level of credibility for the elite media to consider them as a legitimate topic of inquiry. As a consequence, this story was not pushed strongly by the media, nor by the President's opponents, and appeared, on the surface at least, to have a limited shelf-life. Not all however were content that the story disappeared so readily. *Los Angeles Times* reporter Bill Rempel expressed his dissatisfaction with the media's conduct. He believed that Troopergate constituted: '[an] abuse of office and deceit: It is the kind of story the press ought to be aggressively pursuing, rather than running from or hiding or knocking down.'[69]

Conclusions

Clinton's involvement in scandal preceded the Lewinsky episode. It proved to be a constant distraction, and periodic surges of attention on scandalous activity attuned the American people and the Congress to Clinton's past activity. More often than not Clinton shrugged off the allegations of malfeasance. The Comeback Kid reputation appeared, initially at least, to outweigh the Slick Willie reputation. Clinton's involvement with scandal encouraged the search for more revelations and, consequently, a wide net was cast in the hunt for presidential wrongdoing. Gennifer Flowers set in motion a familiar pattern of events. The opportunity to profit financially encouraged further sexual, not to say profitable, revelations about the President's private life. Not all of Clinton's activities were scandalous in nature, but the accumulation of allegations across time, in combination with periodic political ineptitude, necessitated a semi-permanent damage limitation exercise which often seemed to impinge upon the President's ability to concentrate upon the administration's legislative agenda.

Despite claims about Whitewater and previous wrongdoings while Governor of Arkansas, the President's job approval figures did not fluctuate markedly. They declined through the 1992–4 period, but mainly because of public policy problems and the appeal of a new right-wing agenda advanced by the GOP [Grand Old Party] in 1994. Although poll samples thought Clinton untrustworthy on Whitewater, the American people appeared prepared to grant him the benefit of the doubt. He might not be sufficiently forthcoming, and may have been involved in questionable investments while Governor of Arkansas, but as long as the American economy was strong and Clinton was doing a satisfactory job as President he retained the confidence of the American people. This was underscored by a convincing win in the 1996 presidential election. In advance of the Lewinsky scandal, the American people had seemingly distinguished between Clinton the politician and Clinton the person. Indeed, it is plausible to argue that this had already taken place in advance of the 1992 election when scandalous allegations had but a marginal impact upon the fortunes of candidate Clinton.

For all the efforts of the Independent Counsel and the Republican-controlled Congress to promote Whitewater as a meaningful political issue, the investigation of the Clintons' Arkansas legacy had a disinterested audience which remained relatively uninformed as a consequence of the complexity of the matter and the nature of media coverage. The impact of Whitewater in Washington was therefore markedly different from its impact around the country. This served as a precursor to the Lewinsky affair. Try as it might, the Republican party could not substantiate charges against the Clintons, nor transform allegations against the administration into meaningful political capital. Clinton attempted to appear cooperative with the investigative mandate of the OIC and the Congress. Deflecting attention from the scandal he urged the American people to focus on a conventional public policy agenda. Neither those prosecuting Whitewater nor those resisting the investigative onslaught found that it was resolved satisfactorily. It persisted with no proven or substantive charges being leveled at the President or First Lady. For the Congress, and Senator D'Amato in particular, the failure to get hard evidence of Clinton wrongdoing essentially nullified the long-term efforts to capitalize upon the Clintons' Arkansas past.

2
The Lewinsky Affair

Prior to the revelations about Clinton's relationship with White House intern Monica Lewinsky, the Clinton administration was experienced in defending the President against accusation of scandal. And yet, for all the expertise of the White House in suppressing accusation of presidential wrongdoing, the Lewinsky scandal presented a host of new problems. The sudden explosive disclosure of the President's affair, in conjunction with his initial denials about a relationship with 'that woman', suggested that this episode was another overblown and over-hyped media exercise fuelled by Clinton's opponents. For the Republican party it offered a golden opportunity to undermine the President's credibility. Furthermore, the timing of the Lewinsky accusations was important. They came after an elongated effort by Paula Jones to sue the President for sexual harassment, and it initially appeared that Lewinsky might have fallen victim of the President's reputation for womanizing. In a short period of time, the President found himself in a predicament which would test his own political judgement, and transform a discreet affair into a Constitutional crisis, with the attendant chance that he might be convicted and removed from office by the Senate, following impeachment by the House of Representatives.

This chapter considers the Jones sexual harassment case against President Clinton, and how it eventually led to charges of perjury and obstruction of justice. Clinton's strategy during this pivotal period, in the prelude to the Lewinsky scandal, influenced his political fortunes during 1998. As outlined in Chapter 1, the substantive section of a scandal is the foundation upon which a procedural phase rests, the latter being the period where initial wrongdoing is addressed. Via the unlikely route of the Jones case, Clinton's relationship with Monica

Lewinsky was exposed and attendant damage limitation measures were necessary. Although it was resolved in 1998, the Jones case, particularly in its later stages, was damaging to Clinton's credibility. By the time it concluded, the Lewinsky matter posed a more serious political threat. This chapter concludes with a review of the onset of Clinton's Lewinsky-related problems, with the damage limitation measures initiated to deal directly with the Lewinsky matter, and Clinton's role in them, reserved for Chapter 3.

Clinton's damage limitation exercise, during both the Jones and Lewinsky episodes, was critical for his presidency and for the integrity of the presidential office. His decision to initially deny a relationship with Lewinsky, and later admit that his comments were misleading, cast negative aspersions upon his character and set the foundation for a controversial OIC investigation and impeachment proceedings in the Congress. This only occurred because the President chose to contend a case of sexual harassment originating in Arkansas, and was challenged by an individual who demanded a hefty financial settlement. Clinton's inability to anticipate the multitude of problems posed by the Jones case is understandable, but ultimately led to serious political repercussions which elevated scandal to the forefront of political debate.

The Jones harassment case

The Troopergate allegations, outlined in Chapter 1, precipitated a series of events that were, in the long term, to cause substantial problems for the Clinton presidency. The Troopers alleged that, in Arkansas, Clinton had been to hotel rooms to meet with women and, while they guarded the location and were consequently aware of the Governor's exploits, they were later offered further employment in return for their silence. This in itself was potentially damaging but, as mentioned previously, the Troopers appeared to lack the credibility to seriously challenge the President and the mainstream media were unenthusiastic about covering the story in late 1993. Lingering questions remained however. Who were the women with whom Clinton had met, and were they willing to speak about their experiences? The question was answered in early 1994. On 11 February, Paula Corbin Jones charged Clinton with harassment, claiming that he subjected her to unwanted sexual advances in a hotel room in 1991. He was not President at the time of this alleged incident and this was in its essence a 'he said–she said' event. This played marginally into the hands of those making the accusations, as it was impossible for Clinton to disprove and, as a consequence, it pitted his word against that of an individual who played upon the familiar Clinton theme of adultery and sexual malpractice.

Jones contended that her civil rights had been violated and initially requested an apology from the President for the trauma caused by his action. Her case and cause were supported and funded, in part, by conservative elements. She made her initial charges against Clinton at the Conservative Political Action Committee convention.[1] As with previous Clinton scandal allegations there appeared to be an underlying partisan motivation to the charges, and differentiating between a just case and a politically inspired lawsuit proved difficult. In May 1994 Jones filed a 700,000 dollar suit against the President for sexual harassment. Clinton, in turn, hired a legal team to defend himself against Jones's charges, including an individual who would take a leading role in the Lewinsky damage limitation exercise at a later stage, Robert Bennett.

The Jones case hinged, in many respects, upon when it would proceed. Was it prudent to have Clinton defend himself against charges of such an individual nature, allegedly committed when he was not President, and thereby sidetrack him from conducting the duties of the presidential office? Court battles ensued as the President's team argued for delay, ideally until Clinton left office and was able to give his full attention to the case and its ramifications. Bennett also queried 'whether a sitting President may be sued for alleged events that took place before he entered office'.[2] In response, the Jones team argued that no person was above or beyond the law, and in the interests of equality Clinton should, as with any other citizen, be required to answer the charges brought against him. Initially the matter seemed to favor Clinton as delays and court decisions suggested that the litigation might be postponed sufficiently to allow the President to continue in office unhindered. However, in an overriding decision in January 1996, the US Court of Appeals permitted proceedings on the grounds that the President was subject to the same laws as other American citizens. It did however recognize the special position and circumstances faced by Clinton, acknowledging that sensitivity should be given 'to the burdens of the presidency and the demands of the President's schedule'.[3]

Following an appeal, the case of *Jones* v. *Clinton* was heard by the Supreme Court in 1997. This was a decisive moment for Clinton, and for the American presidency in a wider context. The central issue was whether the case could proceed while Clinton held office.[4] Initial discussions had taken place against the backdrop of Clinton's re-election campaign in 1996 and could have appeared overly political. Clinton's victory reduced the political overtones. The decision of the highest Court in the land to review the case made for a judgement of weighty proportions. The Court ruled by nine to zero to allow the case to continue while Clinton was in office. There was, however, a tacit recognition of the unique nature of Clinton's position. While he was a citizen who was not above the law, Justice John Paul Stevens nevertheless acknowledged: 'The high respect that is owed to the office of the chief executive, though not justifying a rule of categorical immunity, is a matter that should inform the conduct of the entire proceeding.'[5] Stevens also stated, erroneously, that the case 'appears to us [the Supreme Court] highly unlikely to occupy any substantial amount' of the President's time. He grounded his opinion on the fact that only three sitting Presidents had been subject to litigation while in office, and the historical disruption to the office of the presidency had, at best, been marginal. In this instance the intrusion was significant as the President was investigated by the Jones legal team. University of Virginia law professor John C. Jeffries Jr. later remarked: 'recent events [the Lewinsky scandal] suggest that the court's optimism might have been misplaced. What's going on now is rich evidence of exactly the kind of distraction that we feared.'[6] Clinton's immediate response to the decision was to declare: 'It must be an interesting opinion if it's nine to zero.'[7] In keeping with his strategic approach to Whitewater outlined in the previous chapter, the President and his advisers stressed a need to focus upon the public agenda and to consider the legislative mandate for the country. White House press spokesperson Mike McCurry downplayed the decision of the Court: 'I believe the opinion appears to have distracted all of you, but the President continued to conduct the nation's business ...'.[8] There was little the White House could do and its stoic response reflected this fact. The Supreme Court decision cast the President as a normal citizen subject to the laws of the nation while, at the same time, his particular duties and responsibilities were considered only in a token manner. As academic and legal commentator Alan Dershowitz declared: 'The bottom line is that the Supreme Court decision is very good for the country, pretty good for Paula Jones and pretty bad – but far from fatal – for Bill Clinton.'[9]

Throughout the duration of the case, Jones was vilified by Clinton's aides. Bennett described her as 'tabloid trash' while James Carville allegedly declared in late 1996: 'Drag a $100 bill through a trailer camp, and there's no tellin' what you'll find.'[10] For all the comments and public hostility directed at Jones, the problems were not entirely political in nature, nor indeed could they be solved by a simple public relations offensive. These were legal issues which would have to be settled in court or through financial negotiation and settlement outwith that forum. Clinton had several options in the Jones case. Firstly, he could have proceeded and have directly challenged Jones, seeking at the same time to tarnish her reputation, and highlight her substantial financial demands. Secondly, he could also have requested an out-of-court settlement and have negotiated her financial demands, thereby ridding himself of the matter and having Jones appear interested solely in monetary gain. Thirdly, he could simply have defaulted on the case, paying its costs and proceeding no further.[11] None of these options was particularly attractive, but Clinton, on the advice of his legal aides, decided to contest the case. Judge Susan Webber Wright had timetabled the Jones proceedings for early 1998, and Clinton, scheduled to give a pre-trial deposition on 17 January 1998, knew that Jones's lawyers intended to ask about his relationships with other women to establish a pattern of behavior which would enhance the case of their client. Wright stated that an investigation of the President's relationships with women in government was 'within the scope of the issues in this case'.[12] Consequently, Clinton was deposed with more than just the Jones case on his mind. More pressing perhaps was that he would be asked about other liaisons, and, as he knew by the time he entered the room, his covert relationship with Monica Lewinsky was unraveling and she had been asked to file an affidavit concerning her relationship with him.

The Paula Jones case was eventually overshadowed by the Lewinsky affair, and was dismissed by Judge Wright in April of 1998.[13] Although the President was not harshly punished in the legal forum, it acted as the catalyst which exposed the Lewinsky matter. The decision to contest the Jones case was therefore a crucial one which partly determined the evolution of Clinton's second term. This decision was in keeping with Clinton's previous damage limitation strategies. It made him appear honest, forthright, and the victim of circumstance, as opposed to being the perpetrator of any wrongdoing. On this occasion, however, the President was generally unaware of the nature of the evidence and information being amassed about his personal activity. Tapes of telephone conversations between Pentagon worker Linda Tripp and former intern Monica Lewinsky, together with DNA forensic evidence proving a relationship between the President and Lewinsky, would later cast doubt upon Clinton's declarations in the Jones deposition. While the Jones case had important ramifications for Clinton as an individual, it also had a significant role to play in establishing a legal precedent. The Supreme Court ruling which allowed individuals to challenge the President while in office created a presidency which was not beyond the reach of the law. As much as it promoted equality, the conviction of the Supreme Court Justices, as expressed in the unanimous decision, that it would not influence the presidency to a great degree, proved to be misplaced. As much as the Justices recognized the unique institutional position occupied by the presidential office, they understandably failed to take into account the characteristics of this particular President, whose exploits before coming to office were the root cause of many political and legal problems.

Monica Lewinsky

The convergence of the Jones investigation and Clinton's relationship with Lewinsky occurred as a consequence of an unlikely series of events. Linda Tripp drew the attention of the Independent Counsel to a covert affair between Clinton and Lewinsky, and suggested that both intended to lie about it, and conceal it from Jones's lawyers. Thereafter, Kenneth Starr requested that his mandate be expanded to allow him to investigate whether perjury and obstruction of justice had occurred in the Jones case. At the heart of the matter was the affair between Lewinsky and Clinton, an unlikely liaison, yet one which precipitated a Constitutional crisis and struck at the heart of the American government. Several controversial matters characterized the Clinton–Lewinsky relationship. The efforts by both participants to conceal their affair was a principal cause for concern. This involved premeditated efforts to be economical with the truth and thereby allow Lewinsky to visit the President, and permit the two to be alone together. The President engaged in a risky cover-up, one complicated when the affair was investigated by Jones's lawyers and the Independent Counsel. As experienced by Nixon, among others, the charge of a cover-up could be serious, with potentially catastrophic political repercussions. A second matter which permeated the relationship was the desire of Lewinsky to find a satisfactory job, and the President's efforts to help her to this end. When it became clear that Lewinsky was under investigation by Jones's lawyers, the job search, undertaken principally by the President's friend Vernon Jordan, intensified. An emergent question was whether this was a politically inspired move to assuage Lewinsky and buy her silence. A third issue concerned the nature of the relationship. Was it a sexual one? Evidence suggested that it was; a stained blue dress and accounts by both participants clearly suggested that the President and Lewinsky had been intimate together. However, there were complications. Semantics dominated the debate, and the President denied that he had ever had 'sexual relations' with Lewinsky. Later he would contend that it was plausible that she had had sexual relations with him.[14] A fourth matter of importance was that of gifts. The President and Lewinsky exchanged a number of presents. These were subpoenaed by the Jones lawyers, but many were hidden under the bed of the President's secretary, and the President, when questioned under oath, had obvious difficulty remembering whether anything had been exchanged between the two. Again the specter of a cover-up came to the fore, with the associated charge of obstruction of justice. These recurrent and major themes dominated the substantive period of this particular scandal.

Monica Lewinsky arrived at the White House in July 1995 to work as an intern in the office of the Chief of Staff.[15] She developed an in-depth knowledge of the workings of that institution, and had limited access to the President. In November 1995 she was transferred to the Office of Legislative Affairs, and was dismissed from the White House and transferred to the Pentagon, in April 1996.[16] Her tenure at the White House was limited, being confined to a period of less than a year.

Her first contact with the President occurred in late 1995 during a government shutdown caused by a budget impasse.[17] Flirtation and sexual rendezvous followed. There were no conventional sexual encounters between the two, only oral sex. Clinton later recounted that he did not consider this to constitute 'sexual relations', as later defined in the Jones deposition hearing.[18] The two briefly broke off their relationship in February 1996, but it recommenced in late March 1996. The time Lewinsky spent at the White House gave her, and the President, an opportunity to initiate a relationship and conduct it in relative safety, it not being wholly uncommon for staffers to provide documents for the President and have contact with senior officials.

Lewinsky's transfer from the White House in April 1996 necessarily complicated the affair and made contact all the more difficult. She was transferred from the White House because of impressions that she was loitering around the President's office, was an irritant, and posed a potential problem. Evelyn Lieberman, the Deputy Chief of Staff for Operations, received a complaint from a Secret Service official that Lewinsky was a 'nuisance'.[19] No hard evidence was available to suggest that Lewinsky was involved in an affair, and there were only vague suspicions that she might have a crush on the President. Lieberman testified: 'I decided to get rid of her.'[20] Independent Counsel Starr, in his referral to the House of Representatives, contended that Lewinsky was relocated because she maintained close proximity to the President. He stated: 'Most people understood that the principal reason for Ms. Lewinsky's transfer was her habit of hanging around the Oval Office and the West Wing.'[21]

Lewinsky was upset at having been transferred from the White House and expressed her regrets to the President. She desired a better job, or opportunities outside the government sector. During the investigative phase of this scandal, Clinton maintained that he never promised Lewinsky further employment, or to aid her in a job search. The general issue of Lewinsky's employment, and who assisted her in her search, nevertheless became an issue, as it was alleged, in an article of impeachment, that Clinton assisted Lewinsky to maintain her silence. In Clinton's testimony to the Grand Jury in August 1998 he resolutely denied that he ever offered to assist her in seeking further employment: 'But I did not tell her I would order someone to hire her, and I never did, and I wouldn't do that. It wouldn't be right.'[22] Despite her dissatisfaction at being reassigned, Lewinsky had another sexual encounter with the President just before she left the White House, and on that occasion she informed him of her imminent departure.

As a result of Lewinsky's transfer to the Pentagon the relationship dwindled and there were no private meetings between April and December 1996. Lewinsky was now working as a Confidential Assistant to the Assistant Secretary of Defense for Public Affairs. It was during this time that she met Linda Tripp. Tripp was to have a pivotal role to play in this scandal. She provided a wealth of evidence to the Independent Counsel and supplemented his efforts to acquire incriminating material against the President. Tripp had initially been appointed to a government post when President Bush was in office, and had moved to work in the Pentagon in 1994.[23] She befriended Lewinsky and the two discussed the relationship between the President and the former intern across time, with Tripp giving Lewinsky advice on how to deal with emotionally stressful situations. Unknown to Lewinsky, Tripp, under the initial guidance of literary agent Lucianne Goldberg, covertly taped telephone conversations, amassing an extraordinary account of Lewinsky's recollections.[24] Tripp was apparently motivated to act as she had previously been belittled by the White House for having been a source for allegations that Bill Clinton had sexually harassed White House aide Kathleen Willey. To bolster her credibility and, in her opinion, to protect the interests of Lewinsky, during the fall of 1997 Tripp began to tape Lewinsky's accounts of the relationship with the President. Tripp also took written notes, which were later acquired by Starr.[25] Tripp's evidence and determination to assist the Independent Counsel were pivotal in hastening the onset of Clinton's problems. That Lewinsky was unaware of the recordings of her conversations raised ethical and legal questions about the admissibility of the evidence and the nature of its acquisition.[26] While the transfer of Lewinsky from the White House disrupted her contact with the President and removed an irksome figure from that institution, the contact and emergent friendship between Tripp and Lewinsky was significant in the longer term.

Clinton and Lewinsky met several times in a public forum while she was at the Pentagon, but these meetings did not offer any opportunity for the two to continue a private relationship. Phone conversations occurred, but with Clinton's focus on the 1996 presidential election, Lewinsky became increasingly frustrated that she could neither see nor contact the President as frequently as she desired.[27] Following the election, in early 1997, the intimate relationship between the two was resurrected. Lewinsky even went so far as to put a Valentine Day message to the President in the *Washington Post*, appropriately disguised so that it would not be obvious to any person other than Clinton. By this time the President's secretary, Betty Currie, was integrally involved in passing on messages from Lewinsky, and understood the personal nature of the relationship. Currie's centrality as a go-between, and her knowledge of the timing of the meetings between the President and the former aide, made her a key witness once the affair was made public in January 1998.

A critical event occurred at the end of February 1997. The President met with Monica Lewinsky on 28 February and they engaged in oral sex. They also exchanged gifts. Following this encounter Lewinsky noticed stains upon her blue dress. These were stains of the President's semen and constituted critical evidence that proved, beyond reasonable doubt, that the President had engaged in a relationship, of an unspecified sexual nature, with Lewinsky.[28] It was therefore not a 'he said–she said' case, but rather involved interpretations of the precise nature of the relationship, and how accurately it was portrayed to Jones's legal team during the President's 17 January 1998 deposition. Possession of the dress and the request that the President submit a DNA sample to corroborate Lewinsky's claims of a relationship are discussed further in Chapter 4.

Lewinsky claimed that a final sexual encounter took place in March 1997. She also asserted that at this meeting she and the President discussed the possibility of her returning to the White House. This would have made meetings between the two easier and would have partly excised Betty Currie from the role as go-between. Clinton testified about Monica Lewinsky's desire to obtain employment in the White House in his August 1998 Grand Jury testimony: 'She very much wanted to come back. And she interviewed for some jobs but never got one. She was, from time to time, upset about it.'[29] Clinton appears to have entertained doubts about the relationship from this point onwards and, privately at least, did not make himself available for meetings with Lewinsky, much to her frustration. Around 24 May 1997 the intimate relationship was terminated at the behest of President Clinton.

The sexual affair between Clinton and Lewinsky was, for a period, a private one, with only Betty Currie, the President's secretary, seemingly knowledgeable of it in the White House. Lewinsky was less reserved. She regularly e-mailed friends and intimated towards a troubled relationship, and also, as already mentioned, discussed her liaison in detail with Linda Tripp.[30] According to the *Starr Report*, between 1995 and 1998, eleven of Monica Lewinsky's associates and friends were aware of her relationship with Clinton.[31] The likelihood of exposure was high, not only from Lewinsky herself, if she felt neglected by the President, but moreover, because of the motivations of others who may have entertained the possibility of financial gain, and indeed blackmail, with regard to the illumination of the affair. Clinton was overtly concerned about who Lewinsky had informed of the affair, asking her directly about whether she had discussed the issue with her mother.[32] Clinton's concerns were clear, as he suggested in his August 1998 Grand Jury testimony:

> After I terminated the improper contact with her, she wanted to come in more than she did. She got angry when she didn't get in sometimes. I knew that might make her more likely to speak, and I still did it because I had to limit the contact.[33]

According to Lewinsky's recollections, Clinton also, on an occasion when Lewinsky wanted to resurrect the relationship, warned the intern that it was 'illegal to threaten the President of the United States'.[34] This was a fabrication, but it nevertheless suggested that the President exploited his influence and position to intimidate the intern. Despite the risks of disclosure, and the obvious fear that others might come to know of a matter with serious public relations consequences, it remained essentially private, until Linda Tripp approached the OIC and informed it that Clinton had been involved in an inappropriate relationship. When the relationship was terminated, there existed sufficient evidence to prove that the President had engaged in an intimate relationship with Lewinsky over time. It had included meetings, the exchange of gifts, phone calls and sexual encounters. According to Lewinsky's recollections contact was frequent. A summary provided by Starr's investigation is displayed in Table 2.1. The efforts of Lewinsky to acquire her preferred employment dominated her relations with President Clinton for some time. She wished to exploit his influence and return to the White House or, barring that, have him assist her in getting a job of her choice or one that would advance her career prospects.[35] Inquiries about employment at the United Nations or in New York initially proved fruitless, and eventually the President's close friend and aide Vernon Jordan interceded to assist Lewinsky in refining her options. There were still telephone conversations between Clinton and Lewinsky, but these were not intimate and involved practical matters, with the President encouraging Lewinsky to continue her search for satisfactory employment.

Investigation and revelation: Clinton, Jones and Lewinsky

In November 1997, following the Supreme Court decision on the Jones case, President Clinton received written questions from Jones's lawyers requesting the names of women, other than his wife, with whom he had 'had', 'proposed having', or 'sought to have' sexual relations. He

Table 2.1 Clinton–Lewinsky contact, 1995–8

Contact type	Number of contacts
Sexual encounters	Ten: eight while Lewinsky worked at the White House, and two following her relocation to the Pentagon
Phone calls	50: including phone sex
Gift exchange	Lewinsky sends about 30 Clinton sends about 18

Source: Lewinsky recollection; *Starr Report*, pp. 39–42.

declined to answer the questions given that their scope was so broad. Lewinsky was unable to secure satisfactory employment during November, the search seemingly becoming more urgent at this time, with increased involvement from Vernon Jordan. Whether this was at the direct behest of the President, or motivated in part by his urging, remains unclear. This again raised questions about whether there was an attempt, at the presidential level, to buy Lewinsky's silence and obstruct justice in the event of her being approached by the Jones lawyers. The increasing focus of the Jones investigation on Clinton's private sexual activity and the urgency of the job search were certainly irksome for the President, but Clinton had previously expressed concern for Lewinsky's employment and, added to this, his direct involvement at this time was limited.

In early December a list detailing witnesses in the Jones case contained the name of Lewinsky. The President knew before Lewinsky that she was to be called as a witness.[36] She discovered some time later that she was required to testify, and was naturally concerned about why she was on the witness list given the number of women the President interacted with on a daily basis.[37] Lewinsky and Clinton knew of two sources whereby the Jones lawyers could have acquired her name. The President, according to a Lewinsky testimony to the Grand Jury, believed the source of the trouble to be either the Secret Service agents who guarded him, or Pentagon worker Linda Tripp.[38] Both were obvious sources of concern: the agents given their close proximity to Clinton, and Linda Tripp, as a source following rumors of the sexual harassment of Kathleen Willey. Clinton was asked for additional documents by the Jones lawyers on 15 December 1997, specifically that he 'produce documents that related to communications between the President and Monica Lewinsky'.[39] Confusion exists over whether the President and Lewinsky discussed what she should say about their relationship. Should she tell the truth under oath, or should she try to protect the President and conceal the relationship? This dilemma for both the President and Lewinsky underpinned much of the debate in the procedural phase of the scandal. Did the President coach Lewinsky and ask her to lie about their relationship in the Jones case? Lewinsky claimed that there was no explicit discussion about what she, or he, should say. There was a tacit understanding between the two that their previous cover stories would continue and they would endeavor to keep the relationship secret. Clinton was at pains during his Grand Jury appearance of August 1998 to make it explicitly clear that he never encouraged

Lewinsky to falsify information in the prelude to his Jones deposition. He testified: 'I never asked her to lie.'[40] Lewinsky was also asked to surrender all 'letters, cards, notes, memoranda, and all telephone records' between her and Clinton to the Jones lawyers, an extensive request and one which would, if satisfied, have illuminated the true nature of their relationship.

Presidential aide Vernon Jordan advised Lewinsky that he would assist her in the search for a lawyer. Jordan was, by this time, suspicious about the nature of the Clinton–Lewinsky relationship and asked both parties, on separate occasions, whether they had engaged in a sexual relationship. Both answered in the negative. Clinton testified: 'I do remember that I told him [Jordan] that there was no sexual relationship between me and Monica Lewinsky, which was true.'[41] In December 1997 Clinton was asked once again by Jones's lawyers to list the names of women with whom he had had sexual relations, barring his wife. Judge Wright forced him, on this occasion, to answer. He replied: 'None.'

Final meetings between Clinton and Lewinsky took place in late December. The two exchanged several gifts on 28 December, including six items given to Lewinsky by the President.[42] This was a rather bizarre scenario, since she had been subpoenaed by Jones's lawyers to turn over objects received from the President. Clinton appeared to have difficulty remembering the detail of this meeting during the Jones deposition, a matter of some concern given that it came a mere three weeks later. For example, Clinton was asked in the deposition:

> Q. Well, have you ever given any gifts to Monica Lewinsky?
> A. [Clinton] I don't recall. Do you know what they were?[43]

Under questioning Clinton vaguely recalled some of the gifts that might have been exchanged, but his memory was hazy. In his Grand Jury testimony on 17 August 1998 he claimed that he informed Lewinsky that she would have to surrender any gifts requested by Jones's lawyers. He stated: 'And I told her that if they [Jones's lawyers] asked her for gifts, she'd have to give them whatever she had, and that's what the law was.'[44] On 28 December 1997, Betty Currie, the President's secretary, went to Monica Lewinsky's apartment and collected a box of gifts which she later deposited under her own bed. The attempt to conceal the gifts, although amateurish, was a deliberate effort to deny Jones's lawyers evidence of the relationship between the

Table 2.2 Key events: Clinton and Lewinsky, 1995–8

Date	Event
1995	
July	• Lewinsky begins work at the White House
15 November	• Relationship begins between Clinton and Lewinsky
1996	
5 April	• Lewinsky is transferred to the Pentagon
1997	
29 March	• Last intimate meeting between the President and Lewinsky
Summer/Fall	• Linda Tripp learns from Lewinsky of the presidential affair and begins to tape phone calls
5 December	• Lewinsky is named as a witness in the Jones case
8 December	• Vernon Jordan is asked to assist in the search for a job for Lewinsky
11 December	• Lewinsky meets with Jordan and is assisted in her search
19 December	• Lewinsky is served with a subpoena to testify in the Jones case and turn over all presents received from the President
28 December	• Lewinsky visits the White House and receives gifts from President Clinton. These are later taken by Betty Currie and deposited under her bed
1998	
7 January	• Lewinsky signs an affidavit for the Jones case denying a relationship with President Clinton
12 January	• Tripp approaches the Office of the Independent Counsel and claims she has tapes which detail an intimate relationship between the President and Lewinsky
13 January	• Tripp, wired by FBI agents, meets with Lewinsky • Lewinsky is offered a job by Revlon
14 January	• Lewinsky gives Tripp a document which coaches her about what to say about Kathleen Willey sexual harassment claims in her affidavit
16 January	• Starr obtains an expanded mandate to allow investigation of obstruction of justice and subornation of perjury in the Jones case • Lewinsky is detained by the FBI and is offered immunity by Starr in return for testimony
17 January	• President Clinton is deposed and denies 'sexual relations' with Monica Lewinsky

President and Lewinsky. While it was clear that Currie had acquired possession of the gifts, a critical question remained. Who instigated this action? Did the President order Currie to conceal the gifts?

Did Currie act on her own initiative? Did Lewinsky ask Currie to take the gifts from her Watergate apartment? Starr interpreted this episode as a purposeful effort on the part of the President to obstruct justice. The prime source of disagreement was between Currie and Lewinsky, both of whom claimed that the other was the motivating force for this specific action. This issue was debated extensively during the Clinton impeachment hearings. Interestingly, neither Lewinsky nor Currie identified the President as the instigator of this episode, but it was assumed by many, including several Congressmen, that when Currie acted, it would have only been at the direct behest of the President. Clinton dismissed claims of his involvement in his Grand Jury testimony of 17 August 1998:

> Q: ... did you ever have a conversation with Betty Currie about gifts, or picking something up from Monica Lewinsky?
> A[Clinton]:   I don't believe I did, sir. No.[45]

Lewinsky and her lawyer drew up an affidavit to prevent her giving direct testimony to the Jones lawyers. Clinton did not see this directly, although Lewinsky offered to show it to him in advance of his deposition. Vernon Jordan reviewed the document and ensured that it covered a number of sensitive areas and, importantly, denied a sexual relationship with the President. Once it was to Lewinsky's satisfaction, attention turned back to the recurring theme of the search for a new job. Again, the timing of this job search raised questions about the possibility of a quid pro quo agreement between Lewinsky and the President. Lewinsky received the offer of a job from Revlon in New York in the immediate prelude to Clinton's 17 January deposition. Vernon Jordan was instrumental in assisting her, and testified: '[T]hat was no secret, I don't think, around the White House, that I was helping Monica Lewinsky.'[46] Jordan, in turn, kept Clinton informed of events and told him that Lewinsky had received satisfactory employment.

Tripp approached the OIC on 12 January 1998 and informed it of her concerns over perjury and the obstruction of justice in the Jones case. She notified FBI agents that Lewinsky had had an affair with the President, and that a dress, with irrefutable proof of the relationship, was still in Lewinsky's possession. What was more, she offered hope to the OIC that material evidence, to substantiate her claims, might be available: 'Lewinsky won't have the dress dry-cleaned to this day.'[47] Following her surreptitious telephone taping of Lewinsky, Tripp exploited her detailed knowledge of the relationship. In an effort to acquire additional information, on 13 January, Tripp had a lunch meeting with Lewinsky, having been wired by the FBI so she could tape the conversation.[48] The Independent Counsel understood Lewinsky's position in advance of Clinton's deposition to the Jones lawyers, and soon thereafter had an opportunity to examine her affidavit to see if she had misinformed investigators about the relationship. Tripp's decision to approach the OIC, and inform it that Lewinsky intended to lie in the Jones case, cast the Clinton White House into the mire of scandal politics.

Linda Tripp was required to submit an affidavit to Jones's lawyers, as former White House aide Kathleen Willey had named her as a collaborative witness. Monica Lewinsky gave Tripp a three-page document, commonly referred to as the 'Talking Points', identifying points to make in her affidavit, many of which were falsehoods.[49] This was further proof, if any were needed, of an attempt to mislead investigators. Tripp submitted her affidavit to Jones's lawyers on 21 January 1998. It declared that there had been, as Willey had contended, a sexual encounter between the President and Willey in late 1993. It also recounted that Monica Lewinsky had had a relationship with the President. This was in keeping with the information the Jones lawyers desired, as they were seeking to establish a pattern of behavior by the President, and this contributed to their case. Tripp wrote:

> Monica Lewinsky ... revealed to me in detailed conversations on innumerable occasions that she has had a sexual relationship with President Clinton since November 15, 1995. She played for me at least three tapes containing the President's voice and showed me gifts they exchanged ... She said she was going to deny everything, that President Clinton would deny everything and she repeatedly stated that I must lie and deny that she had ever told me anything about a relationship with President Clinton.[50]

Tripp's decision to expose the relationship between Lewinsky and the President brought to the fore several questions about her motivation. She attempted to stifle criticism and justify her action by releasing information that exonerated her from wrongdoing or betrayal. In a statement released on 30 January 1998, shortly after allegations of the affair had become public knowledge, and after Clinton had denied it, Tripp asserted that she was not a Republican with a partisan grudge nor a 'disgruntled White House staffer, with a penchant for involving myself in scandals'.[51] She had 'chosen the path of truth' and had acted to prevent criminal activity. The Clinton administration came in for scathing attack. Tripp had been a background source when accusations by Willey had surfaced in *Newsweek* the previous year. Fearing that she would not be believed if she made allegations about Clinton's sexual activity a second time, and fearing reprisals from the administration for her actions, she chose to contact Starr's office. She denied that she was writing a book and disassociated herself from literary agent Lucianne Goldberg, stating: 'whatever political agenda Ms. Goldberg may have is not mine'.[52] In a riposte designed to counter the damage limitation strategies employed by the Clinton administration, Tripp declared: 'The vicious personal attacks against me by an administration spokesman, and the general climate of threats, intimidation, McCarthyistic tactics and guilt by association can only serve to deter those who in the future may dare to bring information to law enforcement officials.'[53] Through such language Tripp attempted to portray herself as an individual who had risked all to expose an obstruction of justice. The release of taped conversations between Tripp and Lewinsky would later show that Tripp had counseled Lewinsky about the relationship, and had encouraged her to keep a semen-stained dress intact, in case it was later needed to prove that a relationship had taken place.

In advance of Clinton's deposition to the Jones lawyers, the Independent Counsel had information which suggested that Clinton had engaged in a private relationship with Monica Lewinsky. He had been informed that Lewinsky intended to lie about it, and was aware of Clinton's delicate position. Whether it be on the specifics of a relationship, the exchange of gifts, or whether the President encouraged Lewinsky to conceal the affair, it appeared to Starr that there were grounds for an extension of his existing mandate, to investigate violations of law by Lewinsky, and possibly the President. Starr approached Attorney General Janet Reno and asked for expanded jurisdiction.[54] This was granted on 16 January 1998, and enabled Starr to analyze the information submitted by Lewinsky and others in the Jones case. Part of the expanded mandate stated:

> The Independent Counsel shall have the jurisdiction and authority to investigate to the maximum extent authorized by the Independent Counsel Reauthorization Act of 1994 whether Monica Lewinsky or others suborned perjury, obstructed justice, intimidated witnesses or otherwise violated federal law ... in dealing with wit-

nesses, potential witnesses, attorneys, or others concerning the civil case *Jones* v. *Clinton*.[55]

Starr would now investigate the President's efforts to conceal his relationship with Lewinsky, and would, in time, submit a document to the House of Representatives which would recommend grounds for the impeachment of the President of the United States. The private affair between Lewinsky and Clinton had now entered a legal phase, and soon after would become a political issue when media sources reported the expansion of Starr's remit and the new revelations brought about by the Jones deposition. Thereafter, as discussed in Chapter 3, Clinton had to contend with legal battles and political acrimony, and struggled both to retain his own credibility and to preserve the authority of the presidential office.

President Clinton: the Jones deposition

The charges advanced by Independent Counsel Starr against President Clinton, and filed as grounds for the impeachment of the President, arose, predominantly, from the President's deposition to the Jones lawyers. Starr claimed that among the most serious offences, Clinton lied under oath, obstructed justice, and encouraged Monica Lewinsky to file a false affidavit which denied that they had engaged in a sexual relationship. However, Starr's allegations were difficult to prove. While the facts were often not in dispute, and recordings, transcripts, and recollections were generally similar, differences of opinion existed between participants over the interpretation of the factual record. The testimony of President Clinton in the Jones deposition was a crucial piece of evidence in the case presented against Clinton by the OIC. Clinton faced a stern challenge. Generally unaware of the evidence in the hands of the OIC, he entered a critical phase of the Jones case, only to find that a more troublesome concern emerged when he was questioned about his relationship with a former White House aide.

The President was deposed on 17 January 1998, facing questions under oath for about six hours. He was asked about Jones's allegations and, pursuant to the ruling by Judge Wright, was questioned about sexual relations he may have had with government employees. The contents of the deposition were not to be made available for public dissemination, and this is why, even at this stage, there was no immediate flurry of press activity about the nature of the questioning. Consequently, it was several days before leaks about the President's alleged relationship began to openly circulate in Washington. Clinton was aware that former White House intern Monica Lewinsky had submitted an affidavit in which she denied having a sexual relationship with the President.[56] Robert Bennett, his personal lawyer, stated that the witness was 'fully aware of Jane Doe 6's [Lewinsky] affidavit'.[57] In keeping with a prior understanding with Lewinsky to keep the affair secret, Clinton denied ever having had a 'sexual affair', 'sexual relations' or a 'sexual relationship' with Lewinsky.[58] This was important, as Jones's lawyers were trying to establish a pattern of activity on the part of Clinton that suggested he was a habitual womanizer and had made unwanted advances upon their client.

A key issue which influenced Clinton's fortunes later in the year was semantics, and how the President understood specific questions. It could only be established whether he had purposefully lied if it was explicitly clear that interpretations of words and phrases were equally understood by all parties, and were uniformly agreed to. The pivotal discussion and disagreement involved the quest for an interpretation of the term 'sexual relations'. Judge Wright settled on a definition of the term:

> For the purposes of this deposition, a person engages in 'sexual relations' when the person knowingly engages in or causes ... contact with the genitalia, anus, groin, breast, inner thigh, or buttocks of any person with an intent to arouse or gratify the sexual desire of any person ... 'Contact' means intentional touching, either directly or through clothing.[59]

Clinton agreed to this definition. He testified that he had met with Monica Lewinsky several times, but could not recall if he had been alone with her, although he did not rule out that possibility. In a similar vein he remembered giving her gifts, although could not remember what these were or when he had given them. Although he was vague on several issues, many of Clinton's statements appeared categorical, and he resolutely denied having a relationship with Lewinsky, and agreed wholeheartedly with the wording of her affidavit. For example:

> Q. In ... her affidavit, she says this, 'I have never had a sexual relationship with the President, he did not propose that we have a sexual relationship, he did not offer me employment or other benefits in exchange for a sexual relationship, he did not deny me

employment or other benefits for reflecting a sexual relationship.'
Is that a true and accurate statement as far as you know it?
A. *[The President]*   That is absolutely true.[60]

Clinton answered questions about Jones, and also about another
woman who had claimed that he had sexually harassed her, former
White House aide Kathleen Willey.[61] This particular case was seemingly
more difficult for the President. While Jones appeared to have financial
gain as her primary motivation, and Lewinsky never intended to cause
the President political problems, Willey was an aide who, as a
Democrat, seemed to have more complex motives and, initially at least,
a more plausible story. Clinton denied any untoward contact with her.
As recounted in Chapter 3, she became a vocal critic of the President. A
transcript of Clinton's deposition was made public by Jones's lawyers in
March of 1998 as a direct response to Clinton's efforts to have the Jones
case dismissed. Its release merely added to the furore over the Lewinsky
scandal, and made clear that Clinton had explicitly denied a sexual relationship with the former intern.

The Lewinsky affidavit, of which Clinton was aware before he
entered the deposition, was submitted by Monica Lewinsky to avoid
direct testimony before the Jones lawyers. It outlined details of her
employment at the White House and questioned the reasons for her
involvement in the investigative process: 'I cannot fathom any reason
that the plaintiff would seek information from me for her case.'[62] In
keeping with the aforementioned statement cited by Jones's lawyers,
Lewinsky denied having a relationship with Clinton and asserted that
she had the 'utmost respect for the President who has always behaved
appropriately in my presence'.[63] Lewinsky's affidavit was to cause
problems in itself. Although the President had admitted that he knew
of its existence, it remained unclear if he had seen it personally or had
participated in its formulation. In his August 1998 Grand Jury testimony he contended that he only had a general understanding of its
content: 'I didn't talk to her about her definition [of sexual relations].
I did not know what was in this affidavit before it was filled out
specifically.'[64] This subject became a hotly debated issue during the
impeachment hearings of December 1998–February 1999, for if
Clinton had been involved personally, then there was a case for
obstruction of justice and subornation of perjury by the Chief
Executive.

Serious charges against Clinton emerged as a consequence of the
Jones deposition. Starr thought it problematic in several areas, and his

charges were later debated in the House of Representatives when impeachment articles were under consideration. Clinton's first problem as a result of the Jones deposition was perjury. He stated under oath that he had not had 'sexual relations' with Monica Lewinsky. If it could be proven that he had purposefully lied, then he would be guilty of a criminal offense. The House later rejected an article of impeachment (article II) which alleged that Clinton had 'willfully provided perjurious, false and misleading testimony' in the Jones deposition.[65] Ironically, Clinton, on the eve of his departure from office in 2001, would admit that some of his comments about Lewinsky were intentionally false. This, however, was scant comfort or reward for those who, at the height of the scandal in 1998, had struggled to prove that he had knowingly lied. A second problem, directly related to Lewinsky's affidavit, was subornation of perjury, specifically whether the President encouraged Lewinsky to perjure herself in that document. This became a component in an article of impeachment (article III) passed by the House in December 1998: 'On or about December 17, 1997, William Jefferson Clinton corruptly encouraged a witness in a Federal civil rights action brought against him to execute a sworn affidavit in that proceeding that he knew to be perjurious, false and misleading.'[66] A third concern for the President was obstruction of justice, and whether he purposefully impeded investigations and blocked the path of Jones's lawyers. The issue of gifts, given to, and offered by, the President, was a pressing concern, as many were concealed under the bed of the President's secretary, Betty Currie, in December 1997. It was however unclear who originally requested that the gifts be hidden. Nevertheless, this too emerged as an element in an article of impeachment (article III) passed by the House: 'On or about December 28, 1997, William Jefferson Clinton corruptly engaged in, encouraged, or supported a scheme to conceal evidence that had been subpoenaed in a Federal civil rights action brought against him.'[67] A further charge against Clinton included witness tampering. As discussed in Chapter 3, he discussed his testimony with several aides, and with Betty Currie in particular. If it could be proven that he was attempting to influence her future testimony, then he faced additional legal concerns.

For all the problems created as a consequence of the deposition, there existed grounds for hope. It would have to be proven that Clinton had a clear intent to mislead. If he misunderstood a definition, or wrongly answered a question which was vague or open to misinterpretation, then there could be no credible legal penalty. The burden of proof, in legal terms, was firmly upon those investigating Clinton. They had to demonstrate that he purposefully set out to mislead investigators and intentionally influenced the written testimony and recollections of others. There were however several factors which undermined Clinton's position. While he might, in the short term, elude stringent legal guidelines, he would later face a referral from the Independent Counsel which would recommend impeachment and move the scandal firmly into the political realm. Legal issues were therefore only the first of many obstacles between Clinton and the end of this scandal.

Conclusion

The integration of the Lewinsky affair and the Jones case was an unexpected development which threatened the Clinton administration on both a political and a legal front. It involved private activity by the President, political activity by several institutions, and legal moves by an array of lawyers determined to prove the validity of their clients' cases.

Jones's pursuit of her case, alongside her resolute determination, provided the President with a long-term problem which ultimately pitted his word against hers. This left him with several unattractive options. His decision to contend the case, alongside a Supreme Court judgement, had important consequences for the modern presidency. In partnership with the problem of contesting the Jones charges when in office, came the attendant complication of an expanded investigative mandate granted to the Jones lawyers. This allowed an exploration of the private life of the President. Clinton's confidence that he could win the Jones case proved to be misplaced as legal decisions transposed the matter to a forum where he could exert little political control. Although a lawyer by training, the President found that his authority over the development of the Jones case deteriorated across time, exacerbating problems which had remained hidden for a lengthy period, and exposing a relationship that had been terminated almost a year previously.

Clinton's belief that he could maintain a relationship with Lewinsky is initially hard to entertain given the public nature of his job and the lack of privacy associated with the office. Threatening the emotional attachment between the two was the possibility, indeed the likelihood, that the relationship would be exposed. Cover stories were hatched which contended that Lewinsky brought the President papers to sign and that she received gifts, just like several other White House aides. However, her transfer from the White House to the Pentagon demonstrated that there was an observable trait to Lewinsky's relationship with the President that caused visible concern. Contact thereafter was sporadic, with periodic meetings and attempts by the President to terminate the relationship while hoping, at the same time, that Lewinsky would not disclose the affair. This hope was misplaced. Lewinsky shared the news of her liaison with many, including, of course, Tripp. Alongside the recorded information possessed by Tripp there existed written material from Lewinsky to the President, gifts given and received by both parties, and a semen-stained dress which proved that sexual contact had taken place. This was essential to the case mounted by the OIC.

Clinton's deposition on 17 January 1998 marked an important turning point for his presidency. He denied having 'sexual relations' with Monica Lewinsky. The debate over the definition of sexual relations was problematic and later resulted in elongated and, at times, painful debate about whether Lewinsky had sexual relations with the President while, at the same time, he did not have them with her. It reduced the relationship to a bewildering array of legal technicalities, and produced a bizarre scenario which subtly suggested that the President had, in an astonishingly calculated manner, concocted an elusive argument to avoid legal entrapment. His effort failed. Discussion of the relationship provoked legal battles between the President's lawyers and the OIC, as the latter attempted to prove that the President had lied, obstructed justice and had committed subornation of perjury. Clinton's opponents, including Kenneth Starr, claimed that the Lewinsky affair was not the central focus of the investigation, and that sex was not a primary concern. Rather, it was critical to determine, not whether the President had had a sexual liaison with Monica Lewinsky, but whether he had lied about it under oath and had encouraged others to lie. Sexual relations were integrally involved in this matter, but as much as they provided material for the tabloid market and media outlets, they were secondary in Starr's eyes to the President's truthfulness. In this way the Lewinsky affair was frequently perceived as a sex scandal by the American public, but in Washington was very much a scandal which had legal debate at its core.

During the remainder of 1998 the President struggled to maintain his credibility and to continue with conventional political business. Yet, for all his determination and desire to pursue his legislative agenda, he had no choice but to confront the Lewinsky scandal, culminating with testimony to a Grand Jury in August of 1998 and the commencement of impeachment proceedings later in the same year. Clinton's plight was wholly in keeping with the theoretical underpinnings of scandal politics. His initial substantive action, namely the affair with Monica Lewinsky, caused him little problem in the first instance. Indeed, he contained the disclosure of that relationship for a remarkable time. His attempts to deal with the potential fallout from the substantive action, and accurately advance information about Lewinsky in the Jones deposition, was to cause him greater difficulty. Reflecting the experiences of Nixon and Reagan in the realm of scandal politics, Clinton found that his efforts to cover-over the nature of this initial action entailed a procedural phase of immense legal and political strain, elevating the matter from a covert affair to one of significant Constitutional proportions. Only a few days after the 17 January deposition the mainstream media uncovered details about the story, and questioned Clinton directly about his affair with Lewinsky. The President's decisions and damage limitation exercise, examined in the next chapter, produced a series of unexpected turns and twists whereby the 'Comeback Kid' created political problems via his efforts to revive waning credibility in Washington.

3
Protecting the President: Damage Limitation and the Lewinsky Scandal

From the outset, several familiar aspects of scandal politics character-ized the Lewinsky scandal. As experienced by Nixon and, to a lesser extent, by Reagan, Clinton endured a vociferous onslaught on his political office. He faced legal challenges to his authority and found himself immersed in a pitched battle against Independent Counsel Kenneth Starr. To the Clinton White House the tactics used by Starr, and particularly his conclusions and interpretations, smacked of parti-sanship and excess. It appeared as though he possessed an elastic mandate, and would trawl Clinton's past until he found a questionable matter which could be laid against the President. There seemed to be no end to the investigations and no lack of funding either, as the Republican-controlled Congress appeared satisfied that the investiga-tion and cost were warranted ventures. Clinton was saddled with an investigation of his private activity that was immovable and, from the standpoint of the White House, highly questionable. When considered in isolation, the Starr investigation, having begun in 1994 and having achieved little by 1998, appeared to pose few problems, with the Independent Counsel receiving little public enthusiasm or support for his investigation. However, hand-in-hand with a Republican party eager to undermine the position of the President, it held greater force, and resulted in a political and legal assault upon Clinton's position and credibility. When Starr filed a report on the Lewinsky matter rec-ommending grounds for impeachment, the fact that the GOP held the Congress and dominated pivotal congressional committees made the matter all the more serious for Clinton. Irrespective of public opinion and based primarily on a 'he said–she said' interpretation of events, Clinton found himself in the most serious Constitutional predicament since Watergate, and became only the third President, after Nixon and

Johnson, to face impeachment proceedings in the Congress. The rarity of the event made for a thorough search of Constitutional history and precedent, alongside some bewilderment that the President faced proceedings as a consequence of such an unlikely series of events. The partnership between the political and legal, the public and private, and the ensuing interplay between the branches of government demanded a complex damage control strategy of the White House. Additionally, the change of tack by the President in belatedly admitting to an 'inappropriate relationship' necessitated a reconsideration of strategy in the midst of the political drama. With Clinton at the center of events, impressions of the presidential office were inextricably linked to his performance, and his ability to disassociate his own private activity from that associated with the duties and role of the President was severely tested.

The deterioration in Clinton's fortunes appeared, at first sight, to testify to a failed damage limitation effort which had neither stemmed nor dissipated the accusations leveled against the President. Clinton, after all, was eventually confronted by congressional proceedings which had evolved out of legal investigations, and he initially failed to deal adequately with either. When allegations of his relationship with Monica Lewinsky became public in the third week of January 1998 it was important, particularly in the field of public opinion, that Clinton suppress speculation about his activity and, moreover, about his future. The distraction of the Lewinsky affair would cloud discussion about the important State of the Union address, and could, if left unattended, ultimately threaten the Clinton presidency. This scandal appeared particularly problematic. It dealt with an area where Clinton had had previous problems, namely sex. Secondly, it combined legal elements with political and public issues, making political control, via the power of the presidential office, especially difficult. As much as it involved the President of the United States, the power of that office was largely nullified in this instance. It was not a scandal about institutional abuse of power, or the usurpation of power from another branch of government. Rather, it was a scandal where Bill Clinton, the American citizen, was charged with violating several laws.

This chapter evaluates the efforts of the Clinton administration to control the political and legal damage created by the Lewinsky scandal in 1998, in advance of the impeachment proceedings conducted by the Congress. It begins by contextualizing the pivotal episodes of the period in question. It then deconstructs the damage limitation effort into three distinct sections: presidential action, the response of the administration to the scandal allegations, and congressional reaction to Clinton's crisis. These show how the Clinton team modified its approach to the scandal across time. The activity undertaken to deal with the congressional impeachment proceedings, and the White House reaction to that particular event, is evaluated in Chapter 5.

The Lewinsky scandal. Overview: January–September 1998

Following the President's testimony to the Jones lawyers and the decision of the Independent Counsel to request an expanded remit for his investigation, there existed, privately at least, the heightened possibility that there would be a conflict between the White House and Kenneth Starr. Until this time the Lewinsky matter was a bizarre 'he said–she said' issue. It had a twist, however, as both the President and Lewinsky denied that there had been a sexual relationship, and both had advanced information to Jones's lawyers to that end. However, the Independent Counsel possessed information which suggested that both Lewinsky and the President had lied under oath, and as much as the affair might be consensual, it had nevertheless been misrepresented. Even though the Judge in the Jones case had requested that the information and detail of the deposition remain secret, the decision of Tripp to approach the Independent Counsel, in conjunction with the efforts to tape Lewinsky by wiring Tripp and recording conversations, ensured that rumors of a presidential affair would sooner or later seep into the public realm. What was more, a journalist, Michael Isikoff, had details of the Tripp telephone recordings and wished to publish them with *Newsweek* magazine. It initially declined to proceed on the grounds that it might impede the investigation by Kenneth Starr which was ongoing at this time.[1]

Shortly after his deposition on 17 January, Clinton discussed matters pertaining to Monica Lewinsky with several aides. Of paramount concern to investigators was what he said to his secretary Betty Currie on 18 January. According to the evidence accumulated by Starr, Clinton asked her several questions about Lewinsky and about what she knew of the relationship, she being aware of the nature of the intimate affair which had existed between the President and the intern. As she was likely to be called as a witness there existed the possibility that Clinton was coaching his secretary and advising her what to say under oath if she were summoned. Currie stated that the comments made by the President to her were 'more like statements than questions'.[2] According to Currie they included the following remarks:

- 'You were always there when she was there, right? We were never really alone.'
- 'You could see and hear everything.'
- 'Monica came on to me, and I never touched her, right?'
- 'She wanted to have sex with me, and I can't do that.'[3]

Differing interpretations of the President's statements revolved around whether he was asking Currie questions in order to refresh his memory, as he contended, or whether, as Starr maintained, he was attempting to influence her recollections. Starr was left in no doubt that the President was doing the latter, as he made clear in his referral to the House of Representatives:

> In a meeting with Betty Currie on the day after his deposition and in a separate conversation a few days later, President Clinton made statements to her that he knew were false. The contents of the statements and the context in which they were made indicate that President Clinton was attempting to influence the testimony that Ms. Currie might have been required to give in the Jones case or in a grand jury investigation.[4]

Throughout January 1998 Clinton advised his aides, even at Cabinet level, that he not had an affair or sexual relations with Monica Lewinsky. By doing so, Clinton not only involved senior political officials in his cover story, but widened a web of misinformation and ensured that if these aides were called to give testimony they would advance his questionable interpretation of events. The seriousness of Clinton's actions was later apparent when the House passed an article of impeachment (article III) which, in part, contended that he had attempted to influence the testimony of Currie: 'On or about January 18 and January 20–21, William Jefferson Clinton related a false and misleading account of events to a Federal civil rights action brought against him to a potential witness [Currie] in that proceeding, in order to corruptly influence the testimony of that witness.'[5] It also addressed the wider problem of misinformation within the Clinton administration: 'On or about January 21, 23 and 26, 1998, William Jefferson Clinton made false and misleading statements to potential witnesses in a Federal grand jury proceeding in order to corruptly influence the testimony of those witnesses. The false and misleading statements made by William Jefferson Clinton were repeated by the witnesses to the grand jury, causing the grand jury to receive false and misleading information.'[6]

The affair was exposed to the public on 19 January 1998 by the Internet columnist Matt Drudge on his web page, *The Drudge Report*.[7] He advised readers that *Newsweek* magazine had information on a Clinton sex scandal involving former intern Monica Lewinsky.[8] The fact that the Internet was used to disseminate information, and did so in advance of the mainstream news organizations, was symptomatic of this scandal and complicated the White House damage limitation strategies as they had to contend with an unregulated news medium. Mainstream organizations, such as the *Washington Post*, published the story on 21 January 1998, a mere four days after Clinton had given his deposition in the Jones case. This effectively marked the onset of the procedural phase of the scandal, when the focus was not on what the President had done, but on how he would deal with his substantive action, namely his affair with Monica Lewinsky. Public disclosure was an added and irksome distraction, moving the matter beyond the boundaries of legal argument and firmly into the political and public domain. This ensured that the White House had to consider public and congressional opinion whereas, previously, the issue had been a confidential one, understood by only a select few of the President's aides.

January 1998 witnessed a struggle to control the platform of debate. While the White House, and the President in particular, issued forceful denials refuting allegations of presidential indiscretion, Starr and the OIC attempted to grant Monica Lewinsky immunity from prosecution if she would testify to a Grand Jury. In the midst of the mêlée, Clinton delivered his State of the Union address, making no mention of the Lewinsky scandal, unwilling, understandably, to fuel speculation on the matter. Ironically, at the same time the Lewinsky case was erupting and consuming presidential time, the Jones case took an unexpected turn. Judge Wright ruled that the evidence submitted by Lewinsky was superfluous and inadmissible to the essence of that case. From late January onwards a host of Clinton aides and advisers testified to a Grand Jury about their knowledge of Clinton's relationship with Monica Lewinsky. Betty Currie, for example, was called to testify on 27 January, only ten days after the President had been deposed in the Jones case, highlighting, if nothing else, the breakneck speed of the Starr investigation.

The search for the factual evidence to prove that an affair had occurred between the President and the ex-intern continued through the spring. Starr and Lewinsky sparred over the question of immunity, while the President, though rarely volunteering to discuss the scandal, repeatedly denied that a sexual affair had taken place. He did however find that the allegations of sexual malpractice would simply not go away. Former White House aide Kathleen Willey resurrected her claims of sexual harassment in a televised interview on 15 March.[9] This accusation merely exacerbated Clinton's problems, and he was forced to deny publicly any untoward activity with Willey. Thereafter, the White House attacked her, seeking to destroy her credibility via the release of letters from her to the President.[10] Written after the alleged harassment took place these demonstrated that Willey held the President in high esteem, made no reference to the harassment, and suggested that there were no grounds for the charges, which appeared to resurface at a profitable and convenient time.[11]

Clinton's efforts to suppress allegations of wrongdoing in the Lewinsky matter were punctuated by high-pressure press conferences. These were held to address a host of concerns but degenerated into events where the media demanded information about only one issue. This was symptomatic of the President's problem and was characteristic of scandal politics. He could not adhere to a non–Lewinsky agenda at this time and was forced, in both the political and legal arenas, to respond to circumstance rather than direct attention at a matter of his own choice. Media and political commentary was consumed with speculation about the Lewinsky scandal and how it might be resolved. Indeed, the simple question of whether the President was telling the truth had not been determined at this time. Legally, there were more pressing concerns. Having initially claimed executive privilege to prevent Starr interviewing members of the White House, the White House dropped its claims in June 1998. This granted Starr extensive access to members of staff who may have witnessed the President and Monica Lewinsky together, or who might have had conversations with Clinton about Lewinsky.[12] Following elongated debate and several court decisions, Starr had access to most of the witnesses he desired by the summer of 1998. For some time he had been in pursuit of testimony from Clinton and, following extensive discussion between the OIC and the President's lawyers, Starr demanded that the President appear before the Grand Jury and testify under oath about the true nature of the relationship with Lewinsky.[13]

July 1998 was an important month for the presidential office. On 17 July Clinton was served with a subpoena which required him to testify to the Grand Jury. Following negotiations between the OIC and Clinton's lawyer David E. Kendall, he agreed to testify voluntarily and Starr withdrew the subpoena.[14] The date of Clinton's appearance was scheduled for 17 August. Perhaps more troubling for the President were developments that involved Lewinsky and the OIC. On 28 July she reached an immunity deal whereby she would inform Starr of what she knew about the liaison with the President and cooperate with his investigation. This hampered Clinton to a significant degree, for he now knew that his denials of a sexual relationship would be nullified if Lewinsky revealed details of their meetings together.

Table 3.1 Damage limitation: January–October 1998

Date	Event
21 January	The Lewinsky scandal is broken by the main news networks
24 January	A damage limitation team is assembled by the President
26 January	Clinton publicly denies a relationship with Lewinsky
27 January	State of the Union address
	Hillary Clinton alleges a vast right-wing conspiracy is persecuting her husband
15 March	Kathleen Willey reiterates her allegations of harassment by the President
20 March	Clinton invokes executive privilege to prevent aides testifying
1 April	The Jones case is dismissed
1 June	Clinton drops executive privilege claims
2 June	Lewinsky hires a new legal team
7 July	Appeals Court rules that Secret Service agents must testify
17 July	Clinton is served with a subpoena to testify before the Grand Jury
24 July	Clinton agrees to testify voluntarily
28 July	Lewinsky agrees to an immunity agreement with Starr
30 July	Lewinsky turns over a dress to Starr
6 August	Lewinsky appears before the Grand Jury
17 August	Clinton appears before the Grand Jury through a video link
	Clinton makes a speech on national television to admit a relationship with Lewinsky
9 September	Starr submits his Report to the House of Representatives
11 September	*Starr Report* released to the American public
18 September	House Judiciary Committee considers the release of evidence from the Starr investigation
21 September	The President's Grand Jury testimony is released and is played on national networks
24 September	House Judiciary Committee announces that it will consider a resolution of impeachment against the President

With other evidence, such as the Tripp tapes, in the hands of the Independent Counsel, there existed the likelihood that the President's denials would not endure examination. A dress owned by Lewinsky was submitted to Starr's office as part of the immunity agreement. This had stains on it, alleged to be the President's semen, which would prove, when verified forensically, that the President had engaged in a relationship of a sexual nature with Lewinsky.[15] It will be recalled that he had denied, under oath, that there had been 'sexual relations' between the two. The President was asked, on 31 July, to provide a blood sample by the OIC.[16] He did so on 3 August 1998.[17] By 17 August the results of the DNA analysis were known to the OIC, and it was clear that the President had been intimate, in an as yet unspecified manner, with Monica Lewinsky. On 19 August, following the President's confession of an affair, it had become public knowledge that a DNA sample had been requested, and had been donated by the President. This day-by-day trickle of information was characteristic of scandal politics, and ensured that formulating a coherent defense of the President's position across time was a challenging task.

Exacerbating the problems faced by Clinton in advance of his Grand Jury testimony, the submission of the dress posed serious problems. It merely added to the existing evidence that there had been intimate contact between the President and Lewinsky, and suggested that he had been somewhat lax in his descriptions of his contact with her, as outlined in his January deposition in the Jones case. The President now confronted a difficult scenario. If he admitted to intentionally misleading investigators during the Jones deposition he faced charges of perjury, with the attendant likelihood that there would be impeachment hearings in the Congress. His alternative was to argue that the questioning by Jones's lawyers, on 17 January, was vague and imprecise, and he had accurately answered questions as he understood them at that time. This meant that any answers which were imprecise were not necessarily lies, but were unintentionally misleading.[18] Naturally, the focal point concerned the definition of 'sexual relations', a definition agreed to by all parties at the time of the Jones deposition. The pressing question now, and one which would be put to Clinton during his August 1998 Grand Jury testimony, was how he could deny that sexual relations had occurred when there was substantial evidence that he and Lewinsky had been intimate together. As a consequence, the President's Grand Jury testimony assumed the utmost importance, for it would provide both the investigators and investigated with the ideal opportunity to advance their respective cases.

Clinton testified from the White House via a video link on 17 August 1998, and, as discussed later in this chapter, admitted a relationship with Monica Lewinsky. Whether this relationship lay within the boundaries of the term 'sexual relations' as defined in the Jones deposition was open to question. Recognizing the problems posed by his 'inappropriate relationship' with Lewinsky, he repeatedly asserted that he did not commit perjury, did not commit subornation of perjury, and did not obstruct justice in the Jones case.

In anticipation of leaks about his testimony, the President chose to address the nation and candidly admit that an 'inappropriate relationship' occurred. This was a calculated gamble, but one that the President had little choice but to undertake. In a brief speech, analyzed in this chapter, the President apologized to the nation for his error of judgement and admitted that he had acted erroneously. The speech was purposefully depoliticized and the trappings of the presidential office were removed from the visual image, casting President Clinton as an ordinary citizen who had suffered public humiliation. Thereafter, he went on vacation with his wife and family to try and repair the damage inflicted on his marriage.

Starr continued to collect evidence and hear from witnesses through the summer of 1998. He filed his referral with the House of Representatives on 9 September 1998. This report, most commonly known as the *Starr Report*, became a key document, outlining, via an extensive descriptive-narrative, the covert liaison between the President and Lewinsky. It detailed grounds for the impeachment of the President, opening with the blunt comment: '... the Office of the Independent Counsel ... hereby submits substantial and credible information that President William Jefferson Clinton committed acts that may constitute grounds for an impeachment'.[19] It made clear the areas where Starr considered the President's activity and statements to be suspect. Eleven instances were identified as potentially impeachable offenses, although the final decision was to be made by the House of Representatives, that body being granted the power of impeachment by the Constitution. Starr charged that the President lied under oath in both the Jones deposition and the Grand Jury testimony and obstructed justice in seeking to conceal his affair from investigators. He had also attempted to corruptly influence the recollections of other witnesses in the investigation and had abused the authority of the presidential office.[20] These charges were collated from a variety of

sources, and are discussed further in Chapter 4. Many of Starr's allegations appeared in a modified form once the House of Representatives
adopted articles of impeachment against the President.

Following receipt of the *Starr Report* and supplementary material on
9 September, the House began to review the evidence before it. This
was a delicate and sensitive matter and the House Judiciary
Committee held a pivotal role in deciding whether the evidence warranted the action of impeachment. One step undertaken immediately
was to release a significant amount of material into the public
domain. The House released the Starr referral on 11 September and a
week later the Judiciary Committee released Clinton's Grand Jury
videotape and upwards of 3,000 pages of documentary evidence relating to the scandal, including photographs of Lewinsky's stained
dress.[21] This deluge of information both helped and hindered
Clinton's damage limitation efforts. On the one hand the public faced
information overload. Trying to uncover the detail of the scandal and
evaluate the interpretations of Clinton's activities by Kenneth Starr
was decidedly difficult. Additionally, the sexual nature of the descrip-
tive narrative provoked a debate about whether it was in the public
interest to openly discuss the matter and whether there existed a
legitimate need to release all documents in an uncensored fashion.
This served to divert attention from the legal charges and onto the
issues of sex, morality and censorship. For the White House, the
nature and scale of the information release was marginally advantageous. It could, for example, portray Starr as a man preoccupied with
sex and the private life of President Clinton, and cast the whole
matter as an illegitimate witchhunt. However, there were complications. The release of the videotape of Clinton's Grand Jury testimony
was troublesome. The visual image of the President trying to answer
embarrassing questions, and reading a prepared statement admitting
a relationship with Lewinsky removed the aura of the presidential
office and depicted him as a particularly evasive and calculating individual, one who had relied on semantics to uphold a tenuous case.
Nevertheless, some believed that the videotape aided Clinton's position. Tom Korologos, who worked for President Nixon, contended: 'I
thought he did a masterful job.'[22] Thereafter, there existed the possibility of a defection from the President's position by members of the
Democratic party. Having accepted his declarations of innocence
about the affair, many were alienated by his about-turn and his
muted apology. This did not enhance the President's position, and
relations with Democrats in the Congress threatened to fall into a

state of disrepair at this sensitive time. For example, Senator Ernest F. Hollings (D-SC) declared: 'We're fed up ... The behavior, the dishonesty of the president is unacceptable and we'll see with the [Starr] report what course the Congress will take.'[23] With the documentary information in the public realm, the public, at the same time as the Congress, had an opportunity to evaluate Clinton's guilt or innocence. In 1996 the Republican party had maintained control of the Congress, despite the retention of the White House by the Democrats. With the House Judiciary Committee in the hands of the Republican party there existed the likelihood that impeachment proceedings, based upon the charges laid before the House by Starr, would commence.

An overview of the period between the public exposure of the affair and the onset of impeachment proceedings in the Congress highlights the ebbs and flows in the fortunes of President Clinton. Having initially denied a relationship, and encouraged close political aides to believe that one had not taken place, Clinton found that the weight of evidence suggested otherwise. The fact that he was the only person in the White House who knew the full version of events – bar, in the latter stages perhaps, his secretary Betty Currie – placed a particularly heavy burden upon the President. What remains especially difficult to fathom was that he not only misinformed his political aides about the matter, denying a relationship with 'that woman', but he also denied it to his family. His wife, who advanced a vociferous defense of her husband in January 1998, committed herself to a defensive position which was, with hindsight, erroneous. It overtly highlighted tensions within the Clintons' marriage.

This period of the scandal, the procedural phase, contained two distinct sections: a denial period from January 1998 to 17 August 1998, followed by an admission period from 17 August 1998 to the end of the scandal in February 1999. These two periods contained different aspects of damage limitation, and each cast the presidential office and President Clinton in a different light. Clinton's conduct of the defense of his office is questionable, particularly in the denial phase. The damage limitation techniques employed at that time rested upon the stonewall and denial of an affair, in parallel with an effort to cast Starr's investigation as excessive and intrusive. Alongside the activity by the President as an individual, lay an effort by his legal and political teams to endorse the declarations of their leader, and to ensure that the scandal did not wrench itself away from the control of the White House.

Damage limitation: the lost cause

The following sections examine the President's efforts to coordinate a damage limitation exercise. Three specific areas are of interest. Firstly, the statements made by Clinton are evaluated. The frequency of his comments, the nature of his denials, and the about-turn in August 1998 encapsulated the predicament faced by the Chief Executive. Given the nature of his comments in the Jones deposition and tortured discussion about the precise meaning of words in the Grand Jury testimony, public declarations by the President assumed significant weight. They initially attuned the American public to believe that allegations of an affair were mere fabrications. The change in Clinton's rhetoric once it became clear that an affair had taken place, and that he might have lied about it, reflected his concern about a further decline of his already low credibility. What the President said, and when he said it, were therefore elements of extreme importance in shaping congressional and public opinion.

Secondly, the President's efforts to coordinate his administration's damage limitation strategy are considered. Although the President could contain the attack upon his credibility to some extent, he nevertheless required the assistance and support of aides within his administration who might endorse his messages of innocence and provide much needed backup. The President required both political and legal assistance to contend with the Congress and the Independent Counsel, as well as a public relations team which would seek to suppress the charges against him in the public realm. He rapidly assembled an expansive damage control team to bolster his cause. As an added bonus, Hillary Clinton emerged as a pivotal damage limitation coordinator, making prominent public statements and several high profile claims of conspiratorial attacks upon her husband. This focused attention upon those investigating the President and served to identify partisanship as a feature of this scandal. However, Clinton's aides found, much to their frustration and embarrassment, that misleading claims by the President that there had been no sexual relationship undermined the administration's efforts to present a unified and cohesive front in 1998.

Thirdly, Clinton's relations with the Congress between January and September 1998 are reviewed. As much as the impeachment proceedings instigated against the President in late 1998 highlighted institutional tension between the branches of government, they had more complex foundations. As leader of his party, the President could hope, in early 1998, for some support from his partisan allies on Capitol Hill. That was evident until he changed his version of events following his August Grand Jury testimony. Thereafter, it proved to be an arduous task to reclaim the trust and respect of even his own party members in the Congress, and the escalating struggle here was a central feature of the President's damage limitation challenge. This indeed was a vital area for the President to consider, for if it were left unattended, party defections from his position could lead to a difficult scenario, one witnessed by President Nixon some years earlier, where votes in the Congress endorsing impeachment could stack up against him.

(i) Clinton's public statements

As mentioned previously in this chapter, Clinton's public statements were of considerable importance in conditioning the American public, the Congress, and his own White House aides to his version of events. Although allegations of an affair were forthcoming from various media outlets, Linda Tripp, and investigative journalists, it was the President who could exploit the prominence afforded by his office to set the record straight and assert that there had, or had not, been any relationship with Lewinsky. It was impossible to avoid the matter altogether, especially in its initial stages, as it dominated the news agenda and threatened to overshadow the important State of the Union address. If Clinton failed to address the speculation appearing in the newspapers he could be cast as evasive, and of failing to assert his leadership. This, in turn, might be capitalized upon by his opponents, leading to further political complications. It is important to recall that by the time the President began to issue his public denials, the Jones deposition had already taken place, the Independent Counsel had received an expanded mandate for his investigation, and Tripp had informed investigators of the existence of a semen-stained dress, among other things. Even though matters had turned decisively against Clinton in a private and legal forum, the public stage was still unoccupied and, initially at least, the President endeavored to legitimize his position.

Following the unsubstantiated allegations of a presidential affair, Clinton was immediately asked to comment by news organizations. Initial media focus was to have been on the content and meaning of the State of the Union address, due to be given in the last week of January 1998, but the Lewinsky matter dominated the news agenda. In a telephone interview conducted by Roll Call on 21 January 1998, at the very time the Lewinsky story was breaking publicly, the President outlined his strategy to contend with the revelations, one familiar from

Table 3.2 January–September 1998: key public statements by Clinton on the Lewinsky scandal

Date	Interview/event
21 January	Roll Call Interview
	PBS News Hour
22 January	Remarks during Arafat interview
26 January	Remarks following Education Statement
6 February	Joint Press Conference with British Prime Minister Blair
5 March	Exchange with Reporters
11 March	Exchange with Reporters
3 April	Exchange with Reporters
30 April	Press Conference
6 May	Joint Press Conference with Italian Prime Minister Prodi
17 August	Statement following Grand Jury Testimony
4 September	Exchange with Reporters
11 September	Remarks at Prayer Breakfast
16 September	Joint Press Conference with Czech President Havel

the Whitewater affair and other presidential scandals involving Clinton. He asserted, 'I'm going to cooperate with this investigation' and at a later juncture stated: 'But because the investigation is going on and because I don't know what is out – what's going to be asked of me, I think I need to cooperate, answer the questions, but I think it's important for me to make it clear what is not. And then, at the appropriate time, I'll try to answer what is.'[24] In many respects, in his first comments, Clinton portrayed himself, arguably accurately, as a passive observer, contending that it would be the media that would decide the prominence and magnitude of the story. He stated: 'But you guys will have to make that decision [on the importance of the Lewinsky charges]. The press will make that decision.'[25] Clinton immediately found that the press had indeed set its own agenda. On the same day as the Roll Call interview he had an altogether more high-profile appearance. On the PBS *News Hour* show, experienced journalist Jim Lehrer began his interview by addressing the Lewinsky matter, and returned to it twice more to try and entice further information from the President. In terms of agenda-setting this did not prove to be advantageous for Clinton, nor did it assist in his efforts to lay out the administration's policy objectives. Lehrer garnered surprisingly candid denials from the President. When pressed, Clinton asserted that there had been no improper relationship, and when asked to define the exact meaning of the term responded: 'Well, I think you know what it means. It means that there is not a sexual relationship, an improper sexual relationship, or any other kind of improper relationship.'[26] This was an altogether more broad and expansive denial than had previously been forthcoming. Nor was this comment denying an improper relationship an accident, as the President went on to repeat it several times during the interview. The familiar message of cooperation came repeatedly to the fore.[27] Likewise, the President stressed that he would not be diverted by the familiar accusation of scandal emanating from the media and the Independent Counsel: 'But I've been living with this sort of thing for a long time. And my experience has been, unfortunately, sometimes when one charge dies, another one just lifts up to take its place ... I owe it to the American people to put it in a little box and keep working for them.'[28] Whitewater had clearly played a significant role in attuning the President to the mechanisms of scandal politics, and its impact was ironically beneficial in helping Clinton to deal with the Lewinsky scandal revelations.

The President's damage limitation strategy was identifiable within a week of the exposure of the affair to the American people. It followed three paths, designed to court public sentiment and diminish the visibility of this potentially damaging episode. Firstly, he refuted allegations of an affair or of any untoward relationship with Lewinsky. The language he employed was deliberately vague, and left many questions unanswered as to the precise nature of the liaison. This was understandable given the plethora of questions he faced when testifying during the Jones deposition. The second communications strategy called for a full investigation of the facts. This was clearly a political measure designed to disassociate the President from the ongoing events. It cast him as an outside observer, unsure of the exact nature of the relationship. Given that the only two who knew the precise details of the contact were Clinton and Lewinsky, the commitment of the President to an unbridled investigation, and his pledge to assist in the uncovering of the facts, appears superficial at best. A third strategy pledged commitment to a national agenda and sought to nullify media concentration upon the Lewinsky scandal. This was profitable at the time of the State of the Union address, and was worthwhile, particularly in the latter stages of the scandal, when the American public appeared to have grown weary of the event and wished to consider other more pertinent political matters. Following these lines of attack the President attempted to stifle the initial flurry of speculation about his liaison with Monica Lewinsky.

Clinton made several forceful denials about Lewinsky in the prelude to the 27 January State of the Union address. On 22 January, when meeting with Yasser Arafat of the Palestine Liberation Organization, he was again confronted by the Lewinsky scandal, and went through the motions of pledging cooperation and stating he would 'comply' with the investigation.[29] The most memorable and widely replayed of Clinton's early denials occurred in advance of his congressional address, as he tried to stop the scandal from overshadowing the legislative agenda. Clinton's frustrations came to the fore following an address on after-school child care on 26 January 1998.[30] Clearly irritated at the persistent questioning about Lewinsky when he wished to discuss other issues, he made an impromptu statement:

> I want you to listen to me ... I'm going to say this again, I did not have sexual relations with that woman, Miss Lewinsky. I never told anybody to lie, not a single time – never. These allegations are false. And I need to go back to work for the American people.[31]

The irrefutable nature of Clinton's comment indicated his desire to stifle speculation, but it also served to draw added attention to the matter, as the President had now made his public position explicitly clear. Given the nature of the relationship, and the evidence in the hands of the OIC which could prove that one had taken place, this was a gamble, instigated to try and deal with short-term interests. It should be noted however that Clinton adhered to the term 'sexual relations' in this declaration, and this was in keeping with the terminology agreed to at the Jones deposition when a relationship with Lewinsky was discussed. Clinton would later argue that he was justified in claiming that sexual relations, as he understood that term, had never taken place between the two.

The State of the Union address was welcome relief for the President when contrasted with the terse encounters with the news media in the preceding week. He could set the agenda, and as there was no intention of drawing further unwanted attention to the Lewinsky scandal, this was an ideal opportunity for Clinton to outline political issues on his own terms. However, as much as he wished to draw political attention to the legislative agenda, the media speculated about whether he would directly confront the Lewinsky matter. Despite the President's intentions, he was, even in this forum, only partially in control of his own destiny, as *Congressional Quarterly* reported:

> For weeks the White House has been orchestrating a campaign of previews and leaks to build interest [in the State of the Union

address]. Then, in a flurry of headlines about an alleged affair with a 21-year-old intern, Clinton's news value quadrupled. The television audience will watch him coldly, looking suspiciously for bags under his eyes and second-guessing every confident gesture. Routine camera shots of Hillary in the gallery and starry-eyed pages in the aisles will take on second meanings.[32]

The President, unsurprisingly, made no mention of Lewinsky, and would do so infrequently from this time on, unless asked direct questions by journalists.[33] The speech gave Clinton some hope in the midst of an emergent crisis. Playing the political card, he reminded the nation why it elected him for a second time and what he still intended to do to fulfil his promises. This partly explains why his job approval ratings rose and failed to reflect the ensuing scandal. Even Republicans in the Congress had to grudgingly accept that the State of the Union address had been beneficial, rather than detrimental, to the fortunes of the President. Senator Robert F. Bennett (R-Utah) stated prophetically: 'I think the American people have come to the conclusion that they do not want to drive the President out of office just because he's not faithful to his wife, and they turn off all the rest of it.' Trent Lott (R-Miss), Senate Majority Leader, applauded Clinton's ability to shrug off the serious allegations leveled against him: 'The guy is incredible in his ability to come in there and act like everything is just hunky-dory, like there's nothing going on in the world but that speech.'[34] In many respects the content of the speech was that which would have been expected had the scandal not erupted. However, the media, in particular, looked to the scandal as a benchmark for this period, and thus the central focus of Clinton's message was somewhat obscured. Following the address Clinton took his agenda to the country, with a brief trip away from the cauldron of Washington to promote his legislative program. This served to dissipate a siege mentality at the White House. Clinton appeared at La Crosse, Wisconsin, and in Champaign, Illinois, and predictably made no mention of the furore about Lewinsky, although one member of the audience in Wisconsin displayed an 'impeach' sign as a timely reminder of the gravity of the situation. An intense travel schedule was a feature of Clinton's strategy during the weeks following the exposure of the scandal, and permitted him to escape from the Washington press corps and consider the issues which mattered to Americans across the country.[35]

The President avoided comment on Lewinsky, when it was in his power to do so. To justify this silence, lest he be thought to be hiding from a major issue, he claimed it was unwise to comment while a major investigation was ongoing, a strategy reflective of those employed by Reagan and Nixon during Iran-Contra and Watergate. On 6 February Clinton spoke at an annual prayer breakfast, but made no mention of the scandal to the religious audience.[36] The respite did not last however as, on the same day, he faced a press conference, jointly held with British Prime Minister Tony Blair. Clinton was pressed to state the precise nature of the relationship with Lewinsky, and to counter allegations that he had asked her to lie under oath. His answer was in keeping with the developing White House strategy at this time:

> But this investigation is going on, and you know what the rules for it are. And I just think as long as it is going on, I should not comment on specific questions, because there's one, then there's another, then there's another. It's better to let the investigation go on and have me do my job and focus on my public responsibilities, and let this thing play out its course. That's what I think I should do, and that's what I intend to do.[37]

Blair explicitly expressed his support for the President and made clear that he would stand by Clinton at this difficult time.[38] This too was to be a recurring feature of 1998, with a host of world leaders and international diplomats, such as South African President Mandela and UN Secretary General Kofi Annan, making clear their admiration for the President, and highlighting the political accomplishments of the Clinton administration over several years.[39] This aided the President. It stressed the political as opposed to the legal, and drew public attention back to conventional politics and away from scandal. It also made clear that, as much as the scandal might burden American domestic politics, it carried little weight overseas, at least in political terms, and in this area the President could carry on relatively unhindered.

Through the early spring of 1998 Clinton kept a particularly low profile. Tensions between the President and the media corps became tense as a result. The failure of the President to offer any detail of his affair with Lewinsky or even to address the charges, combined with the desire of the media to get at the heart of the scandal, created a scenario whereby a key participant appeared wholly divorced from scandal proceedings. For example, an exasperated reporter asked, 'Sir, you never answered the important questions that I think a lot of people out there would like to hear you on ...', only to be rebuffed by the President.[40] Likewise, in early April, the President held firm when asked about the

Independent Counsel's investigation: I'm not going to comment on that.'[41] The most opportune moment for the media to interrogate the President on the scandal appeared to be when he scheduled a press conference. Even here, when the media could set the agenda, the President was reticent and gave very little away as to his involvement in, or knowledge of, the scandal revelations being reported by the media. Time and again he cast himself as the interested observer, detached and removed from the crime scene, and as eager as everyone else to find out what happened. His frustrations were however obvious when asked about a possible relationship with Lewinsky: 'I have answered it repeatedly and have nothing to add to my former answer. I have repeatedly said what the answer to that question is.'[42] The major brunt of the questions were being answered at this time by the President's aides, and with the attendant possibility that he might be subpoenaed to testify before a Grand Jury there was little reason to have him field extensive media questions. There were however drawbacks to this strategy. It made Clinton appear, at least in the eyes of the media, unforthcoming and somewhat evasive. It was also a problematic long-term strategy, as once he decided to be more open about the precise nature of his relationship, his previous refusal to answer questions made it look as though he had engaged in a cover-up lasting several months.

17 August Grand Jury appearance

Clinton's major opportunity to resolve conjecture about the Lewinsky scandal came when he reluctantly agreed to testify before the Grand Jury, and did so on 17 August 1998. Prior to his appearance, speculation abounded about what he would say, and moreover, the ramifications any candid admission would have upon his political and legal destiny. The President's appearance was of the utmost importance in deciding his fortunes. If he denied an affair then he would contradict the word of Monica Lewinsky, who had already been offered immunity from prosecution in return for her testimony. Hard physical evidence also indicated that at least one intimate encounter had taken place. As Clinton had provided a DNA sample then he knew that his case, in the form of an outright denial, was untenable. His primary aim, therefore, was to narrow the credibility gap which had developed between his testimony during the Jones deposition and the evidence which now suggested that he had in fact had sexual relations with Monica Lewinsky. He had to achieve this without committing perjury and flatly contradicting his deposition in the Jones case.

Dee Dee Myers, former press secretary to Clinton, anticipated his maneuverings in advance of his Grand Jury appearance: 'He lays a trap for himself with language, then tries to get out of it with more language. He's a great communicator, but the [Lewinsky] problem is not about verbal activity.'[43] Similarly, Paul Greenberg, a journalist who coined the term 'Slick Willie', identified Clinton's strategy: 'He's very adept at leaving an audience with the impression that is most advantageous to him at the time, without violating the truth in some semantic sense but violating ... it in any other sense.'[44] Guesswork by the media was not appreciated by the White House, the testimony assuming added weight as substantial airtime and column inches were devoted to its potential ramifications. The President's lawyer, David E. Kendall, issued a dismissive statement: 'There is apparently an enormous amount of groundless speculation about the President's testimony tomorrow ... The truth is the truth. Period. And that's how the President will testify.'[45]

Clinton's testimony to the Grand Jury, delivered via a video link, was the severest test of his version of events thus far, as he was once again under oath to speak truthfully.[46] The testimony proved to be difficult and arduous. He read a prepared statement and then, under questioning, covered several areas already familiar from the Jones deposition; the nature of his relationship with Lewinsky, a definition of sexual relations, the exchange of gifts and material between the two, and whether he had endeavored to influence the testimony of Lewinsky or any other witnesses to the affair. In his prepared statement, Clinton immediately confessed that there had been 'intimate contact' between himself and Lewinsky:

> When I was alone with Ms. Lewinsky on certain occasions in early 1996 and once in early 1997, I engaged in conduct that was wrong. These encounters did not consist of sexual intercourse. They did not constitute sexual relations as I understood that term to be defined at my January 17th, 1998 deposition. But they did involve inappropriate intimate contact.

It was clear that, on this occasion, there could be no concerted or purposeful effort to be economical with the truth. Sufficient evidence was now in the hands of the prosecutors to force him to openly admit a relationship with Lewinsky. In this sense the relationship, and the procedural phase of this scandal, moved from a period of denial, to one of admission. Now the President changed course and, rather than

stonewalling on questions about Lewinsky, confessed to an inappropriate relationship. He consistently argued, in his Grand Jury testimony
and in public, that his previous statements under oath had been truthful, and his error lay in misleading his wife and close confidants by not
being sufficiently open with them. There were additional problems for
the President. As much as he wished to use the Grand Jury appearance
as a threshold to put the Lewinsky scandal behind him, Independent
Counsel Starr used it as an opportunity to probe for contradictions
with Clinton's January deposition and Lewinsky's testimony about the
relationship.[47] Starr found evidence to suggest that the President lied to
the Grand Jury on 17 August in several areas. Firstly, Clinton testified
that he believed that oral sex was not covered by the definition of
sexual relations as outlined in the Jones case. Secondly, he lied about
whether he had touched Lewinsky in an intimate manner, and thirdly,
he stated that a relationship with Lewinsky began in 1996 whereas
Starr understood it to have started in 1995. These interpretations,
among others, were advanced by Starr as grounds to recommend
impeachment.

Following the testimony, and anticipating that his admission of a
relationship with Lewinsky would be released, or would be leaked,
Clinton addressed the nation. This speech was intended not only for
the American public, but also for those on Capitol Hill and at the
White House, with whom Clinton had been less than forthcoming.
This was a critical address, carefully constructed so as to maintain
Clinton's assertions that he had been truthful, if perhaps inadvertently
misleading, during previous statements under oath. Clinton spoke, not
from the familiar presidential forum of the Oval Office, the traditional
location for addressing the nation, but from the Map Room in the
White House, the very room in which he had given his Grand Jury testimony.[48] Clinton began by asserting that he had 'answered their [OIC]
questions truthfully'.[49] He then shrugged off the trappings of the presidential office and cast himself as an ordinary American citizen who
had suffered from a 'critical lapse in judgement'.[50] He declared that he
had complied with the law at all times, but had not volunteered all the
necessary information. What threatened to be particularly injurious
was the likelihood of a demise in his credibility, a matter he confronted in an explicit and direct manner:

> But I told the grand jury today and I say to you now that at no time
> did I ask anyone to lie, to hide or destroy evidence or to take any
> other unlawful action. I know that my public comments and my

silence about this matter gave a false impression. I misled people, including even my wife. I deeply regret that.[51]

This speech contained unbridled attacks on the investigation by the Independent Counsel, which helped to focus public attention on a wider subject than that of individual morality. Clinton pleaded for an end to the investigation, remonstrating: 'This has gone on too long, cost too much and hurt too many innocent people.'[52] In closing, he asked that the American people put the scandal to the back of their minds and cast aside negative impressions: 'I ask you to turn away from the spectacle of the past seven months, to repair the fabric of our national discourse, and to return our attention to all the challenges and all the promise of the next American century.'[53] The speech was brief, left several questions unanswered, and left doubts about exactly what Clinton had actually done; after all, the transcripts of the Grand Jury testimony were not immediately available to the American people. With respect to damage limitation, Clinton attempted to explain his silence by citing several motivating factors:

- A wish to avoid personal embarrassment
- A desire to protect his family
- The fact that the Lewinsky investigation was part of a 'politically inspired lawsuit'

These explanations rested mainly upon personal considerations, and blurred the line between Clinton's personal life and the political issues which now emerged as a result of his admissions. There were no words of apology to the American people and little to suggest sincere regret.[54] Rather, Clinton avoided a definitive explanation of why he had stonewalled for several months and had attempted to use the powers of the presidential office to prevent aides and Secret Service officials from testifying. His damage limitation intentions were clear; he aimed to protect his legal standing and trust that his political performance outwith the realm of scandal would outweigh the damage afflicted upon his credibility and integrity. Accordingly, Clinton maintained before the Grand Jury, and before the American people, that his responses during the Jones investigation were always true, and that the questions as he understood them were answered accurately.[55]

Beyond a media clamor for the new revelations, there existed a wholly different atmosphere. The President's televised statement was delivered largely in a political vacuum. The First Lady and Chelsea

Clinton were both absent, the Vice-President was on holiday in Hawaii, and several of the major Republican figures in the Congress, including House Speaker Newt Gingrich (R-Ga) and Senate Majority Leader Trent Lott (R-Miss), kept an uncommonly low profile. Moreover, the Chairman of the House Judiciary Committee, Henry Hyde (R-Ill) was unavailable for comment, and senior Democrats, predictably, were generally reluctant to volunteer rash opinions on the presidential u-turn.[56]

In the days following the address several individuals issued statements of condemnation, affirmation or regret about the President's action. Vice-President Gore declared his continuing faith in the President and emphasized his desire to see the back of the scandal. Trent Lott was predictably critical of Clinton: 'The President, not the Independent Counsel, must bear the full responsibility for his lengthy relationship with Monica Lewinsky and the pain he has caused his family, his friends, his supporters and the American people since January.'[57] These considered comments, coming after a brief delay, were however outweighed by the immediate rush to judgement by the media and several members of the Congress in the aftermath of the President's speech, as outlined in the congressional relations section of this chapter.

Clinton avoided the media and political spotlight by going on a brief vacation following his televised confessional speech. This permitted him to leave Washington and allow a media debate to rage without him having to face numerous questions about the precise nature of the inappropriate relationship. It also granted him, in accordance with his emphasis upon the delicate and sensitive nature of his private life, time alone with his wife and daughter and allowed him to consider revision to his damage limitation strategy in the light of the changed political circumstances. Clinton appeared at Worcester, Massachusetts, on 27 August 1998 and ended his temporary silence. In keeping with his strategy before the 17 August address, he remained reticent on the Lewinsky matter and considered political concerns such as education, terrorism, and the problems posed by Hurricane Bonnie.[58] A few protesters attempted to raise the Lewinsky issue, but Clinton ignored them and used the occasion as 'a tentative step toward normalcy ... [sic]'.[59] He continued the new phase in his credibility war in early September 1998 when he openly apologized for his conduct with Lewinsky during a photo opportunity with Irish Prime Minister Bertie Ahern. He stated: 'I've already said that I made a big mistake, it was indefensible and I'm sorry about it. So I have nothing else to say except that I can't disagree with anyone else who wants to be critical of what I have already acknowledged is indefensible.'[60] Following brief apologetic comments during a fund-raising tour in advance of the congressional mid-term elections, the President again addressed the Lewinsky matter at a breakfast with religious leaders on 11 September, an occasion which provided a perfect opportunity to exploit a confessional scenario and emphasize repentance.[61] It coincided with the public release of the *Starr Report*. He read a prepared statement, and hinted at a revised political and legal defense. He conceded: 'I agree with those who have said that in my first statement after I testified I was not contrite enough. I don't think there is a fancy way to say that I have sinned.'[62] Playing to his audience and aware of the attention his statements would receive from the media and members of Congress, the President expressed his regret in a forthright manner:

> It is important to me that everybody who has been hurt know that the sorrow I feel is genuine: first and most important, my family, also my friends, my staff, my Cabinet, Monica Lewinsky and her family, and the American people. I have asked all for their forgiveness.[63]

Clinton's emotive recitation to a select audience exploited a prime public relations opportunity. As much as those in the room were important, the viewing public held as much, if not more, importance. While public opinion was not the sole consideration, it had a significant part to play in this scandal, and Clinton's repeated apologies served to ensure that Americans would clearly understand that he now acknowledged his mistake. He pinpointed three areas which were deserving of his attention. Firstly, he would ask his 'lawyers to mount a vigorous legal defense'. Secondly, he intended to 'continue on a path of repentance', and, thirdly, he would devote his time and attention to leading the nation and improving the fortunes of the country.[64] The modified strategy emphasized a more apologetic tone, but the desire of the President to contest the interpretations reached by Kenneth Starr continued unabated, as did his focus upon the public policy agenda. Naturally, the advantage now lay with the Independent Counsel, and the political impact of his referral to the House of Representatives reflected this fact. Nevertheless, the President was intent on capitalizing upon his reputation as the Comeback Kid, and had clearly decided to fight his corner in both the legal and political forums.

In a press conference, jointly held with Czech Republic President Havel on 16 September, Clinton was again questioned by the media about the Lewinsky matter, particularly about his ability to lead the nation. An obvious concern was whether he would face impeachment proceedings, and, at the least, emerge from the crisis as a lame-duck President. Clinton argued: 'I have never stopped leading this country in foreign affairs in this entire year, and I never will.'[65] He then reiterated the apologies which now characterized his damage limitation strategy:

> I have said for a month now that I did something that was wrong ... I also said then, [at the prayer breakfast] and I will say again, that I think that the right thing for our country and the right thing for all people concerned is not to get mired in all the detail here but to focus – for me to focus on what I did, to acknowledge it, to atone for it, and then to work on my family, where I still have a lot of work to do, difficult work, and to lead this country, to deal with the agenda before us ...[66]

Starr's referral to the House of Representatives was submitted on 9 September 1998, and released to the public on 11 September. On 18 September the House Judiciary Committee decided to release documentary evidence, including a videotape of the President's Grand Jury Testimony.[67] This was available for public consumption on 21 September. In all of these episodes Clinton was essentially powerless to affect the decisions and actions of others. Damage limitation strategies had only a limited impact and Starr and the Congress had significant leeway to act without direct interference from the President. The release of the Grand Jury videotape produced little change in the overall development of the scandal as the *Washington Post* reported:

> There was an obvious sense of relief among some Democrats that the release of Clinton's testimony had not produced another moment of devastation for the President – or for them as they look to the midterm elections. But at the same time, there was no indication that the airing of the videotape had any effect on slowing the momentum that has been building for a formal impeachment inquiry in the House Judiciary Committee.[68]

The videotape showed Clinton at the top of his game, and may actually have contributed towards his damage limitation effort in a constructive manner. The *Washington Post* observed: 'the President's videotaped appearance represented the most sustained – and, his aides now assert, the most effective – defense to date of his behavior in the Monica S. Lewinsky controversy'.[69] Clinton appeared to be a besieged underdog, assailed by aggressive interrogators and subject to prying questions about his private life. Although this did not cause undue damage in the public realm, the public relations effort was, at this juncture, of secondary importance, as political attention focused increasingly upon the House Judiciary Committee, a committee in Republican hands and one which would ultimately decide whether the President would face impeachment proceedings in the Congress.

In the period from January to September 1998 President Clinton advanced his case in the Lewinsky matter on few occasions. His strategy was underpinned by legal and political considerations. Firstly, until August 1998, with unspecified evidence in the hands of the Independent Counsel, his aim was to covertly stonewall, yet overtly promise complicity with the investigations. He cast himself as an impatient observer, eager to find out what had occurred, and placed himself in the position of scandal observer, as opposed to that of scandal participant. This position was, in effect, a misleading one, as only Clinton and Lewinsky actually knew the detail of the affair and how each had approached the Jones case during late 1997 and early 1998. For the President to cast himself as a passive observer, while at the same time seeking to assert executive privilege was, at best, a public relations exercise designed to portray a business-as-usual approach within the White House. This was sustainable until it became clear that in the legal forum a weight of evidence had accumulated which made its continuation untenable. Thereafter, with his 17 August testimony before the Grand Jury as the turning point, the damage limitation strategy employed by the President altered. Instead of maintaining his claims of innocence, Clinton argued that the nation should accept his confessions of wrongdoing. This was a wholly different President, one who threw himself at the mercy of an American public which had rightly assumed that a relationship had gone on for some time and, more importantly, had grown increasingly tired of the scandal. New revelations were of no real surprise, and consequently opinion-poll statistics did not alter significantly as a consequence of the events in August, nor as a result of the evidence uncovered by the Independent Counsel.

The damage limitation strategy employed by Clinton was a clear continuation of that employed during the Whitewater episode, and given that it had worked satisfactorily in that instance, there was little reason to initially look to a radical alternative. Scandal issues were sidetracked and the President concentrated on pursuing a conventional public policy agenda. His aides thereafter assumed the burden of scandal, albeit armed with incomplete information about the true nature of the affair. This was attributable to the decisions, actions, and words of the President himself. It was he, and he alone, who knew the precise nature of the relationship with Lewinsky and his guidance on how to proceed following the Jones deposition thrust the administration into a damage control crisis.

Historically, Clinton's efforts to resolve the matter had more in keeping with the scandal experiences of Nixon than they did with those of Reagan.[70] Reagan had contended during Iran-Contra, somewhat dubiously, that he had remained aloof from operations, and thus was not wholly liable for their consequences. Nixon, by contrast, had personally orchestrated the evolution of Watergate. Senator Robert Byrd, former Democratic Leader in the Senate, compared Watergate and the Lewinsky episode: 'Former President Nixon, in an earlier tragedy for the nation and for all of us who were here and lived through it, tried the same thing – delay, delay, delay and counterattack, attack, attack ... Time seems to be turning backwards in its flight. And many of the mistakes that President Nixon made are being made all over again.'[71] In Iran-Contra, hard incriminating evidence to implicate the President in criminal wrongdoing was not forthcoming. In Watergate, via the Oval Office tapes, evidence existed to prove that the President had lied, and played a vital role in bringing the matter to the level of impeachment in the Congress. Clinton's efforts to disassociate himself from events, and to accommodate an investigation, were thrown into disrepair by the fact that Monica Lewinsky had kept a dress for some considerable time, and hard evidence, including tapes, was available to prosecutors. Clinton had few damage limitation alternatives by the end of August but to admit a relationship with Lewinsky and contend that the previous questions asked of him were answered truthfully. This was hardly a premeditated defense, but rather emerged as a consequence of Clinton's decision to contest the Jones case, his attempts to resist Starr's investigation, and his failure to voluntarily declare the precise nature of his inappropriate relationship.

(ii) The Clinton administration: protecting the president

In conjunction with the public proclamations of the President came the broader thrust of the administration damage limitation war, and the efforts of presidential aides to downplay the importance and meaning of the scandal. Individually, the President could only contain the scandal to a limited extent, his words and actions alone being insufficient to set an alternate political agenda. The First Lady, legal and political advisers, and a number of individuals came to the aid of the Chief Executive, albeit when the scandal had broken and had achieved considerable momentum. They advanced his version of events to a waiting public, only to find that, by August, circumstances had changed and they had committed themselves to a leader whose version of events was, at best, misleading. Consequently, many of Clinton's aides had to retract previous comments, yet remain visibly loyal to the President.

Clinton initially dealt with the breaking news stories about Lewinsky on his own terms and asserted that there had been no sexual relationship. Close aides were informed that the allegations were a fabrication, and discussion ensued about how they might be refuted and their political impact minimized.[72] The lack of truthful and frank information from the President naturally impeded the ability of the White House staff to rally to his cause, and left many unsure as to the exact nature of Clinton's relationship with Lewinsky. One senior White House official, cited by the *New York Times*, complained: 'Nobody here knows what's going on.'[73] One of the first to become involved in alleviating the crisis was the First Lady, obviously a close, if not the closest, confidant of the President. In this instance she was merely another individual who was not fully versed in the facts. In the short term, however, she emerged as one of the leading damage control advisers for the President, having endured accusations of philandering by her husband on previous occasions.[74] A former White House official stressed the positive and negative effects of Hillary Clinton's management style: 'Her instincts are when there's a crisis to come forward, if she feels that it's not being handled right ... It's both good and bad in terms of staff. It still is a little disconcerting when the first lady comes into a meeting and tells them what to do.'[75] At this time there was a noticeable absence of Clinton's former aides who had steered him through his previous political and personal predicaments, the so-called 'rapid response' team.[76] Many aides had moved on to other jobs and left the administration, including senior adviser George Stephanopoulos, troubleshooter David Gergen, and press spokesperson Dee Dee Myers. Clinton still had several senior aides upon whom he could call for assistance, among them external adviser James Carville and White House press spokesman Mike McCurry, both of whom had a weighty task before them. They lined up alongside the President's legal team, principally Robert Bennett and David E. Kendall, and attempted to refute the accusations leveled at the President. They also waged an offensive campaign against the OIC which, they believed, was engaged in a vendetta against this particular President. Clinton also called upon the assistance of former aides to bolster the defense of his presidency. Mickey Kantor, a former US Trade Representative and Commerce Secretary, arrived in late January 1998 to assist in the damage limitation effort.[77] A key task for Kantor was to integrate the legal and political strands of the President's defense, as there threatened to be conflict between the President's legal and political advisers about how best to proceed. One anonymous official at the White House was forced to concede that Kantor's appearance was hardly a confidence-boosting measure: 'You can tell we're in deep, deep trouble when Mickey is called off the bench.'[78] By mid-February 1998 the President had assembled an expansive team of trusted political and legal advisers to contend with this crisis, a point noted by the national media. *U.S. News and World Report* observed: 'The sheer size and scope of Clinton's crisis management operation are unparalleled in presidential history ...'.[79]

The objective of the White House damage limitation team in the aftermath of the Lewinsky revelations was to coordinate a response which would allow a legal and political defense to be advanced in unison. This proved to be problematic from the outset, with a legal need to consider how the evidence might be best marshaled to defend the President against the Independent Counsel investigation. Politically, it was necessary to address the possibility of a slump in public opinion statistics, the reaction of members of Congress, and the attendant likelihood of impeachment proceedings. Intra-branch considerations and conflict were an impediment to a smooth and efficient damage limitation process.

Clinton's newly assembled damage limitation team were overshadowed in late January 1998 by Hillary Clinton. She appeared on national television to conduct a vigorous defense of her husband.[80] In the absence of frequent appearances by the President, aside from the brief and forceful exoneration on 26 January 1998, a more detailed discussion by the First Lady allowed a greater understanding of prevailing sentiment at the White House. Although Hillary Clinton considered several themes, from the state of her marriage to the Whitewater deal, her comments on Lewinsky were of particular note. Her damage control strategies relied firmly upon her husband's admonitions:

> But there's nothing we can do to fight this firestorm of allegations that are out there ... The important thing now is to stand as firmly

as I can and say that the President had denied these allegations, on all counts, unequivocally, and we'll see how this plays out.[81]

By adopting this position, Hillary Clinton later suffered when the President's story changed, and it became obvious that he had been less than forthcoming with her. Beyond the confines of the Clinton's marriage, however, other statements by the First Lady made plain the existence of a siege mentality in the White House: 'I do believe that this is a battle. I mean look at the very people who are involved in this. They have popped up in other settings. The great story here ... is this vast right-wing conspiracy that had been conspiring against my husband since the day he announced for president.'[82] This aided the White House, as it put the focus firmly upon the motives, tactics, and interpretations adopted by the investigators, and accentuated the onset of an aggressive strategy directed at Kenneth Starr and his investigation.[83] As the immediate furore concerning the scandal subsided, the White House damage limitation team was refined and placed under the control of White House Counsel Charles Ruff, an individual who was later to play a central role in the conduct of the President's defense at the impeachment hearings of January–February 1999.[84] Legally, Clinton's defense was managed primarily by Bruce Lindsey, a long-time Clinton aide and 'captain of the defense'.[85]

A strategy employed by both sides, Starr's and Clinton's alike, was to attempt to portray the other as employing inappropriate and improper tactics. This visible and acrimonious conflict between investigators and investigated was a clear deviation from the strategies employed by the White House to deal with previous Clinton scandals. While it may not have been forthcoming with documents nor have offered witnesses on previous occasions, the overt public relations strategy was to pledge compliance with investigators. Throughout the spring and summer of 1998 the White House waged an increasingly open and hostile war with the OIC and did not seek to hide its contempt for the investigation. Aide James Carville announced that 'There's going to be a war', while one anonymous White House official talked of the damage limitation effort as 'part of our continuing campaign to destroy Ken Starr'.[86] Although Starr contended that the White House was purposefully impeding the investigation, and was employing executive privilege to prevent access to Clinton aides who might recall important facts, the Clinton administration, in turn, believed that the OIC was leaking information to the media to undermine the validity of its political defense.[87] Partly because of leaks, and partly because of the

President's failure to comment clearly about the precise nature of his relationship, the White House was only able, in the main, to react to events as they unfolded. The lack of direction was not resolved satisfactorily in the longer term. For example, on 11 February 1998, an unnamed Clinton political aide stated, 'I don't think there's some kind of long-term road map.'[88] Several months later, on 17 September 1998, the *Washington Post* reported that a congressional Democrat believed the White House damage limitation strategy to be so bad that 'There is no strategy at all', while another believed, 'I think their only strategy right now is to get through the day.'[89] Moreover, it was difficult, in the spring of 1998, to advance an unqualified defense, as Monica Lewinsky was seeking an immunity agreement with Starr, and it was possible that the President might be called to testify under oath. Insecurity influenced the White House throughout the year, and until Clinton testified on 17 August, the nature of this scandal, specifically that it was rooted in individual wrongdoing rather than institutional abuse, was to have a major bearing upon the fortunes of the Clinton presidency.[90]

An additional problem encountered by Clinton was that many of those who were part of his inner circle were also potential witnesses for Starr, and were integral to the Independent Counsel's efforts to establish whether Clinton had lied at the Jones deposition. Presidential aide Sidney Blumenthal, secretary Betty Currie, friend and confidant Vernon Jordan, Director of Oval Office Operations Nancy Hernreich, and several of the President's legal aides were summoned by Starr to state what they knew of Clinton's affair.[91] This merely complicated the damage limitation effort as it quickly became clear that the nature of the President's private conversations with his aides and colleagues was a focus of inquiry for Starr, and some of the aides, in particular Vernon Jordan, were indispensable to the satisfactory development of the investigation.[92]

While the President invoked and then retracted executive privilege, and failed to prevent the OIC from calling witnesses during the spring and summer of 1998, efforts to forestall the investigation became increasingly complicated when Lewinsky accepted an immunity agreement, and the President was requested to give a DNA sample. Starr had, in his possession, forensic evidence which undermined the position held by the administration. This forced the President's hand and he was compelled, as related previously in this chapter, to modify his version of events. The most profitable strategy for the President to follow, in anticipation of his Grand Jury testimony, was, as might be expected, a subject for rigorous debate within the White House, as ex-Clinton aide David Gergen observed:

> With the stakes higher than at any time in his presidency, Bill Clinton will now step forward and do the right thing in the Monica Lewinsky affair. It may not be easy for him. Hard-liners in the White House argued early last week that he should keep his head down and stick to his story, even if it is misleading or untrue. As evidence mounted against him, some aides shifted and said that if a forensic test of Monica's infamous dress shows signs of a relationship, he should be more forthcoming but otherwise hold tight.[93]

Debate about strategy was rife and was sufficiently visible that it became a matter which was reported openly.[94] The lack of authoritative leadership from Clinton, when placed alongside the delicate balance between protecting him from legal action and political fallout, made the formulation of damage limitation strategy problematic. The opinions of members of Congress, and the background influence of public opinion, compounded the problems of mounting a coherent defense.[95]

In the aftermath of Clinton's testimony to the Grand Jury, Clinton's advisers, although disillusioned, maintained the attack upon Starr's investigation. Similarly, the President continued to consider public policy issues. White House Press Secretary Mike McCurry stressed the President's determination to remain focused, despite Starr's probe: 'He [Clinton] believes he will restore faith with the American people by demonstrating to them that he remains committed to doing the work that he was elected to do.'[96] Clinton also had to repair his credibility within the Executive branch of government. Internal dissent and unhappiness within the administration was apparent. Clinton apologized to members of his cabinet for his action on 10 September, only to be rebuked by Health and Human Services Secretary Donna E. Shalala. She, in turn, was reprimanded by the President who advised her of the benefits of his moral leadership. Senior aides were generally supportive. A spokesperson for Secretary of State Madeleine Albright stated:

> Secretary Albright believes it was a very moving meeting. She indicated that it was a sad and difficult time for all concerned. She believes that the president's actions were wrong, as were his statements misleading the American people and the Cabinet. But she has accepted the president's apology to the Cabinet.[97]

With internal cohesion at a discernible low, the President faced internal as well as external concerns.[98] The influence and power retained by the White House was a tangential concern given the release of a referral to the House by Kenneth Starr. Senior aides were particularly downbeat about future prospects. One stated, 'We're passengers on the bus, and someone else is driving the bus', while another declared that 'There's no great amount of, shall we say, organization ... What power does this White House have?'[99] The report submitted by Starr was pivotal in shaping perceptions of the President's actions, was negative in its interpretations, and was pivotal in determining the mindset of wavering and undecided members of the Congress.[100] White House lawyers wished to see the *Starr Report* in advance of its submission to the Congress, in order that a defense of the President's position could be accurately assembled.[101] Starr, alongside the House Rules Committee, was not compliant, and the request for the report was rejected. The White House was forced to issue a 'prebuttal' to the *Starr Report*, as outlined in Chapter 4 of this text, without having first seen the document. This again demonstrated that the administration was, in many respects, powerless to halt the momentum gained by this scandal or influence the decisions and actions of others.

As detailed in the next section of this chapter, Clinton's admission of an affair hastened discussion of impeachment proceedings, and he concentrated upon ensuring that congressional Democrats were acutely aware of his political and legal standpoint. In the legal forum attention similarly turned to the Congress. It was that institution which would assume the responsibility of removing the President from office via the high crimes and misdemeanors statute of the Constitution.

The damage limitation strategies employed by the Clinton administration between January and September 1998 were undermined by internal dissention, doubt about the position held by the President, and a day-by-day approach to the evolution of the scandal. Clinton's attempts to assert executive privilege, and to prevent testimony by Secret Service agents were unsuccessful, deepening the problems faced by the White House and setting problematic precedents for future Presidents. Two factors lay at the heart of the predicaments faced by the administration.

Firstly, there was tension between the legal and political advisers in the White House. Political advisers, in particular, were concerned that a strategy designed to legally extricate the President from the scandal could prove crippling, if not fatal, to the Clinton presidency in terms of public and congressional opinion. Legal advisers were concerned that any evidence of illegality would result in severe problems for Clinton above and beyond those associated with political sparring or a slump in the polls. Ultimately neither side prevailed in the quest to control the agenda. This was down, predominantly, to the fact that Clinton, while maintaining that he was legally consistent, had not been sufficiently forthcoming about his relationship and, consequently, no cohesive long-term strategy evolved. Politically, the administration's damage limitation strategies were relatively successful in the realm of public opinion, as discussed in Chapter 7, but failed to assuage many in the Congress, and failed to prevent the onset of impeachment proceedings in the fall of 1998. Legally, the administration had little control of its own destiny and ultimately the President endured the quasi-legal proceeding of impeachment, with the Chief Justice of the Supreme Court presiding over a trial in the Senate.

A second explanation for the inability of the administration to terminate the Lewinsky scandal was the failure of the President to adequately brief his aides on the true nature of the scandal, and avail them of the most pertinent course of action to avert political crisis. His initial public claims that he had not had sexual relations with Monica Lewinsky were accepted by his aides as a legitimate interpretation of his position. That the President maintained these claims for some time after his initial denials naturally allowed many leading aides to advance and endorse the misleading cover-up. This was to the detriment of intra-branch relations and severely impeded the administration's ability to recover quickly and efficiently from this scandal. Nevertheless, many close aides rallied to the President following his confession of an inappropriate relationship and sought to present a unified front.

As the final section of this chapter makes clear, Clinton's admission only served to alienate many in the Congress and hastened the onset of impeachment proceedings. In this sense the damage limitation strategies employed by Clinton were somewhat reminiscent of those employed by Nixon, with a general seepage of negative information about the role of the President in scandal emerging across time.

(iii) Damage limitation and the Congress: January–September 1998

Although attention is understandably drawn to the role of the Congress in the impeachment and trial of President Clinton in 1998–9, the attitude of members of the Congress in early 1998 was no less important in determining the fate of President Clinton. Several critical issues dominated the debate about which punishment should be meted out to the President, and the twists and turns in the story advanced by Clinton made it particularly difficult in the long term for members of the Congress to come to a clear decision to this end. Some qualification is necessary in evaluating congressional opinion. Firstly, it is difficult to neatly sum up the attitude of the Congress, as the 535 members of that institution held a broad spectrum of views on the nature and evolution of the Clinton scandal. Rather, several pivotal coalitions came to the fore and key committees such as the House Judiciary Committee, passed resolutions which determined Clinton's fortunes. Secondly, as the matter involved the private life of the President, many members of the Congress were reluctant to pry and probe, for fear that they would be treated in a similar manner, and the private lives of politicians would be subject to media and legal investigation.[102] Ironically, this occurred in 1998 when discreet affairs by several prominent members of the Congress, Henry Hyde and Speaker-elect Bob Livingston among them, were reported by the media. Thirdly, there was hesitancy in discussing the scandal, especially in the spring and summer of 1998, as investigations were incomplete, and it was considered somewhat ill-advised to discuss material based largely on rumor, leaks, and innuendo. This hesitancy was partly resolved when Starr filed his report and it became clear, particularly to Republicans, that there were legitimate grounds for the impeachment of the President. Fourthly, a complex variable, and one pivotal in the early stages of the denial period, was public opinion. When the public seemed unmoved by the Lewinsky revelations, and Clinton's job approval statistics remained remarkably stable, members of Congress were predictably hesitant to condemn his actions. Circumstances changed once Clinton's confession arrived in mid-August. A key issue here was the onset of congressional mid-term elections, scheduled for November 1998, during which all members of the House and one-third of the Senate faced election. The Clinton scandal was deemed an issue which might prove instrumental in determining voter choice, with the potential for a backlash against the President's party. This heightened debate and discussion, and encouraged members of the Congress to assume clear positions on the Clinton scandal during September, in advance of the election season.

As the scandal was disclosed to the American people, congressional attention focused upon the important State of the Union address to be given by Clinton at the end of January 1998. The scandal was, therefore, at its outset, an irksome distraction from the legislative agenda.

That said, within days of the scandal's exposure, discussion of the possibility of impeachment commenced. Chairman of the House Judiciary Committee, Henry J. Hyde (R-Ill), upon hearing of the allegations of perjury and obstruction of justice, announced: 'Telling people to lie and obstructing justice are serious charges. I would not say he is immune from consideration of impeachment should these allegations prove to be correct.'[103] Hyde was, however, in the minority in being so forthright about his interpretations of the scandal. Given the lack of evidence, the elongated nature of Starr's investigation, and the plethora of allegations made about Clinton's private conduct in previous years, there existed a natural reluctance to comment for fear of being seen as overly aggressive towards the Clinton White House. As Charles T. Canady (R-Fla) commented: 'Most members are sensitive to the fact that it is not responsible to have a knee-jerk response to a matter that is as significant and important as this ...'.[104] Frank Luntz, a Republican consultant to the Congress, distributed a memo to Republicans in late January 1998, advising how to approach the emerging scandal:

> The facts will speak far louder than any of your voices. If you comment, you will take a non-partisan, non-political situation and make it both partisan and political. Do not speculate. Do not hypothesize. Too many Americans justify the President's behavior because they dislike his accusers. Please don't add to that justification.[105]

Given the unpopularity of Starr's investigation of Whitewater, alongside the congressional hearings conducted by the Republican party, it was, primarily because of public opinion, prudent to refrain from a zealous partisan assault upon Clinton. Personal attacks had previously proven fruitless and it was more judicious to wait and allow developments in the legal realm to take their course before weighing-in with a concerted political attack. Democrats conceded that the charges against the President were serious in nature, and that if true, the President would face difficulty. This was a strategic position to adopt. If they alienated themselves from the White House they risked a lack of presidential endorsement in the congressional mid-term elections. Conversely, blind support of the President might lead to severe credibility problems if he were found guilty of the charges raised by Starr. Following the State of the Union address members of both parties struggled to address legislative matters as opposed to the scandal revelations.[106]

Congressional focus in the early weeks of the scandal concentrated upon the bitter disputes between Starr and Clinton. Few were willing to break ranks and condemn Clinton in an overt manner. A more tactful approach, adopted by Hyde (R-Ill), was to suggest that if Starr failed to uncover adequate evidence, then investigative hearings would follow to employ the congressional oversight power. Thereafter, impeachment hearings might commence if sufficient evidence of wrongdoing were uncovered.[107] In the second week of February 1998, discussion about the feasibility of impeachment proceedings began in an open manner in the House. Even then, members of that chamber downplayed speculation. Too many variables existed at this early time to consider impeachment as a foregone conclusion. Representative John Conyers Jr. (D-Mich), ranking Democrat on the House Judiciary Committee, summed up the prevailing atmosphere: 'A foolhardy attempt to impeach an overwhelmingly popular and successful President on inconsistent and highly suspect circumstantial evidence is one way to ensure a Democratic Congressional majority next November.'[108] Media attention at this time focused increasingly upon the House Judiciary Committee, with its charismatic Chairman Henry Hyde, principally because it would be the location for the initiation of impeachment proceedings if they were to occur, and consequently the opinions of its members were of particular note.[109]

As the evidence against Clinton accumulated in the summer of 1998, so did the inclination of members of Congress to speculate on the probable outcome of this scandal. Censure of the President was advanced by some if the evidence proved to be incriminating, while others began to look at the historical records of impeachment inquiries to evaluate the vague term 'high crime and misdemeanors'. When Starr demanded testimony from Clinton, congressional interest became ever greater, as it was clear that presidential comment under oath would prove meaningful in resolving the remaining questions about Clinton's conduct. In July, senior Republican Senator Orrin Hatch (R-Utah), a veteran of the 1987 Iran-Contra hearings, asked that Clinton testify before Starr, because refusal to do so might constitute an impeachable offense. Hatch commented: 'if he doesn't come in ... tell the truth about what has happened, then I think that's a very serious problem ...'.[110] An individual who was to cause untold problems for Clinton in the Congress spoke in early August. Senator Joseph Lieberman (D-Conn) wished to avoid a constitutional crisis, but let it be known, as a foretaste of future commentary, that he harbored frustrations about the impact of scandal upon political life: 'This episode is sorry, and it is sordid, and it has brought down not only our government and the head of our government, but the whole country.'[111] Recognizing the seriousness of the situation, former Clinton aide George Stephanopoulos offered advice to Clinton on how to minimize disaffection within the Democratic party: 'Democrats believe the best thing for him to do right now is to go forward and tell the story and people will forgive it.'[112] Acknowledging the importance of congressional opinion, Clinton met with members of his own party in early August, at the onset of the new congressional term.[113] The atmosphere was cordial and agreement was reached to concentrate upon the upcoming legislative term, and to endorse the President's prior message, one repeated many times, that a national agenda was of far more importance than the politics of scandal.[114]

Clinton's admission of an inappropriate relationship enhanced the likelihood of impeachment hearings and brought congressional opinion to the fore, although as stated earlier in this chapter, few senior members of the Congress were willing to comment upon the President's predicament for some time after Clinton's 17 August public address. Following the speech, Erskine Bowles, White House Chief of Staff, began calling Democrats in the Congress to ask for their continued support at this difficult time.[115] Of those congressional members who were willing to comment immediately, opinion was divided, principally by partisan affiliation. Senator John D. Ashcroft (R-Mo) was downbeat and gloomy about future prospects for Clinton: 'I think we've witnessed the effective end of this presidency ... he's lost his moral authority to lead.'[116] House Republican Christopher Cox (R-Calif) was dismissive of the President's *mea culpa*: 'The President was defiant and asserted, improbably, that it is private and nobody's business – a fantastic notion, that having sex with an intern on the job in the Oval Office is private.'[117] Democrats, by contrast, were more considerate of the President's strategic and semantic defense. Representative Martin Frost (D-Tx) downplayed the latest twist in a long-running story: 'I don't think there is anything for the Republicans to gain by turning this into a campaign issue. The American people are tired of this.'[118] Not all Democrats held the party line, however, and one of Clinton's most important post-August tasks was to marshal the party and convince colleagues that he deserved continued support, particularly if impeachment hearings commenced. This was no small matter, as the fate of the Clinton presidency hung in the balance. The harshest reprimand, albeit an extreme and isolated one within the Democratic party, came from Representative John

McHale (D-Pa), who called for Clinton to resign his position.[119] Many party members felt let down by the President. Senator Dianne Feinstein (D-Calif) expressed her dismay: '... when the president categorically denied any sexual involvement with Monica Lewinsky, I believed him. His remarks last evening [17 August] leave me with a deep sense of sadness that my trust in his credibility has been badly shattered.'[120]

Other respected party members expressed concern about the separation of powers and how the political system might be affected by Clinton's actions and admissions. Senator Daniel Patrick Moynihan (D-NY) observed:

> We want to be careful with the institution of the presidency. A wounded President cannot govern well. I think we are being much too casual about this matter. Even though he's a lame-duck President, popularity and prestige can make him a formidable negotiator. But if he's diminished, he will not have the influence he needs with congress. Legislators won't be afraid of him, [and] won't want to help resolve a problem.[121]

Breaking a brief silence on the matter, House Speaker and long-time Clinton foe Newt Gingrich (R-Ga), was circumspect about condemning Clinton following his admission of an affair. There was good reason for his hesitancy. Clinton's admission of a relationship had thrown the Democrats onto the defensive, and had seemingly made the re-election prospects for many of that party's candidates in the upcoming midterm elections all the more difficult and complicated. There was no benefit in being seen to gloat over the President's problems. What was more, Gingrich shared Moynihan's understanding that institutional change, via impeachment, was problematic. While action by the Congress to remove Clinton might be justified, the presidential office might, in the process, be irreparably damaged. Gingrich's concerns are worthy of reflection:

> There's a high value to stability in our system. I don't like the idea of changing who the president is capriciously. It's very hard to pick a president. It's very expensive. It takes an enormous amount of the nation's energy, and once the nation has made that choice, whoever that choice is, there should be an overwhelming presumption that they serve out their term. The mountain is all on the side of those who say there's a case. It's not just a presumption of inno-

cence, there's a presumption of stability, a presumption of authority, a presumption of the way the nation runs.[122]

Gingrich's comments are particularly instructive, and were heartily endorsed by many members of the Democratic party.[123] They highlighted the institutional advantage held by Clinton. As President, despite the questionable activities undertaken in an individual capacity, he retained political authority because the institutional position he held was viewed with high esteem and was a pivotal lynchpin within government. A core issue therefore, particularly for Republicans, was that as much as they might want to remove Clinton, they also had to beware of harming the presidential office he occupied. There also existed the important consideration of overturning the sovereignty of the people, as expressed in the 1996 presidential election. This factor, in particular, was advanced as a pivotal argument by the President's allies during his impeachment and trial in late 1998 and early 1999. For all the problems encountered by Clinton, the Republican party faced as many in deciding how to approach a scandal which touched upon sensitive issues such as popular sovereignty and presidential privacy, and held little resonance among the voting public. It remained to be seen if scandal would influence the result of the November elections, and whether there would be any capital forthcoming from the problems faced by a President with exceptionally high job approval ratings, gained despite the preponderance of scandal discussion within Washington.

Clinton's efforts to court congressional Democrats continued through late August and into September 1998. While Republican disaffection and criticism was an expected part of political life, the importance of the opinions of the Democratic minority in the Congress was of prime significance. Clinton, aware of the impeachment regulations as outlined in the Constitution, had to ensure that a sufficient number of Democrats adhered to his position, as defection to the opposition camp would mean the end of his presidency. As a consequence, with Clinton riding high in the public opinion polls in the fall of 1998, the opinion of a select band in the Congress became the overriding preoccupation of those coordinating damage limitation in the White House. In this sense the American people were observers of scandal politics. While public opinion was an important factor, this scandal was, in essence, very much a Washington scandal, with the key players and opinion-makers to be found in the Congress and in the White House. A former administration official, cited by media sources, believed that prospects for the President were far from upbeat and that congressional relations were the key to the retention of the presidential office: 'He doesn't have a choice. The only hope he has in having the playing field level is to solidify his [Democratic] base. Republicans aren't going to stand up for him. He needs to have his base energized and at a minimum not criticizing him.'[124] Clinton's popularity in the nation assisted him in the prelude to the November elections, although the support he received was not derived from his scandal activities. Congressional Democrats had a choice to make. They could distance themselves from a popular President and face alienation and resentment from the core Democratic voters in the mid-term elections. Alternately, they could accept Clinton, warts and all, and assume the burden of scandal alongside the President, seeking to minimize its impact and cast it as marginal to the fortunes of their fellow Americans.[125]

Congressional leaders began to vocally criticize Clinton in advance of the release of the *Starr Report*. Senate Majority Leader Trent Lott (R-Miss) accused the President of being a liar, and branded the scandal as 'disgusting'.[126] Lott drew attention to a 'moral dimension to the American presidency', suggesting that the President should uphold unspecified ethical standards. Again this was a precursor to more extensive discussion and debate during the impeachment proceedings about the role of the American President, the duties imposed upon that office, and whether the private moral conduct of the President was a matter for public concern. In early September Clinton received a severe body blow when a senior member of his own party spoke against him on the floor of the Senate, drawing attention to internal party dissatisfaction. To Clinton's detriment it also brought additional unwanted and negative media attention to party dynamics within Washington. Senator Joseph Lieberman undermined Clinton's damage limitation strategies by condemning his 'immoral' behavior.[127] Lieberman's forthrightness precipitated other harsh words from Democratic heavyweights such as Bob Kerrey (D-Neb) and Daniel Moynihan (D-NY). This was not a pre-election ploy by Lieberman for more votes. He was re-elected to the Senate in 1994 and was, as a consequence, not due to contest his seat again until 2000. His comments came because of concern about Clinton's actions, rather than interest in a tight election race. They simply exacerbated the tense relationship between the White House and Capitol Hill and complicated Clinton's damage limitation strategy. They also suggested that there might be some emergent bipartisan consensus which could ultimately undermine Clinton's efforts to portray this event as a partisan-inspired witchhunt. Intra-party relations were, as a consequence, of great importance to the con-tinuation of the Clinton presidency.

Clinton rearranged his schedule in early September to allow consul-tation with Democratic leaders and improve relations with his own party – another indicator, if any were needed, of Clinton's increasing desperation and anxiety about his political support. Appeals were made to members of the Congress to 'Hold your fire' until the contents of Starr's referral were known, as any comments founded upon specula-tion and rumor might be nullified by Starr's conclusions.[128] Clinton's position was precarious, but he possessed advantages which were not of his own making. Traditional partisanship in the Congress meant that Democrats were as suspicious of the motives and actions of Republicans as they were critical of their own party leader. Divergent opinion within the House Judiciary Committee and the likelihood of conflict within that forum once Starr's referral was filed enhanced Clinton's cause, as internal disagreement increased the chance of a simple partisan split, with Democrats lining up alongside the President. There were also several decisions to be made over whether to release documents to the public, including Clinton's videotaped testi-mony before the Grand Jury. Congressional disagreement bolstered Clinton's cause. For example, Senator John F. Kerry (D-Mass) com-mented, in advance of the release of the videotaped testimony: 'The nation is being ill-served by this political water torture that's taking place in a highly calculated, highly partisan way.'[129]

The *Starr Report* was submitted to the House on 9 September, and released to the public on 11 September. This intensified congressional desire to comment on Starr's conclusions. Having downplayed the meaning of the scandal, and cast Clinton's confession as a suitable conclusion to the matter, the White House now faced a Congress ani-mated by Starr's report, consumed by discussion about possibility of impeachment, and eager to speculate on the probable future of the Clinton presidency. Widespread debate about the content of Starr's report and the associated evidentiary material highlighted broad but essentially partisan viewpoints about whether the scandal concerned sex or law. Democratic Senator Robert G. Torricelli (D-NJ) contended that Starr's conclusions were flawed: 'The misjudgments of the President are nearly equaled by the need of Kenneth Starr to provide a level of sexual detail beyond what was necessary to make his point or establish his case. His own lack of perspective and tendency to go to excess undermine his credibility. This level of sexual detail is clearly intended to inflame public passions.' Consider the contrast with the opinions of House Republican Lamar Smith (R-Tx): 'The allegations are far more serious than I had anticipated. You've got five allegations of lying under oath; four allegations of obstructing justice. I think it's more likely than not that the Judiciary Committee as a whole would recommend that the House consider initiating the impeachment inquiry.'[130]

Clinton's fortunes in advance of the onset of formal impeachment proceedings in the House Judiciary Committee were varied and appeared to alter on a day-to-day basis. Suggestions were made that he appear before that Committee and testify about his actions. Likewise, there were discussions about an apology by the President, the payment of a fine, the means by which impeachment proceedings would commence, and the viability of a censure.[131] Republicans played down the censure option, contending it was not a valid constitutional alternative to impeachment, and that Democratic discussion of the matter was 'the perfect marriage between pure spin and public plea bargaining'.[132] Clinton was now, however, entering a more customary forum. With the *Starr Report* submitted to the Congress, and the OIC probe of the Lewinsky matter largely complete, Clinton could play to his strengths, sparring with Republican members of the Congress and working in a largely political, as opposed to legal, environment. The impeachment proceedings had a quasi-legal basis, but Clinton could employ his powers of persuasion to appease Democrats and marshal his forces. Former Clinton Chief of Staff Leon Panetta observed a more upbeat atmosphere in the Clinton camp once the *Starr Report* had been filed, and Clinton's video testimony had not harmed his reputation further:

> There's a lot more hope that he [Clinton] can really win this thing. This is no longer about waiting for the lawyers. This is now a game taking place in an arena they understand, which is the political arena, where they are much more comfortable with the conversation.[133]

Clinton commenced the fight to retain his presidential office with a complex scenario before him. He endured condemnation as a consequence of his changing story, his failure to be forthright with the nation, and the moral problems posed by his affair with a woman many years his junior. The recommendations for impeachment outlined in the *Starr Report*, although controversial, gave Congress a critical interpretation of the President's action which alleged that he had lied under oath, obstructed justice and abused his office. The President's best opportunity to defend himself against Starr's allegations would come in the Congress when his legal team would challenge Starr's conclusions. Although the Republican party controlled congressional committees and retained a majority in both chambers of the Congress, Clinton knew that even if he were impeached in the House, a two-thirds majority vote in the Senate was required to oust him from office. If he could retain the support of his own party then his future would be secure. Additional elements played heavily upon the congressional mind. Firstly, the President faced a rare proceeding, that of impeachment. Only Presidents Nixon and Johnson had previously confronted impeachment proceedings and an urgent review of precedent was necessary to ensure an orderly and just proceeding. Secondly, public opinion was a meaningful factor and influenced proceedings in an indirect, but nevertheless consequential, manner. The congressional mid-term elections granted the American people an opportunity to express their opinions on the scandal and how the House was conducting presidential impeachment. The Congress faced the problematic issue of challenging the will of the people and expelling a popular national leader. Thereafter, there existed the possibility of a popular backlash if it were thought that Clinton had been treated unfairly by opponents whose motives might be considered partisan. Public opinion increasingly became an element of note. Although the public could not express its opinion directly and vote the President out of office at this time, its influence on the scandal became an important consideration for Clinton and Congressmen alike. Thirdly, Clinton was the President of the United States. How could the Congress remove this individual from the presidential office and subject him to Constitutional punishment without harming the office itself, and thereby set a dangerous historical precedent? Did the alleged crimes warrant the label of 'high crimes and misdemeanors', and, more important, what was the threshold by which this level of criminality would be reached? These questions would have to be addressed and resolved by both chambers of the Congress when deciding the future of this President. Lastly, there was the sensitive matter of whether the investigation by Starr and the impending congressional impeachment proceeding comprised a legitimate public concern or constituted a gross invasion of Clinton's private life. Put simply, was the scandal about sex, or did it comprise a violation of the law by the President of the United States? As the President and the Congress approached a pivotal period in the history of both institutions, it was clear that historic decisions would resolve a scandal which had evolved from an inappropriate affair to a Constitutional crisis.

Conclusion

Clinton's damage limitation exercise aimed to convince the Congress and the public that he had not lied under oath when questioned by the Jones lawyers in January 1998, and had not committed perjury or obstructed justice by modifying his testimony to the Grand Jury in August 1998. He faced imposing adversaries. The OIC undertook an extensive and probing investigation of the President and clashed openly with the White House when it sought evidence and testimony to substantiate its case. It conformed to its initial mandate and worked to assemble a case to recommend grounds for the impeachment of the President. Similarly, congressional criticism of the President proved an irksome distraction and added to concerns that if impeachment hearings were to begin, the White House faced a challenge to ensure that Democrats maintained their support of the President. Republicans were predictably critical of the President's words and actions. With the Republican-controlled Congress and the OIC as elite adversaries, Clinton had to battle to create a cohesive and effective damage limitation strategy which would avert impeachment and maintain his high job approval ratings in the polls.

Clinton's long-term strategy in 1998 aimed to diminish the visibility of the scandal, and focus the attention of the nation on familiar issues such as the economy, law and order, and foreign affairs. In advancing this agenda the President spent a considerable time away from Washington, failed to address the scandal allegations he faced on numerous public occasions, and maintained, when pressed on the issue, that the charges leveled against him were groundless. His habit of arguing that he wished to delay comment until investigations by the Independent Counsel were complete was a familiar strategy from previous presidential scandals. It granted him leeway and allowed ample consideration of the evidence before a response to the allegations was issued, and also, more importantly, suggested that the President was an observer of scandal politics rather than a perpetrator of it. What complicated the damage limitation strategy was the wealth of evidence amassed against him, the nature of this evidence, and the fact that on several occasions the President was unaware of the detailed material in the hands of the Independent Counsel. This undermined Clinton's position and encouraged him to alter his version of events in August

1998. This was not portrayed by the White House as a manifest change in the President's story, but rather it subtly refined its stance. Legally, there was no realistic choice but to maintain that there had not been sexual relations with Lewinsky. Clinton argued that while she might have had a sexual relations with him, he did not have any with her. This played heavily upon semantics, but advanced a plausible legal case. Politically, it had an altogether different impact. It appeared that the President had misled the nation, his wife, and his political aides, and, what was more, he now faced the public spectacle of impeachment. Clinton's damage limitation strategy, in advance of impending impeachment proceedings, failed to derail the investigation of Kenneth Starr. This however was of no surprise, as the legal forum was an arena in which he could exert little control.

The President faced a challenge in maintaining cordial relations with members of both parties in the Congress. A feature of the scandal was the initial reluctance of congressional members to discuss it in an open and forthright manner. Concern existed that the problems faced by the President might hinder the legislative program, and condemnation of Clinton in advance of a referral from Starr might be premature and commit congressional members to an unsubstantiated version of events. Clinton's change of tack in August 1998 encouraged discussion of the wisdom of his action, and inspired members of both parties to comment openly, particularly upon the morality of the inappropriate relationship. A focus upon moral issues aided Clinton's cause. On the one hand Republicans were pointing out that the scandal was not about sex, yet, on the other, condemnation of Clinton on moral grounds suggested that sex was a major feature of this debate. Previous illicit relationships by members of the Congress, exposed by the media, made it clear that several of those who put themselves forward to judge the President held no higher moral standards than the President himself. This only served to cast doubt upon the validity of any condemnation. Additional factors such as the November 1998 mid-term elections, cleavages in public opinion, the nature of Starr's investigation, the evidence assembled, and traditional partisan suspicion complicated congressional procedure. While the onset of impeachment proceedings would never be a smooth process, the multitude of questions raised by Clinton's actions ensured that while the charges leveled against him were relatively easy for the Legislators to comprehend, whether they equated squarely with high crimes and misdemeanors was difficult to ascertain.

A rush to judgement by the Congress in the fall of 1998, under-pinned by a conviction in the quality of the evidence offered by Starr and a perceived weakness in the position of the President, induced the onset of impeachment proceedings against the President. This, as shown in Chapter 7, appeared to conflict with public opinion, and threatened to overturn popular sovereignty as expressed in the 1996 presidential election. It was a controversial route to follow, but one taken after several Democrats had suggested a lesser punishment of censure, an option which was ultimately rejected. Clinton's damage limitation strategies worked sufficiently well in the public forum so as to ensure that there was no groundswell of public enthusiasm for impeachment. It was, in effect, a remedy suggested by an elite circle within government, and one which left no room for a compromise position.

Damage limitation measures failed to avert impeachment proceedings. The President and his assembled team of legal and political advisers found that on too many occasions events were beyond their control. Starr decided when his referral to the House would be filed, and declined to allow the White House to see the document in advance. Likewise, the House Rules Committee declined to give the White House advance access to documentary material, placing those defending the President at a distinct disadvantage in the public relations war. Clinton appeared more assured and confident once the focus of attention moved from Starr's investigation to the chambers of the Congress. Here he could call upon partisan allies to stand by him at a troubled time, and could exert some political pressure upon those who would finally decide his fate. By this time however the President had created a scenario whereby he had damaged his own standing to such a degree that it was by no means certain that he would automatically draw support from party colleagues. While his attempts to remain aloof from the scandal and focus on legislative matters appeared to mollify public opinion, elite interpretations of the scandal were not so easily revised by damage limitation tactics which downplayed the legal ramifications of Clinton's actions.

4
The Starr Investigation

Independent Counsel Kenneth Starr was instrumental in the development of scandal politics in 1998, coordinating the investigation of Clinton's alleged perjury and obstruction of justice during the Jones deposition. Having played a central role in the investigation of the Whitewater matter, and possessing a long-term knowledge of the Clinton White House, the personality of the President, and the role and function of the Independent Counsel, Kenneth Starr held a decisive role in determining the fortunes of the Clinton presidency. His investigation provoked controversy however. A constant stream of criticism emanated from the White House, alongside several questions about the cost, duration, and conduct of his probe into Clinton's discreet liaison. For all the public commentary about Starr's investigation, he held his ground stubbornly, and ensured that a vast amount of evidence was delivered to the House of Representatives in order that it make an informed decision about whether to impeach the President. To many, including those at the White House, it appeared that Starr's motivation was a partisan hatred of the President. His appointment in 1994 had been greeted with some suspicion and his long-term tenure proved a constant distraction for the President.

This chapter considers the nature of the Starr investigation, with a particular focus upon the *Starr Report* and the White House response to that particular document. It opens by evaluating the controversies over the nature of Starr's investigation and then studies the White House arguments presented when the *Starr Report* was filed. The need for the White House to counter the charges leveled against the President by Starr was clear. If they were left unattended or unchallenged, then Starr's viewpoint might dominate the platform of debate. Accordingly, the White House issued two documents which challenged the *Starr Report*. Given that Starr would not let the White House or the President see the referral to the House before it was filed with that institution, the White House issued a dismissive 'prebuttal' to the Starr charges, without having first seen them. When the *Starr Report* was available to read, the White House then issued a more detailed response to the accusations and highlighted weaknesses, omissions, and flawed argument in Starr's document. The debate about the Starr investigation, the report, and the White House rebuttals reflected the wider discussions about Clinton's affair, with the familiar argument over whether the scandal was about sex, or about obstruction of justice and perjury, coming to the fore. Starr's actual involvement in the Lewinsky matter was brief. His initial mandate was granted by the Attorney General in January 1998, and the referral to the House submitted in early September of that same year. Within this period Starr made a substantive impact upon the presidential office and emerged as a vociferous critic of Clinton, both as a man and as a President.

Starr's investigation

The role of the Independent Counsel was, and remains, a controversial one in modern American politics. The position held some repute following the efforts of Archibald Cox, in the then-called position of Special Prosecutor, to expose illegality by the Nixon administration. Having been fired by Nixon during the Saturday Night Massacre in 1973, Cox entertained popularity during and after the Watergate scandal for having assisted in exposing wrongdoing by the President. Thereafter, however, the role of the Independent Prosecutor has proven questionable, partly as a result of both Democratic and Republican Presidents having now endured investigation by this institution.[1] The contemporary role of the Independent Counsel was created during the 1978 Ethics in Government Act, enabling an individual to be appointed to investigate possible illegalities by the Executive branch of government.[2] Until Starr's investigation made the headlines in 1998, the Independent Counsel investigating Iran-Contra, Lawrence Walsh, was perhaps the most notable individual who had entertained prominence since Watergate. Walsh pursued Ronald Reagan, Oliver North and John Poindexter among others, but found it exceptionally difficult and expensive to get any matters to court, and eventually his elongated and extensive investigation of that scandal bore little fruit.[3]

The individual appointed to the post of Independent Counsel is granted both their position and their investigative mandate by the Attorney General who is, in turn, granted leave to appoint a prosecutor by a three-judge panel.[4] The Independent Counsel position is created by an act of Congress which lasts for five years. As Starr received endorsement and substantial funding from the Congress in 1994, he was assured of retaining his position until the Independent Counsel act expired in 1999, well after the conclusion of the Lewinsky scandal.[5] The Independent Counsel has the power to investigate whether the President, or others in the Executive branch, 'may have violated any federal laws'.[6] This naturally gives the individual in the post a wide mandate, but any specific investigation must again be ratified by the Attorney General. Leeway does exist however. The Counsel does not have to prosecute a case at hand, but can hunt for information to show that there may be grounds to prosecute. This has given the Independent Counsel substantial power to investigate wide areas in order to uncover incriminating information. This explains why Starr, initially granted his position to probe the Whitewater dealings involving the Clintons, eventually found his attention drawn to a largely unrelated affair and appeared, at first sight, to have initiated a totally new investigation. There are fears that this has undermined the power of the modern presidency, as it has unbalanced the separation of powers, with the same level of expansive investigation not being leveled at the Congress. Members of Congress recognized the multitude of problems posed by the Office of Independent Counsel (OIC), problems made all the more obvious by the Lewinsky matter. By way of example, Senator Patrick Leahy (D-Vt) believed that Starr's probe into the President constituted 'the most partisan, unjustified, demeaning investigation that I can ever remember in my life'.[7] Nevertheless, in the judicial realm the OIC had previously held its ground. In the case of *Morrison* v. *Olsen* (1988) the Supreme Court upheld the Independent Counsel Statute by 7–1.[8] Supreme Court Justice Antonin Scalia, the lone dissenting opinion, believed that the Independent Counsel law was problematic. In 1989 he wrote: 'I fear the [Supreme] Court has permanently encumbered the Republic with an institution that will do it great harm'.[9]

Starr's attention was drawn to the Lewinsky matter when Linda Tripp alerted his office that Monica Lewinsky intended to commit perjury in the Jones case, and Lewinsky had asked Tripp to do the same. Moreover, Lewinsky had received advice on the case from presidential confidant Vernon Jordan.[10] Starr's initial mandate to investigate Lewinsky appeared to have only an indirect linkage to the President. However, as the President was due to be deposed by Jones's lawyers on 17 January, there existed a probability that the President might be an accomplice in any effort to present a misleading version of events. Starr, having approached the Attorney General, received an expanded mandate, detailed in Chapter 2, allowing him to investigate obstruction of justice in the Jones case. Emphasizing the controversial nature of Starr's investigation, there were immediate and pronounced deviations from convention in his investigative procedure.[11] He recorded, surreptitiously, a conversation between Lewinsky and Tripp, and did so in advance of receiving permission to expand his investigation from the Attorney General.[12] Addressing the covert taping of Monica Lewinsky, Cass Sunstein, a law professor at the University of Chicago, observed: 'This kind of Colombo maneuver is not consistent with the role or authority of the prosecutor . . . It is peculiar and inappropriate behavior on his part.'[13] Starr also questioned Lewinsky for several hours when she had no legal representation, prompting an outburst from her lawyer, William Ginsburg: 'That's as close as you can get to a constitutional breach. She was never detained or arrested, but there was enough intimidation by the process, as well as words said to her about the imminence of prosecution, that she did not dare to leave.'[14] At the outset, therefore, questions and criticism beset Starr's investigation.[15] His motives had been thought suspect by the White House on previous occasions, but here, it seemed, the unexpected opportunity to investigate possible illegality by the President prompted Starr to violate conventional procedure.

One of the key battlegrounds between the White House and the OIC was the fight to win over public opinion and to dominate the platform of debate. This was as important when the investigation was ongoing as it was when the referral was filed with the House. Suspicion of leaking and inappropriate investigative procedure prompted many in the White House, and also in the Congress, to call for Starr to be reprimanded or removed by the Attorney General. Public opinion was swayed by this interpretation, with a majority of those polled in the spring of 1998 believing that Starr was 'involved in a systematic campaign to leak information in order to damage Clinton'.[16] Suspicion existed in the Starr camp that the White House was leaking information to the detriment of Starr's office.[17] Congressional Democrats rallied to the President, providing much-needed reinforcement. Representative John Conyers Jr. (D-Mich) charged Starr with 'repeated instances of alleged misconduct and abuses of power'.[18] Similarly, Senator Robert G. Torricelli (D-NJ) expressed his concern over the trickle of information, about the Clinton case, from Starr's office: 'Occasional leaks are understood, but the pattern and level of purposefully leaking information is raising this to the level where a criminal investigation may be required.'[19] Starr, in response to a barrage of criticism, defended his Office and denied that leaks characterized his investigation. He contended that, in terms of the rule of confidentiality, 'I [Starr] respect it scrupulously, and so does my staff' and 'I regret that there have been instances so it would appear, when that rule has not been abided by'.[20] White House spokesman Joe Lockhart immediately hit back: 'It's hard to square the comments of the respect for the secrecy of the grand jury with news reporters directly quoting the independent counsel's office.'[21] During his news conference with Prime Minister Tony Blair, held on 6 February 1998, Clinton attacked Starr publicly. This, of course, as outlined in the previous chapter, followed on from critical comments made by Hillary Clinton about Starr's investigation in interviews given in late January. President Clinton declared that 'someone is leaking unlawfully out of the grand jury proceeding'.[22] Maintaining the intensity of the attack, his legal aide, David E. Kendall, launched a scathing assault upon Starr for leaking information, but did not advance specific information to substantiate his claim. Kendall alleged: 'The leaking of the past few weeks is intolerably unfair. These leaks make a mockery of the traditional rules of grand jury secrecy. They often appear to be a cynical attempt to pressure and manipulate witnesses, deceive the public and smear persons involved in this investigation.'[23]

The leaks from the Starr investigation, at first sight, might be considered minor issues, but they were important to the development of this scandal.[24] The media relied upon leaks from the OIC, and also from the White House, to form a basis for storylines, and to keep up to date with the latest developments in the scandal. Leaks served to shape media interpretation, potentially influenced the testimony of witnesses to the Grand Jury, impacted on public opinion, and forced the White House to adopt a defensive mode on several occasions. They played a meaningful role in increasing the tension between the White House and the Starr investigation and soured the atmosphere to a considerable degree. However, public opinion, a prime target of the leaks, was largely unmoved by the sporadic release of information and, in many respects, leaks only exacerbated the wounds which already existed within the political community in Washington. Starr did find, however, that as a consequence of Clinton's aggressive damage limitation exercise, he was identified by the public as the prime culprit in the battle over leaks, as highlighted in Table 4.1.

Table 4.1 Leaks and the Office of the Independent Counsel

Is Starr leaking information to harm Clinton politically?	
Yes	50%
No	37%

Source: CNN/*USA Today*/Gallup Poll, 13–15 February 1998.

The plethora of leaks prompted Starr to pledge an investigation into their source, but the matter was not one that was resolved to the satisfaction of any of the major players in the drama.[25]

Accentuating the concerns over leaks, Clinton faced an irksome distraction when his January deposition in the Jones case was leaked to the *Washington Post* in March. The deposition was supposed to be confidential, and Clinton, although he was not legally barred from discussing its content had not, as related in the previous chapter, been particularly forthcoming about its substance. As the content of the deposition upheld, rather than contradicted, his prior statements about Lewinsky, there existed suspicion that the White House had itself leaked the information. Robert Bennett, Clinton's legal aide, responded to these allegations with ferocity: 'The releasing of the deposition, the leaking of it, was a reprehensible and unethical act by the antagonists of the President.'[26] The President's 'antagonists' however were quick to declare their innocence. Starr countered: 'This office has received questions about whether we were the source of today's Washington Post story. We categorically deny that we were directly or indirectly the source of the story.'[27] These leaks did little to enhance the ability of the White House to advance its case, even if they endorsed the President's public version of events. The leaks were unexpected, brought further attention to events and issues generally detrimental to the Clinton administration, and pushed the White House into spin-control to stifle potentially damaging material. This was not wholly unexpected however, as a recurrent historical feature of scandal politics has been the often disorganized way in which information has been released into the public domain. In this scandal the presence of the unregulated Internet did little to help. Naturally, the media were eager to accept information and to publish it, leaving the White House in a predominantly defensive mode, and adding to administration concerns that, in this particular scandal, salacious evidence proving that an affair had occurred might be released inadvertently. This assists in explaining why Clinton promptly admitted an inappropriate relationship with Monica Lewinsky on 17 August 1998. He had to make a public announcement on his own terms, as the likelihood of a leak of his Grand Jury testimony was strong, and if information were released via a leak, then accusations of a White House cover-up would arise, this being one of the most damaging scandal accusations.

A further contentious matter between the Clinton White House and the OIC was executive privilege. This involved a claim by the President that he could rightfully withhold information from congressional or judicial investigation, as there existed an assumed zone of privacy created by the separation of powers. This allowed the President and his advisers the opportunity to discuss political material in confidence. The problem of this presidential power is that it is not explicitly granted by the Constitution and, as a consequence, it has aroused debate about the validity of its usage, culminating in the Supreme Court case *United States* v. *Nixon* (1974).[28] In that case the Court held that the need for evidence relating to potentially criminal acts overrode the right of the President to withhold information from investigative parties. Here lay the problem for Clinton. While he claimed that there was no criminality and that he had not obstructed justice or committed perjury, Starr's investigation assumed the opposite, and Starr wished to question Clinton's aides to gather as much pertinent information for his case as possible. This brought an assumed presidential power into direct conflict with a controversial investigation by a widely despised Independent Counsel. While executive privilege was not a critical factor in Clinton's defense armory, it nevertheless constituted an element of presidential power which would inevitably be tested. Clinton initially advanced executive privilege to prevent testimony by his aide Bruce Lindsey, and thereafter by his close confidant Sidney Blumenthal, an individual who had discussed the Lewinsky matter with Clinton following the Jones deposition in January.[29] The *Washington Post* summarized the core essence of the executive privilege matter with regard to the President:

> The claim of executive privilege in this case raises the constitutional questions of whether its use extends beyond cases involving the national interest to the president's personal interest. Three areas traditionally considered protected are: law enforcement matters, military or diplomatic affairs, and information that goes to the deliberative process of making public policy.[30]

Executive privilege was invoked in a discreet fashion, it not being a subject that held great sway in the public domain. President Clinton did not publicly acknowledge that he had asserted this presidential power. Its presence evoked comparisons between Nixon and Clinton, comparisons particularly harmful to the Clinton White House, as they cast the President as a participant in a case of comparable severity to that of Watergate. Starr raised this matter, emphasizing his belief that Clinton's use of executive privilege echoed that of the Nixon era.[31] The White House also attempted to extend privilege claims to cover conversations between Blumenthal and First Lady Hillary Clinton, a novel idea given that she held no officially titled political office.[32] This once again raised a host of new questions about the implied powers of the presidential office. Hillary Clinton was eventually recognized, by the courts, as an official who was covered by executive privilege, a significant advance in the scope and grasp of the privilege function. The President was nevertheless dismissive of reporters' questions about executive privilege, and distanced himself from it during questions on 24 March 1998:

> Q.   Mr. President, we haven't yet had the opportunity to ask you about your decision to invoke executive privilege, sir. Why shouldn't the American people see that as an effort to hide something from them?
>
> *The President.*   Look, that's a question that's being asked and answered back home by the people who are responsible to do that. I don't believe I should be discussing that here.[33]

The White House was ultimately to lose in its efforts to invoke privilege, the matter being decided in the courts. A federal judge, Norma Holloway Johnson, ruled that Starr's need to collect evidence in his probe outweighed the right of Clinton to assert privilege.[34] Judge Johnson wrote: 'If there were instruction from the President to obstruct justice or efforts to suborn perjury, such actions likely took the form of conversations involving the President's closest advisors, including Lindsey and Blumenthal . . .'.[35] Speculation abounded about whether the President would seek to appeal against the decision, and whether there would be a showdown in the Supreme Court. This was a prospect which again resurrected harmful comparisons with the plight faced by President Nixon. Clinton dismissed talk of Watergate, asserting: 'The facts are quite different in this case.'[36] The US District Court decision was released in a redacted form on 28 May 1998.[37] While discussions about an appeal were ongoing, Starr requested that the Supreme Court immediately take on the case, in order that his investigation be brought to a swift conclusion.[38] Clinton was granted a short time by the Supreme Court to consider whether he wished to agree to a prompt ruling on the matter.[39] There were political problems for the White House in deciding whether to force the issue. If it contested the case, there was the chance that harm might be done to an assumed presidential power and that the White House would be distracted by a hastily arranged Supreme Court case. Alternatively, if the President declined to take the case immediately to the Supreme Court, then it might, through the elongated judicial appeals process, end up there anyway. Clinton would then be accused of delaying Starr's inquiry, and might suffer political as well as legal problems. Clinton decided, on 1 June 1998, to abandon an appeal of the decision of the lower court on executive privilege. This avoided involving the Supreme Court in the process, avoided a delay of the Starr investigation, and meant that Clinton accepted the ruling of the US District Court on the issue. This court had acknowledged the existence of executive privilege, recognized its extension to some aspects of the First Lady's conversations and, if anything, had expanded the scope of the privilege power. It had based its decision against the President on the grounds that the need for evidence in this particular case outweighed the interest of the President to assert his rights. In the narrow area of executive privilege there appeared to be no outright winner, and the creation of yet another area of dispute and acrimony between the White House and Starr's investigation.[40]

This continued when Starr challenged attorney–client privilege matters involving the President and his legal aides, and struggled to acquire testimony of Secret Service officials who might have witnessed meetings between the President and Lewinsky.[41] An interpretation of the nature of the investigation was a pivotal factor in the legal realm. If it were seen as partisan in nature or merely a probe into a private affair, as the White House contended, then there were no grounds to challenge presidential claims of confidentiality. However, the courts could not take the risk that a claim of privilege by Clinton might leave the matter unresolved or allow a cover-up to occur and Starr was generally successful in acquiring the several testimonies he desired. Consequently, key presidential aides testified to the Grand Jury about their knowledge of the President's affair, and about his statements to them on that particular subject. The nature of the evidence, exposed following Clinton's confession, provoked questions and criticism about Clinton's executive privilege strategy. Although Clinton ultimately survived the Lewinsky scandal and received an endorsement of the continued existence of executive privilege from the courts, political science professor at the University of Pittsburgh, Mark Rozell, contended: 'I think much of the Clinton strategy has weakened traditional presidential power with respect to executive privilege. In part, that's because they have sent up losing argument after losing argument for what appears to me to be attempts to delay the Starr investigation.'[42]

Starr, having acquired the testimony of Clinton's aides, now turned his attention to the President. Starr asked him to testify voluntarily about his involvement with Lewinsky several times after the scandal broke.[43] Clinton declined to appear.[44] There were several Constitutional problems for Starr in compelling the President to testify. If Clinton simply refused to testify then Starr faced a quandary. Constitutional experts appeared divided about whether Starr could serve a subpoena to Clinton and force his appearance. Akhil Reed Amar, a Yale law school professor, believed that Starr would encounter grave problems in enforcing a subpoena if Clinton refused to comply: 'The true grand jury of the United States when it comes to the President of the United States is the House of Representatives'.[45] Conversely, others, such as Gerard Lynch, a Columbia University law school professor and prosecutor during the Iran-Contra scandal, believed that Watergate set a notable precedent which curtailed presidential power in this realm: 'It's clear from U.S. v. Nixon that the president is not immune from having to testify about matters related to a criminal investigation and that puts the president in a very difficult position.'[46] Clinton's aides, in the expectation of a subpoena, had not only to consider the Constitutional and legal ramifications of blocking testimony, but additionally had to consider the public relations fallout if Clinton declined to appear. The White House assumed a public posture which suggested some degree of compliance with Starr's demands. One senior aide stated: 'We wanted to head off stories that there is going to be a constitutional confrontation', while Mike McCurry, a spokesperson at the White House, declared that David E. Kendall, the President's lawyer, 'will work with Mr. Starr's office to try to ensure that the grand jury gets the information that it needs'.[47]

The OIC served a subpoena to the President on 17 July 1998.[48] Under increasing pressure to appear before the Grand Jury the President agreed to testify, and Kendall informed the OIC, on 24 July, that: 'The President is willing to provide testimony for the grand jury . . .'.[49] Starr thereafter withdrew the subpoena served upon the President. Several factors influenced Clinton's decision to appear, and nullified the threat of a further Constitutional dispute.[50] Firstly, Judge Johnson had threatened to set a date for Clinton's testimony if he did not comply with Starr's subpoena. Clinton, if he had to appear, wanted to do so on his own terms and therefore engaged in negotiations with the OIC about the nature, timing, and location of his testimony. Publicly, he put a brave face on events, stating on 31 July: 'I'm looking forward to the opportunity . . . of testifying. I will do so completely and truthfully.'[51] Secondly, his appearance proved a necessary step because Starr had by late July agreed an immunity deal with Lewinsky, and had in his possession a dress which could prove that a relationship, of an as yet unspecified sexual nature, had existed between the President and Lewinsky. This might contradict Clinton's statements under oath in January 1998 that there had not been any sexual relations between the two. It was imperative that the President ensure that his interpretation of events was understood by the OIC and he was not perceived to be embroiled in an untenable cover-up. Thirdly, Democrats on Capitol Hill were concerned that a refusal to appear before the Grand Jury might be construed negatively by voters and lead to complications in the November elections. Intra-party concerns therefore had a part to play in the President's appearance.

Confusion existed about whether the President would willingly give a blood sample to allow cross-checking of the forensic evidence acquired by Starr, a first for the presidential office. The OIC wrote to Clinton's lawyers in terse language at the end of July stating: 'Investigative demands require that President Clinton provide this Office as soon as possible with a blood sample to be taken under supervision.'[52] The White House was at first reluctant to bow to the unspecified nature of the term 'investigative demands'.[53] However, the OIC threatened to raise the stakes if the President failed to comply with the request:

> Because of the President's pledge to cooperate with this investigation and out of respect for the Presidency, we have not issued a subpoena for this [DNA] sample. We do not wish to litigate this matter, and we wish no embarrassment to the President. Yet, we have substantial predication for our request, and we must do our job.[54]

Aware, once again, of the likelihood of perceptions of a cover-up if the President refused to accede, the White House, in early August, allowed a blood specimen to be taken.[55] The stains on Lewinsky's dress corresponded with the DNA sample and made clear that relations of a sexual nature had taken place between the President and Lewinsky. This underscored the need to define the President's understanding of the term 'sexual relations', as used during the Jones deposition.

A wealth of legal evidence, political and public pressure, and concern about interpretations of the President's statements under oath during his 17 January Jones deposition, forced the President to appear before the Grand Jury and confess to an inappropriate relationship on 17 August 1998. This was not a path or route chosen by the President, but rather a scenario which had been forced upon him by the tactics employed by Starr, and the evidence accumulated by the OIC. As detailed in Chapter 3, Clinton employed semantics to uphold a tenuous legal case before the Grand Jury, and was forced into a humbling public confession of an inappropriate relationship. Damage limitation strategies had neither prevented nor hindered Starr's probe and, public opinion aside, they had proven largely ineffectual in containing Starr's legal assault.

The *Starr Report*

The *Starr Report* was submitted to the House of Representatives on 9 September 1998. It consisted of a long descriptive-narrative, alongside 11 grounds for the impeachment of the President, as displayed in Exhibit 4.1.[56] Starr also filed extensive evidentiary material, in paper and video form, allowing the House Judiciary Committee to later release hard copies of testimony and evidence alongside the videotape of the President testifying to the Grand Jury.[57] A significant amount of information was released on the Internet. Recognizing the importance of the *Starr Report* to the fortunes of the Clinton presidency, the White House mounted a vigorous campaign to dismiss its charges. This was done in a public forum, and was intended to influence the opinions of the members of the House Judiciary Committee and others in Congress who now held the power to decide the President's fate.[58]

As related in the previous chapter, the impending submission of the *Starr Report* increased activity by the President in Washington as he attempted to shore-up party morale. This was only partially successful, as legislators wanted to gauge public reaction to the Starr referral before supporting or condemning the President. With direct reference to the *Starr Report*, the White House asked to review the document in advance of its submission to, and release by, the House, so that it

Exhibit 4.1 The *Starr Report*: grounds for impeachment

There is substantial and credible information supporting the following eleven possible grounds for impeachment:

1. President Clinton lied under oath in the Jones deposition when he denied a sexual affair, a sexual relationship, or sexual relations with Monica Lewinsky
2. President Clinton lied under oath about his sexual relationship with Monica Lewinsky during his Grand Jury testimony
3. President Clinton lied during the Jones deposition about being alone with Lewinsky and about the exchange of gifts
4. President Clinton lied in the Jones deposition about his discussion with Lewinsky regarding the Jones case
5. President Clinton conspired with Lewinsky to conceal the truth about their relationship and conceal subpoenaed gifts
6. President Clinton obstructed justice by lying under oath and encouraging Lewinsky to lie and file an affidavit to prevent her testifying
7. President Clinton attempted to obstruct justice by aiding in a job search for Lewinsky which encouraged her to continue to withhold information about the relationship
8. President Clinton lied under oath in the Jones deposition about his discussion with Vernon Jordan
9. President Clinton tampered with a witness by attempting to influence the testimony of his secretary Betty Currie
10. President Clinton tried to obstruct justice by misinforming his aides and refusing to testify for seven months – and did thereby deceive, obstruct, and impede the grand jury
11. President Clinton abused his constitutional authority

Source: Adapted from: 'Grounds for Impeachment', *The Starr Report*, pp. 154–5.

might compile a reasoned response to the charges advanced by Starr. This request was rejected. The House Rules Committee voted on 10 September along party lines to deny the White House advance access to the report before it was released publicly, and unanimously to recommend that the House make public the report.[59] Thereafter, the House voted by 363–63 to release the report, and it was posted on the Internet on 11 September.[60] As a consequence, the White House legal team initially compiled a response to the Starr allegations without having seen them. Entitled *Preliminary Memorandum Concerning Referral Of Office Of Independent Counsel* (hereafter *Preliminary Memorandum*) this document outlined the defensive stance adopted by the President, and was influential in shaping both contemporaneous and future strategic positions.[61] Several matters of the utmost importance in the upcoming impeachment hearings were addressed, giving a foretaste of the nature of the debate for and against the President. The White

House pointed to the confession of wrongdoing by the President, and stressed that he had publicly apologized to the nation for his actions. As an extension of previous claims that private activity was no business of the Independent Counsel, the *Preliminary Memorandum* argued that the President's actions did not warrant impeachment, nor did they meet the Constitutional term 'high crimes and misdemeanors'.[62] The White House lawyers, while defending the President's position in principle, also went on the offensive with critical observations about how Starr had acquired his evidence, how he had interpreted that same evidence, and how the President's efforts to employ the powers of the presidential office did not constitute an abuse of power. With regard to the aforementioned power of executive privilege, for example, the *Preliminary Memorandum* asserted:

> Invocation of privileges was not an abuse of power. The President's lawful assertion of privileges in a court of law was only made on the advice of his Counsel, and was in significant measure *validated* by the courts. The legal claims were advanced sparingly and as a last resort after all attempts at compromise by the White House Counsel's office were rejected to protect the core constitutional and institutional interests of this and future presidencies.[63] (italics in original)

All charges which might be considered to be impeachable offenses by the President were brushed aside. The core of the defensive case was presented in a forthright and simple manner:

> The President himself has described his conduct as wrong. But no amount of gratuitous detail about the President's relationship with Ms. Lewinsky, no matter how salacious, can alter the fact that:
> 1)   The President did not commit perjury;
> 2)   The President did not obstruct justice;
> 3)   The President did not tamper with witnesses; and
> 4)   The President did not abuse the power of his office.[64]

The *Preliminary Memorandum* contended that the President had done little more than act in an inappropriate manner, in a private capacity. Consequently, the argument returned to the familiar themes of private morality and public duty, to which this text has already made reference:

This means that the OIC [Office of Independent Counsel] report is left with nothing but the details of a private sexual relationship, told in graphic detail with the intent to embarrass. Given the flimsy and unsubstantiated basis for the accusation, there is a complete lack of any credible evidence to initiate an impeachment inquiry concerning the President. And the principal purpose of this investigation, and OIC's report, is to embarrass the President and titillate the public by producing a document that is little more than an unreliable, one-sided account of sexual behavior.[65]

Written in advance of the release of the *Starr Report*, the *Preliminary Memorandum* was remarkably accurate in pinpointing the areas where Starr would mount his case against Clinton. It played heavily to the Congress, and repeatedly stressed the high standards of criminality and wrongdoing required for impeachment proceedings. It tactfully applauded the Congress for keeping the contents of the *Starr Report* confidential for a brief time after it was filed (even though the White House was not allowed to see the document at that time), and castigated Starr's investigation for the leaks and spillage of information into the public realm. Indeed it was 'based on these illegal leaks, as well as our knowledge of the President's testimony' that the White House claimed to have been able to file such a clear rebuttal without having first reviewed Starr's charges.[66] The *Preliminary Memorandum* sectionalized the President's defense. It addressed the nature and role of impeachment, the fundamental problems posed by allegations of obstruction of justice and perjury, and questioned repeatedly the conduct of Starr's probe, earmarking that investigation as a source of many of the perceived problems confronting the nation. Its communications target was principally the Congress rather than public opinion, although that nevertheless warranted background consideration. The *Starr Report* was created to recommend grounds for impeachment; the *Preliminary Memorandum* was designed to counter that suggestion and to present the Congress with an alternative interpretation of events.

The *Preliminary Memorandum* was released on 11 September 1998, the same day the *Starr Report* was released publicly by the House. A direct White House response to the content of the *Starr Report* was issued a day later, on 12 September. This second document in defense of the President, entitled *Initial Response To Referral Of Office Of Independent Counsel* (hereafter *Initial Response*), directly confronted the 11 charges advanced by Starr which, he contended, constituted grounds for the impeachment of the President.[67] It continued in much the same vein

Table 4.2 The release of the *Starr Report*: the key events

Date	Event
7 September 1998	• Clinton's lawyer David Kendall asks Starr for a preview of his report. His request is rejected
9 September	• House leaders agree that the House Judiciary Committee will conduct hearings to decide on possible impeachment action
	• Starr's report is delivered to the Congress
10 September	• House Rules Committee declines to give White House access to the *Starr Report*
	• House Rules Committee approves a resolution (H. Res. 525) authorizing the Judiciary Committee to take possession of Starr's submission and make sections of it public
11 September	• The House of Representatives adopts the resolution 363–63 and the *Starr Report* is posted on the Internet
	• The White House submits *Preliminary Memorandum Concerning Referral Of Office Of Independent Counsel* to the Congress – written without having seen the *Starr Report*
12 September	• The White House submits *Initial Response To Referral Of Office Of Independent Counsel* to the Congress – written after having seen the contents of the *Starr Report*

Source: Adapted from 'Scandal Chronology: September 5–11', *Congressional Quarterly Weekly*, 12 September 1998, p. 2385; 'Scandal Chronology: September 12–18', *Congressional Quarterly Weekly*, 19 September 1998, p. 2476.

as the *Preliminary Memorandum*, alleging that Starr was overly preoccupied with sexual issues and had failed to substantiate the charges he had raised.[68] It contended that the investigation by Starr had a political bias: 'it is plain that "sex" is precisely what this four-and-a-half-year investigation has boiled down to. The Referral is so loaded that only one conclusion is possible: its principal purpose is to damage the President.'[69] The frequent references to sex in the *Initial Response* helped to distort the focal point of this scandal. They portrayed the matter as a sexual episode and distracted attention from the legal points which underpinned Starr's accusations. This was in keeping with the overarching thrust of Clinton's damage limitation strategies. The *Initial Response* drew attention to the fact that the investigation by Starr had been presented as fact, yet there was no opportunity to cross-examine the witnesses. While this undermined Starr's case, it also had other ramifications. It ensured that when impeachment proceedings commenced there would be demands for witnesses to be called so as to ensure a fair hearing for each side. This complicated matters to some degree, as it threatened to extend hearings across several months and presented the Congress with a task of ever more complex proportions.

While reproaching Starr's conduct, the *Initial Response* played heavily upon interpretation of the President's intent, and similarly upon differences of opinion about the meaning of words and episodes central to the impeachment debate. It built upon the *Preliminary Memorandum*'s understanding of the nature of impeachable crimes and cast Starr's report as 'overreaching in an extravagant effort to find a case where there is none'.[70] For example, the OIC alleged that the President had committed perjury on 17 January 1998. In response to this potentially impeachable allegation the *Initial Response* addressed Starr's selective use of evidence, the prior standards set by courts, the burden of proof required to demonstrate the offense of perjury, and the problems posed by disagreement over the meaning of the term 'sexual relations'. By way of example of the President's defense, the following passage highlights the dual nature of the strategy. On the one hand it conceded personal error, while on the other it attacked Starr on the legal shortcomings of his evidence in relation to the perjury allegation:

> Lawyers' arguments, however well taken, should not obscure the President's admission that his relationship with Ms. Lewinsky was wrong and his acceptance of responsibility for his conduct. But one example will suffice to demonstrate the inherent weakness of the OIC's claim. The OIC argues that oral sex falls within the definition of sexual relations and that the President therefore lied when he said he denied having sexual relations. It is, however, the President's good faith and reasonable interpretation that oral sex was outside the special definition of sexual relations provided to him. The OIC simply asserts that it disagrees with the President's 'linguistics parsing', and that reasonable people would not have agreed with him . . . This simply is not the stuff of which criminal prosecutions – and surely impeachment proceedings are made.[71]

Further attacks were directed at the *Starr Report* and its use of evidence when it was being reviewed by the House Judiciary Committee. The White House expressed its discontent that Starr had selectively used evidence which portrayed the President in the worst possible light. It argued that Starr's report was a 'one sided and unfair manipulation of the evidence and the law' and drew attention to the omission of an important statement by Lewinsky which seemed to demonstrate that the President had not been involved in any conspiratorial act: 'no one ever asked me to lie, and I was never promised a job in return for my silence'.[72]

Citing legal precedent and conflicting evidence, the White House attempted to avert the onset of impeachment proceedings. These efforts, however, were in vain. As Chapter 5 demonstrates, as a consequence of the desire of the Republican majority on the House Judiciary Committee to press on with hearings, alongside a lack of an immediately obvious alternative and agreed-upon method of punishment, Clinton was forced to defend his tenure of the presidential office. The damage limitation measures employed by Clinton's defenders, portraying the scandal as a sexual escapade as opposed to a legal transgression, were insufficient in early September 1998 to sway the opinions of Republicans, many of whom, by this time, were already convinced of Clinton's guilt.

Conclusion

The meandering investigation of the Lewinsky scandal by the OIC created untold problems for the Clinton White House. Beginning in January 1998 and culminating in the submission of a referral to the House in September of that same year, Starr succeeded in initiating impeachment hearings by the closing months of 1998. In a narrow context Starr was successful in realizing his mandate, and his report offered credible evidence which suggested that Clinton had been evasive and had employed semantics and verbal contortions when seeking to conceal his covert affair. He did, however, via his investigative procedure, and zealous pursuit of White House aides, create substantial controversy about the nature and political function of the OIC and how it affected the separation of powers. The cost of Starr's investigation, upwards of 40 million dollars by the time the Lewinsky probe was complete, cast some doubt upon whether this was a prudent use of taxpayers' money. Likewise, the catch-all approach of Starr's remit also suggested that he had discretionary powers to probe and pry into a whole host of issues, including the President's private life.[73] Although Starr received his mandate from the Attorney General, the White House lost no time in complaining and elevating to public view the sheer scope of Starr's 'witchhunt'.

The impact of the OIC upon the presidency is a subject for caustic debate. Starr entertained a high public profile for several months through 1998. This did not however make him a popular figure with the American people. Whereas the Special Prosecutors who investigated the Nixon White House were perceived to be instrumental in the struggle to expose presidential wrongdoing, Starr failed to mobilize public sentiment to his cause, and held low approval ratings throughout the Lewinsky matter. In some respects this did not affect his probe, as he was not popularly elected, and there was little that public opinion could do directly to derail his investigation. There were attempts to court public approval, and to justify an investigation of the President's private life, but Starr continued relatively unhindered because his investigation was solidly grounded in the legal, as opposed to political, realm. Nevertheless, when the opportunity permitted, Starr exploited his prominence. When he submitted his evidence to the Congress, for example, Representative James A. McDermott (D-Wash) complained: 'He [Starr] made a media circus out of it'.[74] Some openly supported Starr's investigation and believed that it had been beneficial to the presidential office, if not to this particular President, while others contended it was Clinton who had wreaked long-term damage upon his own office. Arch conservative and former Supreme Court nominee Robert Bork suggested: 'This [Starr's investigation] begins to demystify the presidency, and I'm not sure that's all bad.'[75] Harold Bruff, Dean of the University of Colorado Law School, was more pessimistic about the whole episode: 'It's just been a disaster for the presidency.'[76] Whether the presidency needed Starr to demystify it is a leading question, as even taking account of the problems faced by previous administrations, Clinton's spate of scandals had, on their own, already made it clear that the person in the Oval Office was not beyond temptation or inappropriate behavior.

The overriding feature of the relationship between Starr and Clinton in 1998 was conflict. This was not always immediately obvious in an overt fashion, but the employment of executive privilege and disagreement about attorney – client privilege and Secret Service testimony ensured that, in the legal realm, the battle was acrimonious. Both investigators and investigated blamed the other for the delays and the bitter disputes. Certainly, Clinton appeared to stall the probe by citing presidential powers, such as executive privilege, in the early stages of the investigation. While such action generated controversy, the courts nevertheless validated its existence, but deemed that privilege could not be invoked if it impeded a legitimate investigation of a possibly criminal act. In this sense both sides could claim victory: Clinton for having executive privilege, an assumed presidential power, recognized in the courts, and Starr for having shown that his investigation was legitimate and warranted an extensive reach. The hostile atmosphere created further problems as claims of conspiracy abounded and leaks were attributed to both sides. Moreover, the White House did not have an opportunity to cross-examine witnesses or to evaluate the *Starr Report* in advance of its submission to the House or its public release. This initially made for guesswork in the creation of a defense, followed by a laborious point-by-point dismissal of Starr's conclusions when the report was available for consultation.

Whatever the longer-term impact of Starr's investigation upon the presidential office, there remains little doubt that it severely damaged Clinton during 1998. While public opinion remained stable and worked to the benefit of the President, congressional disapproval mounted following the President's admission of an affair with Lewinsky and, thereafter, became ever louder once the grounds for impeachment were filed in September. It was Starr's investigation that drove an unwilling President into a public and humbling confession that he had misled his family and the nation. Likewise, Starr's referral pushed the White House into unwanted impeachment hearings and ensured that Clinton's legal team would have to fight to guarantee the continuation of the Clinton presidency. The fact that the House of Representatives ultimately adopted articles of impeachment against the President also suggests, on the surface at least, that there was some justification to Starr's investigation and his interpretation of Clinton's actions. The underlying problem however was that the White House viewed the Starr investigation as partisan and politically inspired. Now it faced a Congress in the hands of the Republican party, which, exploiting Starr's evidence, threatened to terminate the Clinton presidency, overturn popular sovereignty as expressed in the 1996 election, and bestow upon Clinton an unenviable historical legacy. As discussed in the next chapter, Clinton's damage limitation effort now turned from challenging Starr, to persuading the House that the 'awful step' of impeachment should be avoided.[77]

5
Impeachment and Trial

Clinton faced a grueling political challenge when the Congress began to consider the *Starr Report* and contemplate the grounds for impeachment advanced in that document. It was however no easy task to weigh up the evidence presented and identify an appropriate form of punishment. With the irritant of Starr's investigation dispensed with, Clinton's attention naturally turned to persuading members of the House of Representatives to vote against articles of impeachment and drop all the charges suggested by Starr. If he failed to achieve this aim, then his presidency might come to a premature end and, given that he had rejected the route of resignation, he would face conviction by the Senate. At stake therefore was the future of Clinton's presidency. The Congress too faced pressure, as it attempted to resolve an issue forced upon it. Not only did it have to set aside its normal political agenda, but it also faced an added complication as mid-term elections occurred in the midst of this political crisis. Above and beyond these inconveniences lay the challenge of what to do with Clinton. It was too easy to refer to the Constitution and assume that any questionable action by the President warranted his impeachment and removal from office. Thereafter, if the President was not impeached, it might set a precedent whereby the Chief Executive was considered to be above the law and able to conduct himself in a manner which would cast moral aspersions upon the presidential office. Clinton's actions, and in particular his apology to the nation, appeared to demonstrate that he felt that the scandal was over. The Congress had to convince the nation that any further action was warranted and necessary, discipline the President in an appropriate way and, in many respects, convince itself that any punishment would not harm the presidential office and damage the American political system in the longer term.

The President did not involve himself extensively in the impeachment phase of the scandal. Rather, he allowed his legal aides to present his case before the Congress, relied on members of the Congress who sympathized with his predicament to defend his cause, and was thereafter aided by public opinion statistics which suggested that the American people had no deep desire to see him removed from office. Clinton's impeachment experience developed and was resolved across three phases. Firstly, the House Judiciary Committee decided, via hearings and investigation, to recommend articles of impeachment to the full House of Representatives. Secondly, the House impeached the President by voting on the articles of impeachment which had been passed by the Judiciary Committee. This decision demonstrated that partisan grievance was a significant feature of impeachment, a notable development because it was not intended as a partisan weapon to be employed on grounds of party disagreement. The House Managers, those advocating the conviction of the President, advanced their arguments to the Senate, heralding the third phase of the Clinton impeachment saga. In the Senate the Chief Justice of the Supreme Court presided over the trial of President Clinton. As much as this was an historic moment for the presidency, Clinton made few public comments at this juncture, and public interest in the trial remained marginal throughout. Discussion of whether to call witnesses also threatened to stretch the Senate phase to several months. However, agreement between those prosecuting and defending the President to limit the submission of new evidence and testimony ensured that the trial period was limited in its scope and duration.

This chapter begins by considering the problems posed by the impeachment of the President. In 1974 President Nixon resigned from office before the impeachment process had been fully enacted. He recognized that he did not entertain the full support of either party in the Congress and, once the House Judiciary Committee had approved articles of impeachment, anticipated that there was little to stop his forced departure from office.[1] Clinton's situation was different. The impeachment process passed through the House and on to the Senate, posing several procedural problems, as this had not happened since the impeachment and trial of Andrew Johnson in the mid nineteenth century. Clinton's experience was also racked by partisan division, and broached new ground in the modern era. The chapter continues with an examination of the three phases of the impeachment battle. Firstly, the struggle to adopt articles of impeachment in the House Judiciary Committee is examined. Secondly, the attempts by the Chairman of the House Judiciary Committee, Henry Hyde (R-Ill), among others, to get the articles of impeachment approved by the House of Representative are discussed. And thirdly, the problems encountered by the Senate are evaluated. It faced the final historic decision of whether to convict or absolve the President, and its decision not to convict Clinton naturally had a significant bearing upon Clinton's legacy. At the core of the impeachment process lay the effort of the President to minimize the damage inflicted upon his own presidency and upon the presidential office in a wider context. That the President took a less overt position during this critical phase of the scandal was a strategic and considered maneuver, designed to show that the scandal was of secondary importance in his mind to the public policy issues which confronted the nation and the American people. As a consequence, this was an impeachment process where the President appeared to be noticeably absent from the major debate about both its causes and its consequences.

Impeachment

Impeachment is a rarely used procedure, enacted to remove the President of the United States from office. The Constitution, the source of the impeachment guidelines, states that a President can 'be removed from Office on Impeachment for, and Conviction of, Treason, Bribery, or other high Crimes and Misdemeanors'. That presidential impeachment has occurred so rarely, in only three cases, testifies, in part, to a degree of hesitancy in using it to punish Presidents for wrongdoing. It is also problematic as a consequence of the ambiguous language employed in the Constitution. While this indeed has enhanced the flexibility of that document, it has ensured that to simply define a high crime and misdemeanor has become a task in itself. This is testament to the desire of the Founding Fathers to ensure that impeachment was only to be wielded when matters were incontrovertible, gained broad bipartisan support, and evoked a widespread consensus about the severity of wrongdoing.

Impeachment is a multi-step process.[2] The term itself is slightly misleading, referring to only half the process of removing a President from office. The House of Representatives has the sole power to impeach the President. This means that in effect it brings charges of wrongdoing against the President, these being contained in articles of impeachment detailing the nature of the perceived transgressions. Thereafter, if the charges are agreed to by a straight majority in the House of

Representatives, the Senate is involved in a trial phase. It examines the charges brought by the House and finds whether these are in keeping with an understanding of the nature of impeachment as outlined in the Constitution.[3] The case against the President is conducted and presented by House Managers who instruct the Senate on the views of the House. The Chief Justice of the Supreme Court presides over the trial in the Senate. This implies that the process is judicial in nature, but it is of note that the Framers of the Constitution located the impeachment process in the political, as opposed to legal, realm and while the trial in the Senate takes on some trappings of a legal process it retains, at its heart, a political element.[4] The Senate votes on the charges brought to it by the House. It must approve charges by a two-thirds majority if the President is to be removed from office, and it must vote on each article of impeachment separately. If any single article is approved by the Senate, then the President is required to leave office. The requirement of a super-majority ensures that, in normal circumstances, any perceived wrongdoing must transcend party division and persuade members of the President's own party that the crimes are sufficiently serious to warrant removal from office.

Clinton faced substantive problems when the Lewinsky matter reached the Congress. Firstly, as related in Chapter 4, Starr had suggested 11 alleged transgressions as grounds for the impeachment of the President. The charges were not restricted to one single area, nor did they concentrate upon one particular event. They were wide-ranging and contained serious charges of perjury, subornation of perjury and obstruction of justice. Whether these reached the constitutional standard of a 'high crime' was for the Congress to decide. Secondly, Clinton faced a Congress where the Republicans held a majority in both chambers. This posed particular problems when a vote to impeach was taken in the House. If it went along party lines, then the President faced the likelihood of a trial in the Senate. Thirdly, the alternatives to impeachment were not at all popular with a broad swathe of the Congress. While Republicans concentrated upon impeachment, several Democrats considered censure to be a viable alternative, an option that was rejected as a non-Constitutional method of resolution in political circles, but received widespread endorsement in public opinion polls. Fourthly, Clinton faced impeachment as a direct consequence of the investigation of an Independent Counsel, this being a notable development and one where he faced an imposing adversary. As is presently discussed, Starr was one of the first witnesses called by the House Judiciary Committee, offering him a gilt-edged opportunity to present his case to the Congress and the nation, in the face of sporadic responses by the President. Indeed, the impeachment process as a whole does not mandate the appearance of the President in the congressional forum, and Clinton, as a consequence, conducted his defense via legal aides and infrequent comments to the news media.

Opening arguments: the House Judiciary Committee

The House Judiciary Committee had to evaluate the *Starr Report* and to establish whether its content warranted the creation of articles of impeachment. The Committee was dominated by the Republican party, its Chairman being the experienced Republican Henry Hyde (R-Ill). The Committee itself was considered to be more partisan than most in the Congress, the members of each party quite diverse in their make-up and ideological thrust, as the *Washington Post* reported:

> The House Judiciary Committee that is on the brink of taking up the impeachment of President Clinton is a kind of flawed mirror of America. Instead of a true reflection of the country's moderate political character, it projects a sharpened and amplified image of the nation's cultural and ideological extremes.[5]

This fact alone aided Clinton's damage limitation exercise. The left-ward-leaning Democrats were unlikely to accede to Republican demands for extensive hearings on the President's predicament. While Clinton attempted to assure the members of his own party of his continued ability to lead, even if impeachment hearings were to commence, members of the Congress began to bicker, in advance of any formal hearings, about how they should be conducted and how long they should last. Internal dissent along party lines made it clear that a motivating factor in this scandal might be partisan animosity for the President. Even if this were not the case, the mere perception that it might be a contributory factor, as suggested by Hillary Clinton earlier in the year, cast a dark shadow over the proceedings and made it more difficult for the Republican party, in particular, to prosecute its case. Clinton could therefore anticipate that the Congress would split along party lines, but he could take nothing for granted, and predictably devoted time and effort to improving White House–congressional relations.

In advance of hearings and impeachment resolutions there also existed additional assurance for Clinton that the creation of impeachment charges might prove arduous and perplexing for the Judiciary Committee. It had to establish whether the allegations leveled by Starr reached the constitutionally required standard of a high crime and misdemeanor. Exactly what the term meant and how it should, or could, be applied to Clinton caused disagreement from the outset. For example, two members of the House Judiciary Committee held clearly divergent views on the role of impeachment. Representative Zoe Lofgren (D-Cal) considered it a redundant measure in the Clinton scandal: 'It's very clear that impeachment was really meant to be a between-elections remedy for behavior that endangered the system of government on the part of the chief executive . . . It's not to punish the chief executive, it's to save the Constitution. Criminal law . . . has nothing to do with this whole process.' Republicans adopted an alternative viewpoint. Representative Bill McCollum (R-Fla) believed: 'A felony crime would definitely constitute a "high crime" . . . If at the end of the day, I were to conclude that the president lied under oath in a deposition in the Paula Jones case with criminal intent and committed perjury, I would vote to impeach him because if we don't do that, he will have broken the rule of law and undermined the rule of law and we would be setting a terrible precedent.'[6] Precedent was indeed an important consideration. The *Jones* v. *Clinton* (1997) case had clearly shown that the President was not considered to be above the law. Here, it seemed, was a second opportunity to demonstrate that all American citizens were equal before the law. Once again the decisions that were to be made with respect to Clinton would have a wider and potentially longer-term impact upon the presidential office. This too was not lost on the members of Congress.

In late September and early October 1998 the Congress, and the House Judiciary Committee in particular, discussed the ways and means of conducting just hearings into the allegations leveled against the President by Starr. Henry Hyde (R-Ill) submitted a resolution which, reflective of that used against Richard Nixon, permitted his committee to investigate the President:

> Resolved, that the Committee on the Judiciary, acting as a whole or by any subcommittee thereof appointed by the chairman for the purposes hereof and in accordance with the rules of the committee, is authorized and directed to investigate fully and completely whether sufficient grounds exist for the House of Representatives to exercise its constitutional power to impeach William Jefferson Clinton, President of the United States of America.[7]

The House of Representatives decided to initiate impeachment proce-
dures on 8 October 1998 and voted by 258 to 176 to investigate
whether the President had committed high crimes and misdemeanors.[8]
Worryingly for the President, 31 Democrats sided with the Republican
party. This was not wholly unexpected, however, as condemnation of
the President had been forthcoming from many Democrats following
his August confession, and a vote to commence an investigation was
entirely different from a vote to impeach. That said, the President faced
a stern challenge if he was unable to convince the members of his own
party that his case was a just one. Attempting to cast Clinton's crimes
on a par with those of Nixon, Republicans were quick to point out
similarities with the Watergate scandal. Representative F. James
Sensenbrenner Jr. (R-Wis) declared that to have voted against the
impeachment resolution would have meant a 'return to the imperial
presidency of the Nixon era'.[9] Conversely, the Democrats who argued
in defense of Clinton cast him as an individual who had 'sinned', not
as a perpetrator of institutional abuse. The emergent cleavage in the
argument was to characterize the congressional debate throughout the
hearings and influenced impeachment votes in both the House and the
Senate. One side argued that there was evidence of abuse of office and
a purposeful attempt to evade the law and obstruct the Independent
Counsel, while the other contended that the President had made an
error of judgement, and had clumsily handled the aftermath of the
scandal's exposure. Ineptitude, they argued, alongside an extra-marital
affair, did not constitute an impeachable offence.[10]

Clinton reacted promptly to the vote in the House to commence
impeachment proceedings. As much as he wanted to remain aloof
from events, it was too important a development for him to ignore. In
alignment with his damage limitation strategy and rhetoric earlier in
the year, and indeed during Whitewater, the President stressed the
need to look beyond the Lewinsky matter and to focus directly upon
the needs and requirements of the nation. On the day the House voted
to initiate impeachment proceedings, he spoke briefly on the matter
prior to a meeting with his economic advisers. He brought attention to
the vote at his own behest, testament to his understanding of its
significance. He stated that he expected a fair process, and one where
party division would not obscure the guidance provided by the
Constitution. Thereafter, he underscored the need to carry on with the
agenda set by the American people, as impeachment lay 'in the hands
of the Congress'.[11] Two themes dominated the comments made by the
President. Firstly, he repeatedly referred to the American people and

the policies which affected their daily lives, such as Social Security and economic well-being. Secondly, mirroring past rhetoric, he deemed it inappropriate to comment further on scandal developments. When asked how he was dealing with the impeachment vote and the scandal personally, Clinton did not drop his political guard:

> Personally, I am fine. I have surrendered this. This is beyond my control. I have to work on what I can do. What I can do is to do my job for the American people. I trust the American people. They almost always get it right and have for 220 years.[12]

Direct reference to public opinion was no accident. As indicated in Chapter 7 of this text, opinion polls clearly indicated a popular reluctance to see the President impeached and forced from office. Clinton's remarks were a timely reminder to those in the Congress that they were apparently acting against prevailing popular sentiment, and that with November mid-term elections only a month away there was good reason to consider all the possible ramifications of a vote to initiate impeachment. Nonetheless, public opinion had no technical place in impeachment, that procedure being reserved for those in Washington acting as the representatives of the people, and not for the people themselves.

The mid-term election results proved to be advantageous for the President. Democrat gains in the House demonstrated to those prosecuting scandal in the Congress that Clinton's predicament meant little to the nation.[13] Votes appeared to be cast on non-scandal concerns such as the economy and public policy issues.[14] This surprising result served to undermine the Republicans who had hoped that the scandal would benefit their party.[15] Henry Hyde, Chairman of the House Judiciary Committee, dismissed the election results as inconsequential to the progress and mandate of his committee and the Congress. He contended: 'The [House Judiciary] committee continues to have a clear constitutional duty to complete its work in a fair and expeditious manner . . . This was just as true before the election as it is today. Our duty has not changed because the Constitution has not changed.'[16] Senior Democrats on the House Judiciary Committee rejected Hyde's viewpoint. John Conyers Jr. (D-Mich), a vocal and prominent Democrat at this time, argued: 'If there was ever any doubt, this election has made it clear the American people do not want President Clinton impeached and to misread that elementary message is really kamikaze politics.'[17] Clinton maintained his accustomed position at this time, repeatedly stating that the matter was out of his hands and he had no further comment. A senior aide succinctly announced: 'The lawyers will continue to handle impeachment stuff and the President will continue to be President.'[18] The elections proved to be surprising and problematic for the Republican party, and an unexpected boon of political fortune for Clinton. The results would not avert impeachment nor minimize its political impact, but public opinion was now a visible ally of the President and a factor which discreetly influenced interpretations of Clinton's predicament and his future fortunes as President.

On 5 November Clinton and the House Judiciary Committee clashed directly. The Judiciary Committee presented the President, under the auspices of its impeachment investigation, with 81 written questions concerning his involvement in the Lewinsky matter.[19] The Committee had declined to call a number of witnesses and the written request circumvented a need to call the President and induce a political and media circus. Clinton was asked to detail his meetings with Lewinsky and the gifts they exchanged, and was asked to illuminate several of the points initially raised in the *Starr Report*. The tone of the document was particularly terse, all of the 81 questions beginning with the phrase 'do you admit or deny . . .?', thereby putting pressure on the President to reply with clarity. Gregory B. Craig, the White House coordinator of the impeachment defense team, argued that there would be no new revelations as a consequence of Hyde's written inquiry: 'I don't think our answers are going to change the dynamics of the inquiry. We're going to work our way through it and make a good-faith effort to respond to it in a timely manner, sooner rather than later.'[20] Clinton's response was delivered to the Committee before the end of November 1998, but did little to appease the demand for fresh information. Many of the answers repeated information previously submitted to the Independent Counsel.[21] A dissatisfied Hyde stated: 'I have reviewed with dismay President Clinton's responses to the 81 requests for admission presented to him on November 5.'[22] This only caused more frustration for Republicans on the Committee who seemed unable to force the hand of the President and sustain the momentum of the scandal. This outcome was, in part, attributable to the adoption of a focused strategy to deal with impeachment. The White House damage limitation team was, by now, a tight-knit unit, working under the auspices of Craig and consisting of lawyers and experienced political aides, including many, such as White House Counsel Charles F.C. Ruff, who would play a prominent role during Clinton's trial in the Senate.[23]

Table 5.1 The House Judiciary Committee: the impeachment proceedings,
October–December 1998

Date	Event
5 October 1998	By 21–16 votes the House Judiciary Committee recommends an impeachment inquiry
8 October	House votes 258–176 to commence impeachment procedures
5 November	House Judiciary Committee presents Clinton with 81 written questions about the Lewinsky scandal
19 November	Kenneth Starr testifies before the House Judiciary Committee
27 November	President Clinton responds to the 81 written questions from the House Judiciary Committee
8–9 December	Witnesses for the defense appear before the House Judiciary Committee
10 December	Summary of argument before the House Judiciary Committee
11 December	Clinton makes another public apology about his behavior and accepts that censure would be an appropriate alternative to impeachment
10–12 December	Articles of Impeachment are debated in the House Judiciary Committee. All four are passed.

In an effort to specify the exact nature of impeachment, the House
Judiciary Committee's Subcommittee on the Constitution held a day of
hearings, and consulted political and historical experts who advanced
their personal understanding of what constituted an impeachable
offense. Nineteen historians discussed the matter and, as might be
expected, came to conflicting conclusions about whether Clinton's
actions warranted removal from office. Direct comparisons with previous impeachment hearings, principally those involving Nixon, proved
limited in their worth. Debate centered on whether there was an alternative to impeachment, whether lying was an impeachable offense and
whether a knee-jerk reaction might harm the political system in the
longer term. Arthur M. Schlesinger Jr., the respected historian, clashed
with Republican members of the panel when he suggested: 'I doubt if
there's anyone in this room who hasn't told a lie at one time or
another about his love life . . . We'd become the laughingstock of the
world . . . [if impeachment were to proceed]'.[24] Other academics dis-
agreed. Stephen B. Presser, from the Northwestern University School of
Law, contended that Clinton had committed an impeachable offense,
and speculated: 'George Washington would have recommended

President Clinton's impeachment, and this would likely have been the view of Madison, Hamilton, Jefferson and Mason, as well.'[25]

Republican disillusionment at this time was a feature of media reports and appeared to permeate the atmosphere in the Congress. Public opinion opposed the efforts of the GOP to oust Clinton, prompting one Republican, Bob Barr (R-Ga), to complain about the influence of this factor: 'Polls are becoming the currency of the political realm. The whole issue of impeachment has not been explained to the American public.'[26] Henry Hyde was similarly disillusioned. The issue of sex appeared to dominate the issue of law. While debate raged about morality and the President's sexual exploits, there was little chance that the core issues advanced by Republicans, on the subject of obstruction of justice and perjury, would entertain attention. This misplaced focus served to undermine the campaign to impeach the President. Likewise, problems abounded about how to proceed. With the impeachment process under way there was little that Hyde could do to halt it without both humiliating himself and casting major doubt upon the role and function of the Independent Counsel.[27] Representative Jack Quinn (R-NY) commented: 'Henry Hyde is in a bit of a bind there. He's started down this track. Now the question becomes how do we stop it.'[28]

The House Judiciary Committee summoned Independent Counsel Kenneth Starr to testify before it.[29] He appeared on 19 November 1998. His appearance was not uniformly welcomed by the Committee members, demonstrating at the outset that there would be no smooth ride through the impeachment process. Democrat John Conyers set a dissenting tone, contending 'that to date our committee process has not been bipartisan nor fair' and that it had dumped 'salacious grand-jury material on a public that does not want it'.[30] Internal dissent only worked to Clinton's advantage, setting Starr's appearance against an atmosphere of partisan rancor and bitterness. Starr used this gilt-edged opportunity to advance his case to reiterate the key themes raised in his referral to the House of Representatives. He repeatedly emphasized Clinton's alleged abuses of his authority and meandered through several areas of his investigative mandate, including Whitewater. There was also heated discussion of whether Clinton's actions were comparable to those of Richard Nixon in 1974.[31] Starr was questioned on whether he held a personal vendetta against Clinton, prompting him to advance his understanding of the core issues of the case:

It has nothing to do with the identity of the occupant of the office. It has everything to do with what the presidency is, and the nature of our relationship to one another as individuals, and whether we are all equals under the law . . .[32]

Starr emphasized a need to look to the facts, and avoid concentration upon individual motivation or character. He contended that the evidence spoke for itself and, if examined in an impassioned and apolitical manner, it was clear that Clinton had abused the power of his office. Starr was questioned by members of the Committee and also by David E. Kendall, Counsel for the President. Kendall took the opportunity to highlight the cost, duration, and questionable nature of Starr's controversial investigation. The testimony did little to alter the path of events. Starr's interpretation of Clinton's actions had been in the public domain for some time, and his comments did little to substantially alter the tone of debate on the impeachment questions.

The House Judiciary Committee continued with hearings into December 1998, calling an array of lawmakers, judicial experts, academics and former government employees, each with their own distinctive interpretations of the Clinton case, and how it compared to past crises endured by the American presidency.[33] Legal expert Alan Dershowitz contended that being President had not absolved Clinton of the responsibility to uphold the law, but rather, because he was President, he faced pressure that would rarely be forced upon a 'normal' citizen. He stated:

> It is clear that the false statements of which President Clinton is accused fall at the most marginal end of the least culpable genre for this continuum of offenses, and would never even be considered for prosecution in the routine cases involving an ordinary defendant.[34]

Again the problem of separating Clinton the individual from Clinton the President begged many questions as to how the scandal could be resolved, and how Clinton might be punished without irreparably harming the presidential office.

The arguments emanating from both Republicans and Democrats, and the arguments forwarded by the new witnesses were generally familiar ones, reflecting debates earlier in the year. Democrats exploited the partisan nature of the hearings, and the lack of a rigorous examination of Starr's evidence and conclusions. Likewise, they drew attention to the nature and role of impeachment, making clear that flawed enactment would do more harm than good, and would, moreover, set a precedent which might cause untold problems in any future allegation of malfeasance by a President.[35] Robert Wexler (D-Fla), for example, downplayed the severity of the President's wrongdoing: 'The President betrayed his wife. He did not betray the country.' With reference to public opinion, Zoe Lofgren (D-Cal) outlined the possible consequences of approving articles of impeachment, not for the President, but for the members of the Committee themselves: 'For those who are out to get the President, shame on you. But beware: next election, the voters will be out to get you.'[36] Republicans, by contrast, elevated congressional duty above and beyond normal political interplay. This issue, they argued, was exceptional, and the onus on the Committee was not to heed public opinion, nor to regard the matter as a sexual comedy, but to enforce the Constitution of the United States and remove a President who had committed a high crime. Henry Hyde pressed the Republican point home as the Committee neared its vote on four articles of impeachment. Seeking to concentrate attention on legal matters he asserted: 'Perjury is not sex. Obstruction is not sex. Abuse of power is not about sex.'[37]

Four articles of impeachment were debated in the House Judiciary Committee. Each was voted on in turn, and each addressed different matters raised initially by Independent Counsel Starr. The articles were extensive and wide-ranging and, as summarized in Table 5.2, covered the broad scope of the allegations against Clinton.

Coinciding with the release of draft impeachment articles was a resolution of censure, crafted by Democrats Boucher (D-Va), Delahunt (D-Mass), Jackson Lee (D-Tx) and Barrett (D-Wis) – all members of the House Judiciary Committee.[38] It argued that the President issued false statements about his relationship with Lewinsky, 'took steps to delay discovery of the truth', should face legal proceedings for his conduct, and should accept the censure as a formal acknowledgement of wrongdoing.[39] The White House gave vocal support for censure, a welcome alternative to the heady process of impeachment. White House Press Secretary Joe Lockhart stated: 'The President's general position is that he's done something blameworthy . . . If members of Congress want to come to him with an idea short of impeachment, it's something he would consider.'[40] Clinton appeared before reporters at the White House on 11 December to make a brief and final plea that an alternative to impeachment be found. He declared: 'What I want the American people to know, what I want the Congress to know, is that I am profoundly sorry for all I have done wrong in words and deeds. I never should have misled the country, the Congress, my friends, or my family.'[41] Clinton's late efforts to sway the Republicans to an alterna-

Table 5.2 Articles of impeachment: a summary

Article I. The President provided perjurious, false and misleading testimony to the Grand Jury concerning:
• The nature of his relationship with Lewinsky
• His testimony in the Jones deposition
• His attorney's comments during the Jones deposition
• His attempts influence the testimony of witnesses in the Jones case

Article II. The President provided perjurious, false and misleading testimony in the Jones case:
• In his answers to written questions by the Jones lawyers
• Concerning the nature of his relationship with Lewinsky, his knowledge of Lewinsky's involvement in the Jones case, and in his efforts to influence her testimony

Article III. The President obstructed justice in an effort to delay, impede, cover up, and conceal the existence of evidence related to the Jones case:
• He encouraged Lewinsky to file a false affidavit
• He encouraged Lewinsky to give misleading testimony
• He encouraged the concealment of evidence in the Jones case
• He assisted in a job search for Lewinsky to corruptly prevent her truthful testimony
• He allowed his attorney to make false statement during the Jones deposition
• He gave a false and misleading version of events to Betty Currie to corruptly influence her testimony
• He made false statements to aides and advisers to influence their testimony

Article IV. The President:
• misused and abused his office by making perjurious, false and misleading statements to Congress
• brought disrepute on the presidency
• betrayed his trust as President
• acted in a manner subversive of the rule of law and justice

---

Source: Adapted from:'House Resolution 611', *The Impeachment and Trial of President Clinton* (1999) pp. 445–50.

tive course of action failed. He had apologized before, and had made clear that he had no intention of resigning.[42] The choice for members of the Committee was starkly clear. They had to censure the President, and allow him to continue in office as a potentially crippled and humiliated individual, or alternatively, push ahead with impeachment, ignore public opinion, and permit the full House to consider whether the matter should proceed to a trial phase in the Senate. The Democrat censure resolution was emphatically rejected, emphasizing, if any further evidence were needed, that the partisan advantage held by the

Republican party would be an impediment to any attempt to forestall the momentum gathered by the scandal.

The articles of impeachment were approved by the House Judiciary Committee on 11–12 December 1998, as shown in Table 5.3.

The partisan nature of the vote gave the White House both concern and hope. The Republicans, holding the numerical advantage, had the power to punish the President and grant the House the opportunity to discuss the articles. However, the more the matter the appeared to be a partisan attack upon Clinton the less credibility those making the attack held, and the greater the damage inflicted upon the Constitutional process of impeachment. While Clinton could not withstand the numerical supremacy held by Republicans on the House Judiciary Committee, he could anticipate, in the longer term, that the super-majority required to ensure conviction by the Senate would be exceptionally difficult for Republicans to acquire and, even at such a late stage, his future would be secure.

The White House mounted a vigorous and acrimonious war of words with the House Judiciary Committee. It presented documents suggesting that impeachment was an overly harsh method of punishment, argued its position before the Committee members and had its defenders in the form of the Democrats on the Committee and numerous expert witnesses. For all the words and actions however there was little to stop the Republican party, armed with an abundance of evidence, to create and pass articles of impeachment against Clinton. The President's direct role in this first period of the impeachment debate was minimal. His defense was conducted principally by senior aides and lawyers. This was a prudent move. There was little that additional comment by the President could do to resolve the situation. He had apologized to the nation, and had indicated that a resolution of censure would be an appropriate and acceptable form of punishment. Furthermore, there existed the remote possibility that he might be called as a witness during a Senate trial, and spontaneous comment might be more detrimental than beneficial to his case. If the Senate decided to call him as a witness, the spectacle of his appear-

Table 5.3 Impeachment articles: the votes by the House Judiciary Committee

---

Article I. Passed by 21–16. All votes strictly along partisan lines
Article II. Passed by 20–17. One Republican, Lindsey Graham (R-SC) dissented
Article III. Passed by 21–16. All votes strictly along partisan lines
Article IV. Passed by 21–16. All votes strictly along partisan lines

---

ance might be calamitous for the American political system. The greater the likelihood of institutional damage, the more hesitancy Clinton could expect from members of the Congress.

Impeachment : the House debate

Clinton's strategy in the aftermath of the vote in the House Judiciary Committee was to attempt to convince moderate Republicans in the House to stop short of a vote of impeachment. The matter increasingly appeared to be one beset by partisanship, and it was Republican members who held the critical votes which would determine his fate. Bitter debate, apparent at the Committee stage of the proceedings, now reappeared during discussions in the full House, where 435 individuals held varying opinions on the severity of the President's actions.

The President was not wholly consumed by the scandal and, in accordance with his oft-repeated pledge to apply himself to the business of the nation, he visibly turned his attention to matters not directly related to scandal politics. Indeed, foreign policy developments at this time appeared to assist the President in a significant manner, and served to divert popular attention from an impending vote to impeach in the House. As soon as the vote had been cast in the Judiciary Committee the President, along with his family, left the country to deal with peace agreements in the Middle East. This removed him from the rancorous debate in Washington and sent a telling message to the American people: that while the House debated whether to force the President to face a trial in the Senate, he was applying himself to more lofty concerns. Upon his return to Washington he initiated a major foreign policy venture, one hatched and discussed when in the Middle East. Iraq was bombed by the United States and Great Britain on 16 December 1998. Clinton appeared on television that same evening to explain his policy decision to the American people. Recognizing that many might consider his action to be a ploy to draw attention away from the impeachment crisis, he confronted the issue directly:

> Saddam Hussein and the other enemies of peace may have thought that the serious debate currently before the House of Representatives would distract Americans or weaken our resolve to face him down . . . But once more, the United States has proven that . . . when we must act in America's vital interests, we will do so.[43]

This did little to convince Republicans that the policy was not initiated as a diversion tactic.[44] Curt Weldon (R-Penn) commented: 'The cynicism is at an all-time high . . . This is the anything-to-keep-my-job game.'[45] Senate Majority Leader Trent Lott (R-Miss) alleged: 'Both the timing and the policy are subject to question.'[46] The action did have an impact upon domestic proceedings. House Speaker designate Bob Livingston (R-La) postponed impeachment hearings for a single day to allow foreign policy matters to be resolved, and to permit members of the Congress to focus intently upon one serious political issue at a time. Clinton's timing of a strike against Iraq raised serious questions about whether the President was attempting to buy time when attempting to persuade wavering members of the Congress to side with him. On a more general front it appeared that the strike upon Iraq only delayed the inevitable, with the impeachment hearings commencing a short time later. If this was a case of the tail wagging the dog, then it had but a marginal effect upon the impeachment process.

A second distraction from the plight faced by the President arose from sexual revelations directed not at the President but at those prosecuting the scandal. In a surprising twist, the Speaker designate to the House, Bob Livingston (R-La), admitted, on 17 December 1998, to past sexual 'indiscretions'.[47] He had initially informed Republican colleagues: 'I have on occasions strayed from my marriage and doing so nearly cost me my marriage and my family.'[48] Livingston decided to resign, partly to avoid a credibility battle with the President, but also to exert additional pressure upon Clinton to follow suit. If the Speaker were to resign as a consequence of inappropriate sexual activity, then why not the President? Clinton's aides argued that the Speaker designate should not resign. Livingston however left no doubt that he saw his own plight inexorably linked to that of the President. He stated, 'I must set the example that I hope President Clinton will follow. I will not stand for speaker of the House on January 6.'[49] Livingston's revelations, and the timing of their exposure, were no accident. Larry Flynt, publisher of *Hustler* magazine, had previously offered a reward of one million dollars to anyone who could provide documentary evidence that a member of the Congress had had 'illicit sexual relations'. Flynt aimed to show the hypocrisy of a Congress determined to investigate and release information about the President's private life. Indeed several Republicans had already been forced to admit marital indiscretion. They included the Chairman of the House Judiciary Committee Henry Hyde (R-Ill), Oversight Committee Chairman Dan Burton (R-Ind), and vocal Clinton critic Helen Chenowen (R-Idaho). The revelations reduced the debate to one about sex, and distracted from discussion about law. This served to undermine the Republican argument that legal issues underpinned the impeachment process. Questions were also raised in the Congress about the timing of the revelations about Livingston. Was the White House damage limitation team at work? Brian P. Bilbray (R-Cal) contended that there existed a White House effort to eradicate meaningful opposition: 'Victims all seem to fall into the same pattern . . . Anyone who is perceived as a threat to the administration is immediately attacked.'[50]

For all the distractions and temporary delays, the impeachment of the President continued. Debate on the four impeachment articles submitted by the House Judiciary Committee, originally scheduled for 17 December, commenced on 18 December. By this time, those who had been identified as moderate Republicans had, almost unanimously, come out against the President and declared that on at least one article of impeachment they would vote in the affirmative. The decision of the House was a foregone conclusion. Given that there had only to be one article passed by a straight majority for there to be a trial in the Senate, and that moderate Republicans and some conservative Democrats intended to vote against the President, it appeared all but inevitable that Clinton's case was a lost one. The debate in the House lasted only two days.

Two broad themes dominated discussion. These generally followed partisan divisions, and reflected well-defined differences of opinion about the meaning and severity of the scandal. The prevailing Republican argument was that the President had violated the law and deserved to be removed from office. Emphasizing the factual evidence and the President's semantic contortions, Sam Johnson (R-Tx) was typical in his arguments before the House:

> It is clear from the evidence that this President committed perjury. It is clear from the evidence that this President obstructed justice. It is clear from the evidence that this President abused the power of his office.[51]

Tom Campbell (R-Cal) attacked the Democrat opposition to impeachment, arguing: 'no speaker has refuted the facts'.[52] Thereafter, Republicans played upon the rule of law, Clinton's apparent reluctance to cooperate with Independent Counsel Starr, and the message that any verdict, other than impeachment, might send to future Presidents. One Republican, Frank Riggs (R-Cal), stated that he had consulted with former President Gerald Ford, and 1996 presidential candidate Bob Dole, and both had stated they would vote to impeach had they been members of the House.[53] While the vast majority of Republican members of the House spoke in favor of impeachment on one or more grounds, there were some dissenting voices. Joseph McDade (R-Penn) identified Starr's investigation as problematic: 'I am gravely concerned about the tactics used by the independent counsel in this matter regarding the President.'[54] Only a few Republicans spoke forcefully against impeachment. Peter King (R-NY) made clear his difference of opinion with Henry Hyde: 'We are driving good people from government. What we are talking about here in this case, the President's conduct, was illegal, it was immoral, it was disgraceful, it was indefensible, but the fact is, I don't believe it rises to the level of treason or bribery . . .'.[55] Despite the limited dissent, the determination of the Republican leadership to press on with impeachment was unabated. Henry Hyde asked members of the House to serve their country and alleged that Clinton was a 'serial violator of the oath [of office]'.[56]

Democrats argued along different lines to the Republicans. Firstly, they contended that impeachment was not warranted by the actions taken by President Clinton, and to employ that device would harm the Constitution and the American system of government. Robert Wexler (D-Fla) argued this point: 'If we dumb-down impeachment and make it easier for future congresses to impeach presidents, we will forever weaken the institution of the presidency.'[57] A second strategy accentuated the importance of public opinion, and suggested that a vote to impeach would alienate the American people. David Bonoir (D-Mich), for example, argued: 'To force an impeachment vote is to completely ignore the will of the American people.'[58] A third strategy cast the matter as one beset by partisan politics and recrimination. Dianne DeGette (D-Col) summed up Democratic sentiment:

> We have divided this House with partisan politics, sowing mistrust and exposing the darkness in our own hearts. It started with the first vote of the 105th Congress to censure the Speaker, and it has continued to this day to the vote to impeach the President.[59]

Public opinion polls had identified a popular belief that the impeachment process was beset by partisanship and had degenerated into a political witchhunt. Democrats exploited this perception, and thereby placed additional pressure upon Republicans to consider partisanship as a hindrance to a just impeachment. A final argument advanced by Democrats was that censure constituted a viable alternative to impeachment. David Obey (D-Wis) made clear that it was an oppressive and legitimate alternative, as historical circumstance had made clear: 'To those who say censure has no bite . . . I come from the State of Joe McCarthy. Tell him censure has no bite. It destroyed him . . .'.[60]

When the debate on the articles of impeachment concluded there was an attempt to introduce a censure resolution as an amendment, designed to force a vote on that issue. However the censure motion was considered 'not germane' and was defeated 230–204, ensuring that the decisions to be made, and votes taken, would be solely about impeachment.[61] The votes in the House, displayed in Table 5.4, ensured that a trial would take place in the Senate, based upon two articles of impeachment.

Clinton responded immediately to the decision taken by the House of Representatives, appearing before the White House media corps following the vote to impeach. Having thanked the Democratic leadership which had fought valiantly on his behalf, he outlined his plan of

Table 5.4 Impeachment, 19 December 1998: the votes in the House of Representatives

Article I	The President provided perjurious, false and misleading testimony to the grand jury regarding the Paula Jones case and his relationship with Monica Lewinsky **Yea 228:** 223 GOP, 5 Dem **Nay 206:** 200 Dem, 5 GOP, 1 Ind
Article II	The President provided perjurious, false and misleading testimony in the Jones case in his answers to written questions and in his deposition **Yea 205:** 200 GOP, 5 Dem **Nay 229:** 200 Dem, 28 GOP, 1 Ind
Article III	The President obstructed justice in an effort to delay, impede, cover up and conceal the existence of evidence related to the Jones case **Yea 221:** 216 GOP, 5 Dem **Nay 212:** 199 Dem, 12 GOP, 1 Ind
Article IV	The President misused and abused his office by making perjurious, false and misleading statements to Congress **Yea 148:** 147 GOP, 1 Dem **Nay 285:** 203 Dem, 81 GOP, 1 Ind

action to contend with a forthcoming trial in the Senate. He pinned the blame for the unusual political scenario firmly at the door of House Republicans and on exacerbated partisan division, and suggested that the Senate might view the charges against him in a different light:

> I have accepted responsibility for what I did wrong in my personal life. And I have invited Members of the Congress to work with us to find a reasonable, bipartisan, and appropriate response. That approach was rejected today by Republicans in the House. But I hope it will be embraced by the Senate. I hope there will be a constitutional and fair means of resolving this matter in a prompt manner.[62]

Following Clinton's customary pledge to work on behalf of the American people and fulfil their political expectations, he also addressed the 'politics of personal destruction', implicitly suggesting that this scandal was not about the rule of law, but rather constituted a vengeful attempt to remove him from office. Thereafter, he bolstered this argument, contending: 'We must get rid of the poisonous venom of excessive partisanship, obsessive animosity, and uncontrolled anger. That is not what America deserves. That is not what America is about.'[63] Clinton concluded the speech with a lyrical passage, asking Americans to rise above the politics of scandal, and overlook the fact that it was his actions that had precipitated the crisis in the first instance. He stated:

> So, with profound gratitude for the defense of the Constitution and the best in America that was raised today by the [Democrat] Members here and those who joined them, I ask the American people to move with me to go on from here, to rise above the rancor, to overcome the pain and division, to be a repairer of the breach – all of us – to make this country, as one America, what it can and must be for our children in the new century about to dawn.[64]

For all the rhetoric, Clinton now faced a trial in the Senate. Impeached for giving false testimony to the Grand Jury in August 1998 and for obstructing justice in the Jones case, he joined Andrew Johnson and became only the second President to face a Senate trial. His efforts, and those of his aides, to halt the process in the House, had ultimately proved futile.[65]

Clinton's inability to persuade the House of the legitimacy of his case was not unexpected. One by one, those considered to be undecided about his guilt declared their support for impeachment and voted in the affirmative on at least one of the charges laid against the President. The numerical superiority of the Republican party in the House, combined with the simple process of a majority vote, meant that for Clinton to have escaped impeachment at this stage would indeed have been an extraordinary feat. Moreover, Hyde and his Republican allies on the House Judiciary Committee held the whip hand, and rallied the party to condemn the President on moral, political, and legal grounds. Damage limitation strategies, enacted by the White House, held little weight in this forum. Clinton's allies in the House argued that a vote to impeach would damage the institution of the presidency, that impeachment was an inappropriate form of punishment in this instance, and that censure would be a preferable alternative, one endorsed by the American public in poll samples. What was more, they argued that the will of the American nation was being neglected and, as further discussed in Chapter 7, the concept of popular sovereignty was being superseded by an elite act of partisan vengeance. Clinton lost the battle in the House. However, the Senate promised to be a more welcoming forum, one in which he could anticipate a more favorable outcome.

The Senate trial

One hundred individuals faced the formidable task of reviewing the two articles of impeachment passed by the House, and deciding whether the President deserved to be removed from office. Although conviction was only a remote possibility, there still existed an atmosphere of trepidation and hesitancy, particularly because the scandal had thus far developed in such an unlikely and often haphazard fashion. The Constitution provided Clinton with a procedural advantage over those prosecuting the scandal. A two-thirds majority was required to remove the President, and this was wholly unlikely in the absence of new evidence or revelations. The 55 Republicans in the Senate needed 12 Democrats to join them to force conviction, and the likelihood of a major desertion by Democrats was small. Following the House impeachment, it was clear that there was little public interest in congressional activity, and to Clinton's advantage, public apathy ensured that there would be no groundswell of support for a decisive conviction. The Senate trial threatened to last for some months if a

tight agenda were not agreed to, and consequently it was in the interest of those who wished to defend Clinton to suggest that an elongated
trial would be a natural progression from the impeachment debate in
the House.[66] This might deter Republicans from calling witnesses and
ensure that an alternative method of resolving the crisis might be
found. What was also advantageous to Clinton was that the Senate
could avoid a trial by simply holding a majority vote, dismiss the
charges, and seek to find an alternative and agreeable solution.[67]
Censure, rejected by the House, offered itself once again as a compromise position. However, there were also several problems for Clinton
in concocting a satisfactory damage limitation strategy at this time.
While public opinion was favorable to Clinton, there was no guarantee
that it would remain so, and any significant change in this area might
cause difficulty, even though it had no formal role to play in the proceedings. Moreover, senior Senators, such as Daniel Moynihan (D-NY)
and Joseph Lieberman (D-Conn), had been vocal critics of Clinton's
activities in advance of the impeachment proceedings. It was possible,
although unlikely, that prior condemnation might be repeated on the
floor of the Senate and culminate with a successful vote to remove the
President. Consequently, Clinton could take little for granted and had
to approach the trial with a degree of caution.

Problems appeared in abundance in advance of the Senate trial. They
included: procedural difficulties, whether to call witnesses, the length
of the trial, and the time assigned to each side to present its case.
Historical precedent was by no means encouraging. President
Johnson's impeachment trial lasted two and a half months, a prospect
not entertained readily by either defense or prosecution.[68] Trent Lott
(R-Miss) scheduled the trial to begin on 7 January, ensuring that the
Christmas period would be a busy one for both sides engaged in the
conflict. There existed, to Clinton's advantage, tension between
the two chambers of the Congress.[69] If the Senate debated the articles
at great length it risked paralyzing the Legislative branch of government for some time and if it called witnesses it risked turning the trial
phase into a media spectacle which might diminish the authority of
the chamber. What threatened to inflict the most intra-branch damage
was the prospect that the Senate might immediately hold a vote to
dismiss the charges, and effectively nullify the effort by the House to
consider and approve articles of impeachment.[70] Ross K. Baker, Rutgers
University political scientist, commented: 'I don't think the senators
should be in the position of having the House members, having done
all the heavy lifting, suffered all the opprobrium, then get up and utter

a few incantations and declare the whole thing over.'[71] Pressure existed for there to be a meaningful trial, but hesitancy also characterized this historic political event.

Clinton's damage control team focused intently upon the two articles of impeachment which now stood between Clinton and the end of this scandal. The matter of partisanship was frequently floated so as to make clear to Republicans that any vote to convict would be construed, by the White House at least, as a politically inspired decision. Special Counsel, and head of the task force on impeachment, Gregory B. Craig, observed: 'These two articles are legally defective, constitutionally deficient and factually without foundation. No responsible prosecutor would consider bringing charges based on the evidence and to consider removing the President on this basis would be the single most destructive act of partisanship in American history.'[72] In advance of the opening arguments in the Senate trial, it was certain that the President's team would mount a vigorous defense of their client and challenge the scope, detail, and factual evidence contained in the impeachment articles, while continuing to challenge the legitimacy and accuracy of the evidence collected by the Independent Counsel.

Negotiations concerning the structure and duration of the trial dominated White House–congressional relations in early January. Witnesses proved to be a particularly problematic concern. House Managers requested as many as 10 witnesses, including Lewinsky, but were opposed by Democrats in the Senate who objected to the unilateral request and the lack of detail about how and when the White House team would be able to follow suit. Tensions between those presenting the House case to the Senate, the so-called House Managers, and members of the Senate became tense and at times bitter. Senate Minority Leader Thomas A. Daschle (D-SD), clearly irked at House interference, commented: 'We didn't involve ourselves in their [House] proceedings and it's very disturbing that they now seem to be intent on involving themselves in ours.'[73] Later in the trial there were suggestions that the Senate 'owed' it to the House to discuss the impeachment articles at length and to call witnesses to clarify contradictions in the evidence. White House counselor Paul Begala mocked the intrabranch sense of duty: 'That's like saying the Titanic owed something to the iceberg.'[74] Clinton could afford, albeit to a limited extent, to sit back and allow the Congress to immerse itself in rancorous debate about the process and procedure of impeachment, detracting from the central concern of why the President faced the Senate in the first place.

Clinton's damage limitation exercise in advance of and during the Senate trial consisted of tactful reserve by the President and a renewed and aggressive attack upon the two remaining articles of impeachment by his legal aides. A business-as-usual approach continued to characterize the President's political strategy, even at this critical stage of the proceedings. Public opinion had responded positively to Clinton's claims that the scandal was sidelining the important business of the nation. His job approval statistics had remained high throughout this phase of the scandal. A revised approach was not warranted. Further to this, the Senate might not respond positively to a barrage of comments and criticism from the President, as an unnamed White House aide made clear: 'We don't want to be in the business of providing theater criticism . . . It doesn't matter what we think about the [GOP] presentation . . . We want to do everything we can to make the case in the court of the public opinion, but we're not going to do anything that hurts our case in the court of the Senate.'[75] The main forum of elite debate was the floor of the Senate, with the President cast as an interested observer, as opposed to an active participant. This permitted him to concentrate upon populist concerns such as planning new economic reforms and crafting a State of the Union address. On 13 January 1999 he made a brief comment on the Senate trial, one wholly in keeping with the general thrust of his damage limitation strategy: 'I think the Senate had to deal with that [the trial]. We filed our brief today. It makes our case. The important thing for me is to spend as little time thinking about that as possible, and as much time working on the [labor] issue we're here to discuss as possible. They have their job to do in the Senate and I have mine. And I intend to do it.'[76]

The arguments on the floor of the Senate were reflective of those presented in the House Judiciary Committee and on the floor of the House. The *Washington Post* reported that the trial commenced with a ' "Groundhog Day" like repetition of the familiar phrases and arguments that have become a staple of the impeachment proceedings'.[77] In advancing its defense the White House issued a 13-page *Response to Trial Summons* on 11 January 1999, followed thereafter by a 130-page *Trial Memorandum* on 13 January.[78] The *Response to Trial Summons* addressed the core themes of the two impeachment articles. The White House contended that the charges did not reach the standard of high crimes and misdemeanors. Each article was addressed in turn, the President's legal team arguing that the factual and interpretive record, as presented by the House Managers, was inaccurate.

Article I charged the President with perjury, and false and misleading testimony under oath, before a federal Grand Jury. In response, the White House pinpointed the factual contradictions which undermined this article of impeachment. The President denied that he made 'perjurious, false and misleading statements' to the grand jury when he testified about

- the nature and detail of his relationship with Monica Lewinsky
- statements he had made in the Jones deposition
- statements he allowed his attorney to make during the Jones deposition
- alleged efforts to influence the testimony of witnesses and to impede the discovery of evidence in the Jones case

The White House roundly condemned the structure, format, and scope of the impeachment articles. Several areas were identified as problematic. Firstly, Article I was considered inappropriate as it 'does not meet the Constitutional standard for conviction and removal'. Secondly, the White House contended: 'Article I is unconstitutionally vague. No reasonable person could know what specific charges are being leveled against the President.' Thirdly, it was thought to be overly expansive, and was 'fatally flawed because it charges multiple instances of alleged perjurious, false and misleading statements in one article'.

Article II appeared similarly deficient to the White House. It charged the President with obstruction of justice and impeding the investigation of his activity. The White House engaged the charges in an uncompromising manner. It asserted that the President:

- denies that on or about December 17 1997, he 'corruptly encouraged' Monica Lewinsky 'to execute a sworn affidavit in that proceeding that he knew to be perjurious, false and misleading'
- denies he 'corruptly encouraged' Monica Lewinsky 'to give perjurious, false and misleading testimony if and when called to testify personally' in the Jones litigation
- denies he 'corruptly engaged in, encouraged, or supported a scheme to conceal evidence' in the Jones case
- denies he obstructed justice in connection with Monica Lewinsky's efforts to obtain a job in New York to 'corruptly prevent' her 'truthful testimony' in the Jones case
- denies he 'corruptly allowed his attorney to make false and misleading statements to a Federal judge' concerning Monica Lewinsky's affidavit

- denies he obstructed justice by relating 'false and misleading statements' to 'a potential witness,' Betty Currie, 'in order to corruptly influence [her] testimony'.
- denies he obstructed justice when he relayed allegedly 'false and misleading statements' to his aides

Reflecting the scathing criticism of Article I, Article II was also deemed insufficient to meet the standard of a high crime and misdemeanor, too vague to allow an evaluation of its specific applicability, and overly broad in its scope.

The White House argued these points repeatedly during the Senate trial, while rebutting new allegations raised by the House Managers. White House Counsel Charles Ruff asserted that the President was innocent of all charges laid against him in the impeachment articles. Clinton's team disputed the facts advanced by the House Managers and made clear that the President contested the recollections of others involved in the scandal. An emergent issue, one of limited importance

Table 5.5 The Senate trial: January–February 1999

Date	Event
7 January 1999	Trial begins in the Senate
11 January	Clinton's defense team delivers a 13-page document, *Response to Trial Summons*, outlining its key objections to the articles of impeachment
13 January	The White House submits a 130-page *Trial Memorandum* addressing the charges against the President
14 January	House Managers begin to present the charges against Clinton
19 January	Clinton's team defend the President
22 January	Senators present questions to the defense and prosecution
25 January	The Senate discusses whether to drop the charges against Clinton
26 January	Arguments presented in favor of, and against, hearing witnesses in the case
27 January	The Senate votes 56–44 to continue the trial, and by the same margin to acquire depositions from three key witnesses
28 January	February 12 set as a projected date for the end of the trial
1 February	Monica Lewinsky deposed
2 February	Vernon Jordan deposed
3 February	Sidney Blumenthal deposed
6 February	Tapes of Lewinsky's deposition are shown before the Senate
8 February	Closing arguments
12 February	Final vote

during the House phase of impeachment, was the calling of witnesses. This would have offered Senators an opportunity to compare conflicting versions of events.

While the House Managers were eager to call witnesses, and their appearance would have brought the President's actions and words to life before the Senate, the issue nevertheless held some advantages for the White House. The appearance of witnesses would inevitably lengthen the trial and this might antagonize an already irritated American public. This, even though interest and viewer figures for the trial were low, could work to the benefit of the President and the detriment of the Senate. One White House official declared: 'Delay is unpopular. It's an enormous political price they will pay.'[79] Clinton aides were also upbeat that witnesses, if called, would provide no new evidence, and might even irk members of the Senate who would have to listen to repetitive information. One unnamed White House source contended: 'The idea that somehow the Republican prosecutors are going to elicit testimony that would be harmful to the President, that somehow Starr and his gang did not because they were too timid or too unthorough is preposterous.'[80] Some degree of hesitancy about proceeding apace became evident on the part of Democrats and moderate Republicans.[81] Even conservative Republicans, such as Richard C. Shelby (R-Ala), expressed concern that witnesses would provide no new information: 'if it's going to be the same old stuff, they're wasting their time'.[82]

The Senate approved a request by the House Managers to call witnesses on 27 January, but in a restricted fashion.[83] Three individuals were to be questioned about key issues of the scandal: Monica Lewinsky, Vernon Jordan and Sidney Blumenthal. The vote went generally along party lines 56–44, with only one Democrat voting with the Republicans. A vote to dismiss the charges against Clinton was defeated by the same margin. Although the trial continued, this provided fresh hope and reassurance for the White House as it emphasized the partisan nature of the proceedings. Special Counsel Gregory B. Craig looked upon the developments as a positive sign: 'Today's events make clear that the votes are not there to convict and remove the President from office. Any proceedings from this day forward only serve to delay the final resolution of this matter and run counter to the best interest of the Congress, the presidency and the American people.'[84] It appeared, to the White House at least, that the Republican party was determined to see the President suffer, and that in spite of abundant evidence produced by the Starr investigation there was a need to talk to Monica Lewinsky yet again. While the Senate was immersed in the trial of the President, the President cast himself as a servant of the nation, one of the few in elected government who was addressing the core issues identified in the opinion polls and at the mid-term election. Clinton increasingly seemed to be in touch with the American people; the Congress did not.

Following the deposition of the three witnesses, there appeared no new decisive evidence to significantly sway a substantial section of the Senate to, or away from, the President's position. Indeed, many of the statements made, in particular by Vernon Jordan, appeared to sub-stantiate rather than refute Clinton's testimony of 17 August 1998. There was an attempt to have Monica Lewinsky appear on the floor of the Senate to give evidence directly, but this was defeated 70–30.[85] This removed the prospect of live drama, and in several respects demonstrated that many in the chamber wished to end the debate and consider the evidence available at that time. Closing argument were presented by both sides on 8 February. The Senate then contin-ued to debate the two articles of impeachment behind closed doors, in the prelude to a final vote.[86]

Clinton's position looked secure in advance of the trial vote. Three prominent Senators, all Republicans, made plain their intention to reject both impeachment articles: John Chafee (R-RI), James Jeffords (R-Vt), and Arlen Specter (R-Penn).[87] This made it explicitly clear that the two-thirds majority required to convict the President would be unattainable. On 12 February 1999, the Senate opened its doors, and the vote to convict the President of high crimes and misdemeanors commenced. The verdict, displayed in Table 5.6, pronounced President Clinton not guilty.

Table 5.6 The vote in the Senate: 12 February 1999

Article I	The President provided perjurious, false and misleading testimony to the grand jury regarding the Paula Jones case and his relationship with Monica Lewinsky Guilty: 45 Not Guilty: 55
Article II	The President obstructed justice in an effort to delay, impede, cover up and conceal the existence of evidence related to the Jones case Guilty: 50 Not Guilty: 50

Source: Adapted from *The Impeachment and Trial of President Clinton* (1999) p. 434.

A motion was introduced to try and censure the President.[88] This was presented by a bipartisan group, but failed to meet Senate stipulations, as only 56 voted to introduce the measure while the Senate was sitting as a court. Therefore, the President was neither convicted nor censured as a consequence of the debates which took place in both chambers of the Congress.[89]

Clinton responded to his acquittal by the Senate with a brief statement, delivered to waiting reporters.[90] He apologized for the words and actions which had served to 'trigger these events and the great burden they have imposed on the Congress and the American people'.[91] Attempting to unite the nation behind a common cause, and as a gesture to the Congress, Clinton laid the foundations for a new era of political partnership: 'Now I ask all Americans, and I hope all Americans – here in Washington and throughout our land – will rededicate ourselves to the work of serving our nation and building our future together.'[92] Reflecting his determination to forget a scandal which had dominated political life for over a year, Clinton's statement lasted barely a minute. While he was ready to dismiss the scandal as a footnote to his presidency, bitterness and acrimony emanated from those who had worked tirelessly to convince the Senate that he deserved a meaningful punishment. The Investigative Counsel for the House Judiciary Committee, David P. Schippers, roundly condemned the Senate for its failure to convict the President on the two articles of impeachment. He stated: 'I feel there was no fair trial. There was no constitutional trial in the Senate . . . it seemed like the whole attitude of the senators was "We don't want to be bothered. We don't want to be annoyed".'[93] While recriminations came from those who had failed to win their case, the Congress returned to the task of passing delayed legislation.

Clinton emerged from the Senate trial phase of the scandal with his credibility damaged but with his position intact.[94] The failure of the House Managers to get a Democratic defection to their cause in the Senate was predictable. This does not however detract from the defense waged on behalf of the President by White House aides. They resolutely pressed home conflicts in the evidence and exacerbated the problem of applying that same evidence to broad and wide-ranging articles of impeachment. The President's participation in the Senate trial phase was minimal. He left most of the commentary to his aides and Press Secretary, and maintained the defensive strategy adopted through much of the Lewinsky scandal. Partisan wrangling in the Congress, and intra-branch tension between the House and the Senate ensured that inter-branch rivalry was not the sole consideration for those weighing up the case in the Senate. Moreover, problems of process, procedure and partisanship cast shadows on the ability of the Senate to carefully consider the evidence. While the House Managers demanded witnesses, and the White House threatened to extend the trial into the unforeseeable future, Senators had to assess the pros and cons of continuing with a trial which lacked widespread public endorsement and had little chance of removing the President from office. Although pressure existed to conduct a fair and balanced hearing, the pressure to complete the trial and end a year-long scandal process encouraged a swift resolution of this political episode. The President, through a consistent but overtly passive damage limitation strategy, continued on in office with, as highlighted in Chapter 7, high job approval statistics and support from the American people.

Conclusion

President Clinton entered the impeachment phase of the Lewinsky scandal in a vulnerable position. The *Starr Report* had chronicled a mass of alleged wrongdoing by the President, and congressional criticism of his actions had been biting, particularly with regard to the moral and ethical standards implicitly demanded by the presidential office. The White House, while clearly concerned that momentum might build against the President, and might induce members of both parties to vote for impeachment and conviction, had several weapons and tactics at its disposal so as to avert the forced removal of the President from office at this time.

Clinton exploited the controversy over the Starr investigation throughout the congressional proceedings. His aides and lawyers argued it was procedurally flawed, was the product of partisan and personal vindictiveness, constituted a waste of taxpayers' money, and that its conclusions were extreme and unreasonable when the evidence was cross-examined. Sympathetic academics and former government employees lined up before the House Judiciary Committee to condemn Starr, the Independent Counsel statute, and the conclusion that Clinton's action warranted removal from office. Consequently, the backdrop to the impeachment process produced little consensus and ensured that even at the outset, partisan acrimony clouded debate.

The partisan nature of the hearings and the debate in both chambers of the Congress made Clinton's task all the easier. Partisan hostility in the House Judiciary Committee ensured that the rift between

Republicans and Democrats on the proposed articles of impeachment was visible from the outset. While a few Democrats voted to pass the articles of impeachment in the House, there existed little chance that the Senate Republicans, if so inclined, could muster a two-thirds majority to convict Clinton. The divisions between the ideologically inspired House Republicans and their more conservative counterparts in the Senate also came in for scrutiny, with Henry Hyde (R-Ill) unable to muster overt partisan support for the House Managers' cause in the Senate.[95] Indeed the intra-branch antagonism became a feature of this phase of the scandal, with the President able to quietly observe the disintegration of the movement to oust him from office. The debate and division about witnesses also served to emphasize the problems faced by the Senate, and the weighty task faced by the House Managers. In this instance, process and procedure clashed with the House Managers' objectives and presented the White House with a gilt-edged opportunity to threaten to subject the Senate to an elongated quagmire of a trial with no determinable end. This was a prospect it was not prepared to readily entertain.

Impeachment clashed with the will of the American people, as Chapter 7 of this text demonstrates. There was little evidence to suggest that the scandal formed the basis for voting patterns in the November 1998 mid-term elections. To overturn the will of the people, as expressed in the 1996 presidential election, was a radical step, and one raised frequently by Democrats in the Congress as a problematic procedure. Many Americans thought Clinton guilty of a variety of offenses, but few deemed his forced removal from office an appropriate or just action. While Democrats emphasized the importance of popular sovereignty, Republicans drew attention to the Constitutional requirement that the Congress decide whether the President deserved removal from office for high crimes and misdemeanors, and not the people. In this sense, the Democrats and Clinton played heavily upon the notion of popular sovereignty, while the Republicans' argument was grounded in the trappings of the Constitution and the powers granted to the legislative branch of government to deal with high crimes in the executive branch of government.

Clinton's legacy, as a consequence of the impeachment hearings and the trial in the Senate, remains a mixed one.[96] Joining Johnson and Nixon in the ranks of those involved in impeachment proceedings was an unenviable burden to assume, and one which will earmark the second term of the Clinton presidency. However, Clinton's political reputation in advance of the scandal, and indeed in advance of his assumption of the presidential office was as a survivor, as the 'Comeback Kid'. His ability to endure and survive allegation of wrong-doing was enhanced by the process of impeachment, and his ultimate survival and political recovery. His capacity to endure condemnation for an affair with a woman many years his junior, to confess to an inappropriate relationship, and to be less than forthcoming to investigators while under oath, yet at the same time survive impeachment and evade conviction in the Congress, says much for his handling and knowledge of the workings of government, and of his ability to exploit contemporary understanding of the impact of scandal upon the presidential office.

6
The Media: Intrigue and Revulsion

The Lewinsky scandal was a newsworthy event, prompting an outburst of stories about the President, his private sexual liaisons, and the impeachment proceedings. While political scandal had, in the modern era, been a prominent subject for discussion among news outlets, both printed and visual, this scandal had an additional component. The Internet offered a new and unrestricted means by which the American public could acquire information about the ongoing scandal drama and, in many respects, it proved to be a revolutionary new tool in the conduct of scandal politics. It offered a further means by which the politicians in Washington, and the media in general, could attempt to sway the public to their respective messages and thereby shape public debate. The Internet, however, did not overshadow the more traditional means of information dispersal, and its availability was restricted at the time to a minority who had access to the appropriate computer technology.

The prospect of a further Clinton scandal offered the media an enticing opportunity, but also served up a problematic issue. The scandal inadvertently became a debate about more than obstruction of justice and perjury, and centered as much on sex and the private relationship conducted by Clinton. This broadened its appeal, but also made the content difficult to present without seeming to be prying into the private life of an individual. Moreover, questions were asked about how the President's private life impacted upon his public conduct, and whether the reporting of Starr's investigation was warranted and in the public interest. These proved difficult problems to resolve. The risk to any news organization of playing down the importance of the scandal was that it might allow competing news outlets to capture public attention, particularly as happened

170

with the Clinton address on 17 August, when unexpected and dramatic events thrust the scandal to the fore. Likewise, the first impeachment trial in the Senate since the 1860s ensured that the main news organizations were confronted with a truly historic event. On the other hand, there were problems if too much attention was given to Clinton's predicament. Firstly, it dragged on for almost a year, involving a select number of narrow issues. Over-exposure threatened to bore the public rather than captivate it. Secondly, the reputation of the media was under scrutiny, and could be tarnished by repetitive concentration upon salacious issues. Thirdly, if the public deemed the scandal unimportant, there threatened to be a perceptible gulf of interests between the elite media and the public. Portraying scandal accurately, in the right measure and on the pivotal issues was therefore no easy task.

This chapter firstly considers the effort by the media to portray the scandal via the different forms of media outlet. In keeping with the central thrust of this text, the problems faced by the Clinton White House and the perceptions it held of media coverage are accentuated, highlighting the tense relationship between the Executive and the media at this time. Internal debates about how to portray the scandal to the American people proved to be an irritation to those charged with presenting this scandal. Dispute played neatly into Clinton's hands and caused distraction among those seeking his removal from office. This was plainly evident during the impeachment hearings and the Senate trial, and this chapter concludes with an examination of media coverage of that particular event.

Delivering the message

The media's involvement with scandal politics has been widespread and pervasive. Indeed the media has been identified as a prime reason for the multitude of prominent political scandals in the modern era.[1] It assumed credit for the exposure of Watergate and stimulated an industry and sub-culture intent on exposing corruption and wrongdoing in politics. Iran-Contra however witnessed a more restrained investigation and more cautious reporting as Republicans charged the media with seeking to destroy yet another President. Accordingly, the media portrayal of that particular scandal seemed more muted and less vociferous than that witnessed during the Nixon years.[2] Indeed the media appeared to thrive, not upon the merits or efforts of those who had attempted to expose wrongdoing, but rather on the notoriety and the words of the alleged perpetrators, such as Oliver North, who were charged with illegal acts and of violating stated government policy.

As discussed in Chapter 1, Clinton had faced several accusations of scandal and wrongdoing by the time the Lewinsky scandal broke. Additionally, the Jones case had been in the public domain for some time and the Lewinsky matter was a direct, if unlikely, follow-on from that particular case. Analysis of news coverage of the Clinton scandals by Lichter and Sabato has however shown that prior to the Lewinsky scandal the media were reluctant to play heavily upon sexual scandal allegations, and were more comfortable with, and favorable to, reporting scandal themes which involved financial corruption and the abuse of power. They summarize their findings concerning the type of coverage granted different manifestations of pre-Lewinsky scandals:

> A detailed examination of the stories generated by the alleged Clinton scandals reveals that (1) Whitewater was heavily covered while the sexual allegations were barely touched by most media outlets; (2) the standards of proof news organizations require for airing Whitewater-related charges were lower than those they demanded for the troopers' and Ms. Jones's accusations; and (3) Whitewater sources often received more respectful treatment than the principal accusers of the other scandals.[3]

Several reasons were advanced thereafter to explain the media's reluctance to probe deeply into allegations of a sexual nature directed against the President. They included: disinterest in the private life of the President, a feeling that discussion of sexual material demeaned the professionalism of media commentators (particularly in the face of tabloid coverage), peer evaluation and standards, and wariness about discussing matters of a sexual nature when they involved the President.[4] Dan Rather, the CBS anchorman, talking of the Lewinsky scandal, declared: 'I didn't get into journalism to chase sex stories. One reason I hate it is that I think this story's bad for the country. I don't think anybody comes out looking good, and very few people feel good about it. I don't have an appetite for looking into people's personal lives.'[5] Furthermore, sexual material was considered problematic because it not only sullied political discussion, but a wrongful allegation or claim might tarnish the reputation of a particular newspaper and might blemish the career of an aspiring journalist.[6]

This backdrop was an unsettling one when the Lewinsky scandal erupted. The theme of sex could not be avoided, and as much as Starr attempted to get his message of obstruction of justice and perjury to the American people, the route by which he would prove his case inevitably led through a maze of sexual allegations and inappropriate behavior. The media had to confront this uncomfortable problem. While the Lewinsky scandal appealed to a vast number of media outlets, it necessarily forced the elite media to consider matters it might normally leave to the tabloid element of the profession, and thereafter the presentation of the information about Clinton's activities threatened to alienate the reading and watching public if it played heavily upon sexual matters.[7] The White House, in its damage limitation exercise, exploited the fears of the journalists and exploited the trepidation they held in covering a scandal of a sexual nature. Clinton's lawyer Robert Bennett, for example, commented teasingly: 'I'm very disappointed that The Washington Post, one of the preeminent newspapers in the country, is becoming a tabloid paper.'[8]

The scandal: exposure

The information in the hands of the mainstream media in early January 1998 would have allowed it to expose Clinton's relationship with Lewinsky before Internet columnist Matt Drudge broke the story on the *Drudge Report* web site. Journalist and *Newsweek* columnist Michael Isikoff had information which would have revealed Clinton's discreet liaison, but *Newsweek* was reluctant to publish unsubstantiated material of this nature without further proof.[9] The Internet story might have held little weight in its own right. The situation changed however when the *Washington Post* understood the revised mandate of Starr's remit granted by Attorney General Janet Reno, and perceived that there might be some validity in pursuing the matter further. The story that the President might have engaged in a relationship instantly became front-page news, receiving credence because of the Independent Counsel investigation, and this, moreover, suggested that there might be an element of criminality involved which could prove harmful to the President.

The scandal interrupted mainstream media coverage of a visit to Cuba by the Pope. This was an important theme of criticism throughout its duration. It seemed to sidetrack other newsworthy items and become the sole focus of news attention, an issue addressed by historian Arthur M. Schlesinger Jr. at a *Columbia Journalism Review* forum on 'How the Press Is Shaping (or Misshaping) Politics':

> Why should the press, which was the champion of the reality prin-ciple at the time of Watergate become the promoter of the kind of obsession with the Monica Lewinsky affair at the expense of all the other problems of the Republic? I wonder whether this isn't associ-ated with a change in the structure, a competitive structure, of the press . . . Everyone is trying to scoop everyone else, and therefore the accountability and the responsibility of the press becomes an immediate casualty.[10]

Several stations immediately cancelled regular program schedules to facilitate extra coverage of the emergent information about Clinton.[11] The aggregate mass of scandal coverage across time did not enhance interest in Washington politics. Rather, its accumulation through the year served to cast the media in an unfavorable light and bored the public, who were antagonized by both the level and the nature of the attention.[12] Clinton himself followed a public oriented agenda throughout the scandal and his decision to do so appeared to strike a popular chord with the American people.

Problems in the media's self-regulation were obvious from the outset and became an immediate source of controversy and debate. Pressure to be ahead of the game and to be first to publish information led to concerns about the unsubstantiated nature of the some of the material printed in the early stages. Leaks, too, would dominate later in the year, with information about Starr's investigation, in particular, becoming a source of irritation for the White House and for those in the media eager to uphold high standards and ethics, whatever the content of the potential story-line. James Fallows, editor of *U.S. News and World Report*, contended that the reporting 'has gotten out of control'.[13] The White House recognized the potential problems faced by the President with a wealth of information, much of it mere specu-lation, in the public domain. White House spokesman Mike McCurry argued that there existed: 'a temptation . . . for the story to outpace what is factually known, and a lot of reporting based on allegations that in other kinds of circumstances, in different kinds of environ-ments, would be put through a lot finer editorial screen before they made it on the air and in print'.[14] A key reason for the speculation was the Internet. The lack of regulation and the ease by which an individ-ual could create a website or report material without editorial control ensured that a mass of stories and leads appeared which relied upon notions of conspiracy. Academic Bill Kovach, of the Nieman Foundation at Harvard University, identified the change brought about by the Internet: 'When Matt Drudge puts it up on the Internet and everyone in town is talking about it, it's difficult to resist at least trying to match what he's put out. So each judgment maker in each news organization is left to design his or her own standards.'[15] The deregulation, at one and the same time, increased the amount of outlets through which the public could access information on the scandal, but also ensured that acquiring reliable and accurate information, and differentiating between fact and fiction, was all the more difficult. Journalists and commentators were aware of the problems, but awareness made the issues no easier to contend with.

Shortly after the scandal broke a study of the mainstream media identified a sea-change in the nature of the reporting during this scandal. The Committee of Concerned Journalists released a report entitled 'The Clinton Crisis and the Press: A New Standard of American Journalism?'[16] The report contended that the type of material published during this scandal tended towards opinion and speculation and away from factual analysis and reporting. It argued that the statistics presented a 'news culture that is increasingly involved with disseminating information rather than gathering it'.[17] There were also concerns about sources and how information was acquired. This aligned well with a problem faced by both Clinton and Starr. Their strategies were affected by leaks of information which derailed investigations and undermined Clinton's credibility throughout the spring of 1998. For example, Clinton's deposition in the Jones case was leaked to the media in March 1998. The *Washington Post*, in printing the document, did not reveal its source. White House spokesman McCurry expressed his frustration: 'as a matter of journalistic principle, most news organizations take seriously the responsibility to alert readers to the identity and motive of anonymous sources . . . The Post chose not to do this . . . and you have to ask them why.'[18]

Public anger about the way the media was covering the scandal was identifiable from an early stage. This might in part have arisen because the media were pointing out their own shortcomings. A more likely explanation however is that there was little public interest in the private life of the President. But this proves problematic when audience figures for television shows and sales figures for printed news sources are examined. *Time* magazine sold 100,000 extra copies when the scandal was exposed, and several news programs including 'Fox News Sunday' recorded their highest ever audience figures.[19] The public seemed intent on watching the media product, but at the same time was not prepared to endorse its coverage or declare openly its interest in this story. *Boston Globe* editor Matthew Storin addressed this apparent contradiction. He remarked: 'People like it [the Clinton story], they're intrigued by it, and they don't like that they're intrigued by it. There's revulsion at their own level of interest.'[20] The public continued to watch the scandal with muted interest, did not become more attracted to it over time, but would periodically tune in, in large numbers, to observe Clinton's latest problems.

While the debate about leaks and problems about the sourcing of information dominated the public forum during the spring, the appearance of Clinton before the Grand Jury in August granted the media a prime opportunity to exploit a public event of significant note. Two developments arose as a consequence of Clinton's testimony. Firstly, he gave an address to the nation following his testimony, allowing extensive media analysis of this climactic episode. Secondly, Clinton's testimony was videotaped and was later released into the public domain by the House Judiciary Committee, giving the television networks an unexpected boon, and placing them at the forefront of scandal presentation.

Clinton's decision to testify, and thereafter admit to a relationship, appeared at first sight to grant some vindication to the media. After all, White House media correspondents had been attacked by the White House for concentrating on the Lewinsky affair at the expense of other issues, and Clinton's admission appeared to show that the attention, and accusations of a presidential cover-up, were warranted.[21] Clinton's evening address received an exceptionally high viewing figure, with 67.5 million people watching his brief speech.[22] It was aired on all of the main channels and cable news networks. Media interpretation of Clinton's admission followed immediately, and was generally critical of the President. On NBC, *Newsweek* columnist Jonathan Alter asserted: 'I'm not sure he has come to terms with how much he has soiled his presidency', while ABC's Sam Donaldson was similarly critical: 'He did not tell the country what that relationship was . . . He didn't come clean with the country.'[23] Ex-Clinton officials, such as George Stephanopoulos and Dick Morris, alongside political pundits of all persuasions, clamored to voice opinion about Clinton's apology. *Washington Post* writer Tom Shales, however, was disparaging about the nature of the coverage:

> Finding people with something to say about the matter has not been hard for TV viewers. Finding people with something worth-

while to say has been very difficult. With so many channels and so much competition, standards are lowered to the very bottom and anybody with an opinion is slapped onto the screen. The clamor to yammer is tremendous and deafening. No President before Clinton has ever had to face such a pervasive and punishing wall of noise.[24]

Similarly, House Speaker Newt Gingrich expressed his concern that media coverage of the scandal was consuming conventional politics: 'The editors, the publishers, the producers of this country ought to put themselves on a diet and not spend more than 20 per cent of their time on the scandal.'[25]

Newspaper editorials at national and state level were as critical of Clinton as the television commentators. Few accepted Clinton's explanation at face value and many rounded upon the President for not telling the truth at an earlier stage, both following the address and particularly after the release of the *Starr Report*. The *San Jose Mercury News* condemned the President in harsh tones: 'Clinton has dishonored the presidency. He has diminished his stature as a leader. He has damaged the trust that united the people who form his administration. He has embarrassed the country he swore to protect and safeguard.'[26] The *Atlanta Journal-Constitution* stated: 'Only one person can spare us further heartache. By resigning . . . By making that sacrifice, Clinton would save the nation from a protracted trauma . . . A President more concerned with the national interest than his own preservation would realize that resignation is his only responsible option.'[27] The response of the White House to a barrage of criticism was to simply state that it had been visible for months, and that following the speech there would be no new strategy to accommodate media negativity. Spokesman Joe Lockhart addressed the barbed commentary: 'I wouldn't say it has no bearing on the discussion going on out there, but I'm fairly certain it doesn't provide compelling reasons to change the discussion over here. A lot of people have been on the bandwagon that the President should be run out of office and they have been on it for seven months now.'[28] Public opinion, as explained in Chapter 7, did not follow the elite demands for Clinton's resignation. Indeed, most appeared tired of the scandal and the unending focus on the private life of the President. At times the public seemed reluctant, if not totally unwilling, to adopt the line championed by media outlets, and felt more aggrieved by the actions of Starr, the Congress, and the media, than it did with the actions of the President. One columnist, writing in *Time* magazine, summed up the imbalance of opinion between public and press: 'You [the media] shoved his sex life in our faces last January, and rubbed our noses in it for eight months more, so by now we're more disgusted with you than with Bill Clinton.'[29]

The media maintained the focus on Clinton's scandal despite the messages provided by the polls. Extracts of the *Starr Report*, released in September, were published in many newspapers and posted on the Internet. The content of the *Starr Report*, and how the media decided to publish it, actually undermined Starr's efforts to make a compelling case for impeachment. It will be recalled that Starr wanted to demonstrate that the President had abused the power of his office and had committed perjury and obstructed justice. He claimed that the scandal was not about sex, but encompassed a violation of the rule of law. However, when the media published and printed the *Starr Report* it was more often than not preceded by a warning about the sexual content of the material, and how it might not be suitable for minors or might be considered offensive by some. The *Los Angeles Times* stated: 'We urge parental guidance for children reading the full report.' The *Washington Post* announced: 'Some material in these unedited texts is inappropriate for children and younger readers, and some of the material will be offensive to some adults.'[30] This emphasized the sexual nature of the material, directed attention at areas where Starr did not want preoccupation, and caused problems for those determining how to present the report. The rebuttals issued by the White House contained frequent references to sexual material. However, this was not entirely problematic, as it drew the debate onto the matter of sex, and distracted attention from the issue of law, an outcome advantageous to Clinton's damage limitation effort. Discussing the problem of sexual references, *Chicago Tribune* editor Howard Tyner observed: 'Which term is too salacious and which isn't? Once you get in to that, you open the door to criticism that you're trying to alter the meaning. The contentious parts are the core of the report. That's what it's about. If you take them out, you may as well not run it at all.'[31] The *Starr Report* motivated the media editorials into yet another round of condemnation of the President and his actions. Again the critical elite opinions were not reflected in the opinion polls.

Clinton's Grand Jury videotape was released into the public domain in mid-September. The House Judiciary Committee decided to release it along with a vast number of evidentiary materials collected by the Independent Counsel. The White House was naturally suspect about the motivations of the congressional committee, and questioned the amount of information the public needed to come to an evaluation of the President's behavior. James Kennedy, White House spokesman, commented: 'Talk about information overload. This will be the mother of all document dumps.'[32] Problems existed about whether to censor the material, given its sexual content. Four hours of Clinton's testimony were aired promptly by the main news networks as soon as it was circulated. Clinton failed to live up to advance expectations that the tape would be detrimental to his political standing. His combative, yet controlled, style portrayed him as an astute and thoughtful individual, besieged by investigators. Indeed the whole event seemed more beneficial than detrimental to Clinton's damage limitation exercise. The *Washington Post* observed:

> While the televised testimony may have revealed little that was new about the ongoing Kenneth Starr investigation, viewers who sat through it may well have emerged with a new or renewed feeling of sympathy for the President. His having to sit there and try to remember whether he gave Monica Lewinsky a box of chocolate-covered cherries, in addition to being prodded for lurid details of their sexual activities, made Clinton seem vulnerable and victimized.[33]

Clinton escaped relatively unscathed from this event, one widely thought to have the potential to inflict crippling damage upon his presidency.[34] Again the media had suggested that the sexual overtones might have a bearing upon the opinions of the watching public, diverting attention away from legal aspects and onto sexual matters. The amount of written material, when placed alongside the four-hour tape made rapid and easy consumption difficult, particularly given that Starr had advanced 11 grounds for the impeachment of the President. As a consequence, it was easier for the watching public to consider the sexual aspects of this scandal, than to compare Clinton's January deposition and August Grand Jury testimony, or evaluate whether Clinton had committed perjury, subornation of perjury, or had obstructed justice. This worked to Clinton's advantage. It simplified the discussion, bored the watching public, took the emphasis off the legal aspects of the case, and suggested that the inappropriate relationship, for which he had already apologized, was a central factor in this scandal.

In the aftermath of disappointing mid-term election results, House Speaker Newt Gingrich (R-Ga) again blamed the media for concentrating excessively on the Lewinsky matter to the detriment of other public policy issues. He commented:

I don't think we [the Republicans] are nearly as obsessed as the press corps . . . Look at all the hours that Tim Russert spent on 'Meet the Press' this year on that topic versus the number of hours on Social Security . . . I don't think hour after hour of details about Lewinsky are very newsworthy . . . It is a little disinguous to spend all this media time on a topic and then turn and say why are these other folks obsessed with it.[35]

Gingrich's attempts to find a reason for his party's failure to capitalize on Clinton's problems were dismissed by the media as a last-gasp attempt to salvage something from a disappointing election. Similarly, Larry Sabato, from the University of Virginia, responded to Gingrich's explanations for the Republican failure: '. . . absolutely absurd. The press is everybody's favorite whipping boy. When it's convenient, it's always the press's fault. Every single one of [the Republicans] was calling around fanning the flames on the Lewinsky matter . . . Their minds are fried. They can't believe they had ended up losing seats.'[36] The failure to exploit the Lewinsky scandal appeared to provoke in-fighting and recrimination about who exactly had failed in their job. Had the Republicans played too heavily upon an issue of marginal interest to the American people? Had the media failed to present the case against Clinton clearly and accurately, and had it, moreover, concentrated too heavily upon a narrow band of issues, and turned the American people off the scandal? As the debate among the elite groups continued, Clinton's two-fold effort to firstly distance himself from the scandal and, secondly, to pledge his intention to continue with the public policy agenda he had repeatedly stressed throughout the scandal-ridden year, appeared to hold greater favor with the nation.

A poll conducted amongst journalists by *Columbia Journalism Review* and *Public Agenda* revealed the thoughts of the elite media and permitted an insight into the disparity between elite and popular opinion on the scandal. Following on from the intense scandal coverage and Gingrich's complaint that the story had been overplayed, 125 senior American journalists were questioned on that particular subject. Linda Lightfoot, executive director of *The Advocate* in Baton Rouge thought that for media editors to follow public sentiment and lessen coverage of the scandal was a losing strategy and one that could not be followed. The media, she claimed, had a duty to follow important constitutional stories, even if they were of secondary interest to the nation. It was the media who should set the agenda in this instance and not the country. She stated: 'I don't think we should let people who are not concerned about important affairs dictate our coverage. The fact that a President of the United States might be impeached is extremely important, whether people are tired of hearing about it or not.'[37] The problem with this outlook, however, was that when it alienated a majority of the watching public it played neatly into the hands of those defending Clinton, and made the matter of prosecuting him all the more difficult. Public opinion, as discussed in the next chapter, was a meaningful factor in determining the outcome of the scandal. It was not the decisive factor by any means, but a lack of public condemnation, aligned with widespread boredom with the scandal, assisted the President in his damage limitation exercise. The poll found that 48 per cent of journalists thought the scandal had received coverage that had been 'about right', while 44 per cent thought that it had been overplayed. Remarkably, 4 per cent thought that it had been underplayed. It appeared that on this occasion the media had one agenda, the people another, and Clinton's public policy agenda aligned more closely with that of the nation than the impeachment agenda advanced by the media and many Republicans in the Congress.

The impeachment hearings were covered on the major television networks and on cable, but the coverage did not captivate the American people. A small proportion of the public did watch the hearings, but they never reached the heady heights of the Watergate or Iran-Contra scandals, despite the fact that this scandal came to the very brink of the removal of the President. One of the reasons for restrained interest was the nature of the evolution of the scandal. The themes advanced during the impeachment debates were very similar to those advanced when the *Starr Report* was issued and when the Clinton Grand Jury videotape was released. The hearings rapidly degenerated into detailed debates about the minutiae of the evidence, and demonstrated, if any further proof were needed, that no clear answers would emerge to reconcile the remaining conflicts in the evidence. This failed to capture the attention of the American people, and members of Congress of both parties were aware of the rather tedious nature of the proceedings. Notably, the major newspaper editorials had shied away from the calls for presidential resignation voiced after the release of the *Starr Report*. A majority of the editorials now called for censure rather than impeachment and conviction, and many demanded that the voice of the American people now be taken into account. The *Los Angeles Times*, for example, stated that censure 'would provide a responsible alternative to impeachment . . . The House should be provided a chance to vote on that alternative.' The

St. Louis Dispatch concurred: 'There is another way, and that is censure. The American people support it. The President accepts it. It is time to turn away from impeachment.'[38] Several editorials however still vociferously demanded that the President either resign or be impeached. *USA Today* demanded in its headline, 'Clinton can still act honorably – He can resign', while the editorial asserted 'It is an option that even Richard Nixon accepted at the end.'[39]

The saturation coverage of the scandal by the media did not appear to curry favor with the American people. The fact that media calls for the punishment of the President did not square with the opinions of the American people showed a distinct cleavage of opinion between the media and the recipients of its message. Furthermore, opinion polls suggested that the media coverage of the congressional investigation was disapproved of by a majority of the American public, as Table 6.1 highlights.

Several discussions during the Senate phase were conducted, following a vote in that chamber, behind closed doors. The open and closed sessions did not make for fluent coverage, nor did the vote in the Senate produce a surge of interest in the death-throes of the scandal. Debate and disagreement existed about whether the public should have the opportunity to observe the impeachment proceedings in full, or in part.[40] Senator Orrin Hatch (R-Utah) wished to preserve a legal atmosphere and urged that the deliberations about the President's future be held behind closed doors: 'I think the reason why that rule [to allow private deliberation] was enacted was to keep it as like a jury, in a jury room, but also to get rid of the politics, because if it's public in those debates then you'll have a number of senators who will use that occasion to play politics, where if it's private, it may come down to really what is right, what is wrong here (*sic*).'[41] This argument entailed more than simple adherence to judicial precedent. Public opinion, as demonstrated in the next chapter, was an irritant to the Republican case. It

Table 6.1 Approval/disapproval of the media coverage of the investigation of Clinton

Do you approve or disapprove of the way [each of] the following is handling the current investigation into the charges against Bill Clinton?

	Approve	*Disapprove*	*Don't know*
The news media	35%	59%	6%

Source: PEW Research Center for the People and the Press. 14–17 January 1999.

strongly opposed impeachment and preferred censure as a method of punishment. Hatch's motivations were therefore more complex and strategic, for the removal of the cameras would in effect stifle public understanding and indeed its tangential participation in the process. The removal of the media, and therefore the public, from the trial would reduce it to a forum where elite opinion would dominate, whilst also allowing members of the chamber to speak openly and frankly without fear of negative public reaction to specific opinions. Television executives naturally desired access to the Senate deliberations. Brian Lamb, of the public affairs network C-Span, wrote to Senate Majority Leader Trent Lott in December: 'Full and direct access of the public to each Senator's consideration of the evidence would be consistent with the openness characterizing each step leading up to the trial, including the President's testimony before the grand jury, the House Judiciary Committee meetings and the debate of the full House on the impeachment resolutions.'[42] The open and closed sessions appeared to appease both sides but satisfied no one. It made viewing the trial phase a frustrating pastime, but ensured that Senators were on view, periodically, to the American people and that public opinion and popular aversion to an elongated trial phase were matters for the Senate chamber to consider. Media reaction to the closed sessions was predictably hostile. It disrupted coverage and deprived newsmakers of hard factual information in a scandal that had come to embrace leaked information. The *New York Daily News* announced 'The Senate has shut out the public it purports to represent', while the chairman of CNN, Tom Johnson, thought the process to be one which 'denies people throughout the world the opportunity to judge the fairness of the proceedings'.[43] As shown in Table 6.2, the public reaction to the exclusion of the media

Table 6.2 Television access to the Senate trial

Do you think it is important that the Senate allow the entire impeachment trial to be shown on television, including all witnesses and final debate among Senators, or is it not important that the Senate allow every aspect of the trial to be shown on television?

	8–10 January 1999
Yes, important to be on television	40%
No, not important	59%
No opinion	1%

Source: 8–10 January 1999, Gallup poll.

was mixed, partly, one might assume, because the viewing figures were low, as was popular interest.

The media struggled to enliven the legal proceedings in the Senate throughout the trial phase. Cameras were only focused on those who were talking at any given time, leading to elongated concentration on individuals, with no opportunity to observe a more general reaction to the speeches and evidence presented. While the event may have been historic in nature, it was not good television.[44] This fact was not lost on several members of the Senate who rebelled against the motion to hold key deliberations behind closed doors. Senator Tom Harkin (D-Iowa), for example, left the Senate chamber and delivered a speech in favor of acquittal to the waiting media, drawing criticism from Trent Lott for his failure to prise himself away from potentially harmful media exposure. The intra-branch antagonism only served to enhance Clinton's chances of survival.

The final vote in the Senate to convict or absolve the President provided some drama, even though it was wholly predictable and failed to capture widespread public attention. Each Senator had to announce their decision on the two articles of impeachment by stating 'guilty' or 'not guilty', adding some theater to the proceedings. The media anchormen on the major networks attempted to add gloss to the event and the vote. Cokie Roberts of ABC News described the proceedings: 'It's not suspenseful, but it is dramatic.' Brian Williams of NBC News stated: 'It was chilling, unexpectedly chilling, to hear the words', and Peter Jennings of ABC considered the proceedings as 'a little anticlimactic for some, but a great, historic civic lesson for others'.[45] The predictability of the Senate decision aided Clinton, reducing the likelihood of a surge of viewers for the final decision, and taking the steam out of the media effort to portray the event as one of significant magnitude. The visible conflict between the media and the Senate about the nature of the coverage, the clash between Republican and Democrat over impeachment and the type of coverage afforded it, and the popular disinterest in the House impeachment and Senate trial, did not make for an efficient or effective process. Clinton, faced by opposition from the elite media and the Republican majority in the Congress, benefited from emergent conflicts between the two, and found that following on from the media spectacles of Watergate and Iran-Contra, this scandal failed to have a similar popular impact. The scandal, in fact, rather than gaining credit for investigative journalists and their tenacious investigation of a presidential cover-up, appeared to diminish respect for the media, as Table 6.3 indicates.

Table 6.3 Opinion on the national media

We're interested in how your opinion of some different groups has changed over the past year of the Monica Lewinsky investigation and impeachment ... has your opinion of the national media become more favorable, less favorable, or stayed about the same?

More	Less	Same	Don't know
5%	56%	36%	3%

Source: *Newsweek* poll, 11–12 February 1999.

Conclusion

Clinton's damage limitation exercise was aided by the problems faced by the media in attempting to cover the scandal. The advantages gained by Clinton were not always of his administration's own making. The sexual nature of this scandal proved difficult, particularly for the elite media, to cover. It appeared more suited to the tabloid market, and created a dilemma about which parts, if any, of Clinton's antics could be presented for public consumption. Starr naturally wanted media and political commentators to concentrate upon the legal aspects of the case, and portray sexual material as a mere backdrop to more serious concerns. However, a central element of the scandal, and an issue which received extensive discussion in the media, was sex and the detail of Clinton's relationship with Lewsinky. Media discomfort with this factor was therefore an internal consideration, and a delicate topic which caused, at the least, a debate about the nature and content of the scandal coverage. Legal matters often appeared to become a secondary consideration. This caused the media to question its own coverage and review its performance. This only served to aid Clinton as the internal bickering distracted from his predicament. Indeed the criticism of the media by discontented Republicans following the November 1998 mid-term elections highlighted that those prosecuting scandal were unsure about how to place additional pressure upon the President.

Clinton was both assisted and harmed by the presence of the Internet during 1998. It exposed the scandal, was unregulated, and thrust stories into the public domain which relied on unconfirmed sources. The constant leak of information, much of it detrimental to the position of the President, proved irksome. This was however an historic feature of presidential scandals and was to be expected. The

Internet merely enhanced the magnitude of the leaks and the unsubstantiated information, and its presence was as much of a distraction for traditional media outlets as it was for the Clinton White House. Public use of the Internet was predictably limited, given the availability of this medium. That said, record access figures on several news websites testified to an interest in this form of information distribution unseen during previous scandals or prominent news events. The decision of the House Judiciary Committee, among others, to release information directly onto the Internet testified to the increasing prominence of the electronic distribution of information.

A prime reason for Clinton's ability to accommodate the Lewinsky episode was the inability of the media to translate its outrage and criticism of the President into any meaningful change in public opinion. This conflict emerged for several reasons, and was ultimately beneficial to the damage limitation efforts of the President. The media appeared to have put itself above the commonplace interplay of politics – much as the Republicans in the House sought to do – and indeed appeared to pay little heed to public opinion. Robert Lichter, of the Center for Media and Public Affairs, identified a new self-appointed role within media circles: 'Journalists now view themselves as the guardians of the political system, not just informing the public but protecting it from politics and politicians.'[46] This partly explains why the public failed to assume the position held by the media, in spite of the extent of coverage and the critical condemnation of the President. Turned off by the scandal, and quickly tired of the overplay on Monica Lewinsky, the American people, as shown in the next chapter, paid little attention to the fourth branch of government and viewed its coverage as overblown and insignificant to the well-being of the nation. In this context the media participated in this scandal as an elite player, and held a position divorced from public opinion and more akin to a branch of institutional government, initially determined to see a discredited President leave office. However, the internal disputes within elite circles, combined with the failure of many media outlets to convey the meaning and consequence of the scandal, ensured that the popular impact of the Lewinsky scandal would be limited.

7
Public Opinion: Reluctant Observers

Public opinion had a meaningful role to play in determining the outcome of the Clinton–Lewinsky scandal. Poll sample results were advanced by both investigators and investigated to validate and support their respective lines of argument, and popular understanding of the nature and meaning of the scandal had a significant impact upon the decisions made in the political realm. Clinton found that his private indiscretions were accepted by the American people, seemingly upon condition that he continued to perform to the nation's satisfaction in the political realm. As this text has stressed, he therefore assumed a conventional political role, emphasizing his determination to press on with a national agenda and to attend to his 1996 election pledges. Whatever Clinton's personal intentions, he had to accept that the Congress and the media would concentrate heavily upon the theme of scandal and exploit it to the full for partisan and profitable gain. This, at the outset, meant that in the public realm there existed a battle to set the political agenda and to interpret the meaning and severity of the scandal. In this respect the American people were immediately faced with a stark choice: to believe the word of the President or to entertain the arguments of his detractors. The fluctuations in public opinion highlighted the relative strengths and weaknesses of each side's case, and accommodated media communication and interpretation of the scandal as it evolved.

This chapter evaluates the meaning of public opinion to each of the main players in this political scandal. Starr, the Congress and Clinton had all to consider the role and impact of public sentiment upon their actions and, moreover, how public opinion might affect the attitudes of their opponents. The Lewinsky scandal was a credibility war, where all sought to bolster their own position and, at the same time, attempted to destroy the public persona of their adversaries. The battle was bitter and acrimonious. Moreover this was a political event where poll statistics were readily available and each of the main participants could observe popular perceptions of their performance. Theoretically, this should have had little or no bearing on the outcome of the scandal. In practice, however, it cast a shadow over proceedings and suggested that the elite players in this scandal might ignore popular sentiment at their peril. The chapter thereafter examines the movement of opinion across time, demonstrating how Clinton's damage limitation policy was integrally tied to popular sentiment, and how public opinion assisted in salvaging the Clinton presidency.

Public opinion

In scandal politics, much of the political interplay takes place at the elite level of government, with little in the way of direct popular involvement in the political or legal processes undertaken to address moments of tension. It would therefore be relatively simple to dismiss the American public as mere observers, with no constructive role to play in scandal development or resolution. This however is far from the case. Public opinion has played an important historical role in shaping the evolution of scandal politics, and the Lewinsky episode proved to be a case in point, whereby it was a material consideration for those in Washington. Several factors made the viewpoint of the American people significant to political interaction during this scandal.

The impeachment and removal of the President was, of course, the objective of many Republicans in the House and the Senate, and also that of the Office of Independent Counsel. Any attempt to remove the President via political means, outside of the expression of popular will at election time, automatically conflicts with the concept of popular sovereignty. In effect, the will of the masses is usurped by a small elite in Washington, technically representative of national opinion. Movement to impeach and remove a President, necessarily restricted to high crimes and misdemeanors so as to curb its usage, revokes popular sovereignty and places a significant political burden upon those in Congress. White House Special Counsel Gregory B. Craig (and coordinator of Clinton's impeachment defense team) contended that the impeachment of President Clinton would, 'disrupt the government of the United States in such a fashion as to gridlock the government, divide the country, and actually defy the will of the people'.[1] The wider the scope of the term 'high crimes and misdemeanors' the more likely it is that popular sovereignty might be overturned in the middle of a presidential term. The correlation between an understanding and interpretation of that particular Constitutional term and the emphasis one places upon the importance of popular sovereignty is therefore significant.

Resolving the conflict between popular sovereignty and scandal politics poses several problems. It is difficult to measure popular attitudes to a specific political episode across time. Obviously the four-year election cycle allows a periodic review of the performance of the President. However, Clinton, having been elected for a second time in 1996, would not have to face any future national election. The next best method of evaluating public sentiment is to employ and evaluate opinion polls.[2] A compelling reason for analyzing poll evidence in this particular scandal is that Clinton employed polls to evaluate and understand prevailing public sentiment. One of his first actions when the Lewinsky scandal broke in January 1998 was to concoct a defensive strategy underpinned by information provided by polls. Opinion poll information therefore had a direct bearing upon the damage limitation strategy and political tactics adopted by the Clinton administration. Indeed, according to former aide Dick Morris, polls were pivotally important to the Clinton presidency in a wider political context:

> For Bill Clinton, positive poll results are not just tools – they are vindication, ratification, and approval – whereas negative poll results are a learning process in which the pain of the rebuff to his self-image forces deep introspection. Intellectually, polls offer Clinton an insight into how people think. He uses polls to adjust not just his thinking on one issue, but his frame of reference so that it is also as close to congruent with that of the country as possible.[3]

Alongside the impact of American public opinion upon the workings of the presidential office lies the influence of public opinion upon those prosecuting scandal. They have several issues to consider before proceeding with a zealous pursuit of the President. Three issues are of particular note in this scandal. Firstly, the November 1998 mid-term elections meant that attention was given not only to traditional local issues, but also to whether scandal politics could be exploited to the benefit of individual candidates. Overplaying the meaning of scandal, particularly if it lacks resonance in the nation at large, has potentially serious drawbacks. Scandal, therefore, is not automatically beneficial for the prosecuting entity when seeking to destabilize the position of the President, and Clinton's predicament in 1998 ultimately did nothing to undermine the fortunes of his party in the mid-term elections. Secondly, members of Congress must observe the ebbs and flows of popular opinion as it applies not only to themselves, but particularly to the President. Persecution of a popular President could lead to a backlash if his party exploits any sympathy generated by an unwarranted attack.[4] Reagan gained valuable leeway during Iran-Contra, for example, by retaining popular support in the realm of personal approval, and thereby making it difficult for Democrats to attack his character for fear of alienating the voting public and generating a reactionary upsurge of support for the President. Thirdly, public opinion can be discounted on specific occasions. Impeachment, for instance, was a power reserved by the Founding Fathers for the Congress, not one reserved for the people nor an instrument of power best wielded by an easily swayed mass. In this respect, the extraction of a potentially volatile public from the impeachment process is a prudent measure. It does however present problems. The removal of the public not only revokes popular sovereignty, but may also allow the contaminating influence of partisanship and institutional acrimony to influence political judgement. The critical step of removing a President from office is held by a mere 535 Americans elected to the Congress, and popular opinion, as much as it might disapprove of the steps taken against any particular Chief Executive, is directly powerless to express its opinion. Naturally, the safeguard of a tight election cycle ensures that popular opinion will be considered by the Congress, for if popular sentiment were wholly neglected, then, via a blinkered approach to impeachment, it might find itself subject to wholesale changes brought about by a disapproving public.

Public opinion clearly has a significant role to play in shaping the outcome of scandal politics. Determining its true impact, given that it is mainly expressed through polls, is a difficult challenge, yet one critical to a true appreciation of the factors determining congressional and presidential action. The value placed upon popular sovereignty in a democratic society further emphasizes the consequential role of public opinion in scandal scenarios. This takes public opinion from the role of observer of scandal politics, into that of participant, even though the actual participation is a tangential factor in the scandal process.

The key players: the influence of public opinion

Each of the key participants in the Lewinsky scandal had to take account of public opinion, but each had to address its impact in a different manner. The legal participants observed public sentiment, but could, in the main, not being subject to popular election, discount the short-to medium-term impact of public opinion on the scandal process. The Congress, an institution able to wait for some time and consider the development of the scandal, could view the long-term evolution of public opinion on Clinton's predicament and react accordingly. This, however, was easier said than done, as the Constitutional burden of the impeachment process, partisanship, and suspicion of Clinton, when placed alongside the complication of a mid-term election, made the task a difficult one. Clinton naturally surveyed public opinion and utilized it to support his precarious position. To this end, he played heavily to popular disposition, exploited his strengths as a political leader and, when times demanded, asked the public to understand that he held deep personal regret over his moral transgressions. The following three sections outline the challenges posed by public opinion to the main players in the scandal.

(i) Kenneth Starr: Independent Counsel

Kenneth Starr had little to gain or lose in the realm of public opinion. His position was not threatened as a consequence of poor poll statistics and this was evident as he stubbornly pursued his investigation despite low levels of public approval. These low figures continued throughout the scandal and suggested there was little public faith in Starr, nor enthusiasm that he advance grounds for the impeachment of the President. Starr, in this sense, was divorced from, but nevertheless judged by, public opinion. One explanation for his negative numbers and poor public standing was that he had been involved in a long-term investigation of the Clintons on several matters, including Whitewater. It superficially appeared as though he was engaged in a witchhunt and was persecuting Clinton. This contributed to the low and declining favorability ratings he gained in January 1998 as the scandal broke, as displayed in Table 7.1.

Table 7.1 Starr's declining popularity: January 1998 favorability ratings (%)

	Favorable	*Unfavorable*	*Never heard of*	*No opinion*
23–24 January	24	24	29	23
24–25 January	26	27	24	23
28 January	20	38	21	21

Source: January 1998, Gallup polls.

Clinton's damage limitation strategists exploited Starr's negative public persona and attempted to portray him as overly vindictive in his relentless pursuit of the President. They also exacerbated perceptions of partisanship and suggested that conventional political division underpinned the Lewinsky scandal. Moreover, they contended that the grounds for Starr's investigation were essentially meaningless. This strategy appeared to entertain some success in the public forum. Following the submission of the *Starr Report* in September 1998, partisanship was firmly identified by the public as a motivating factor in the Independent Counsel's investigation, as Table 7.2 makes clear.

Starr had to consider public opinion to a limited extent, as it would, in time, influence the action of the Congress. While he could continue unhindered with his own probe for presidential malfeasance, he was also aware that when he submitted his referral to the Congress, if he had lost all credibility as a consequence of White House attacks, then the Congress, with one eye on public opinion, might decide to drop the matter and dismiss the suggested grounds for impeachment. Starr's popular credibility was integrally tied to the future fortunes of his report. This ensured that the Congress watched Starr's conduct carefully, and how he played to the public gallery. Starr, of course, was assisted by events, particularly when the President was forced to concede that he had participated in an 'inappropriate' affair. Nonetheless, Starr faced an uphill battle throughout his investigation and found it difficult to cultivate public enthusiasm for his cause, irrespective of Clinton's actions. This was not unexpected. If he had played overtly to the public then questions would have arisen about how public posturing squared with his investigative mandate. Similarly, total silence by Starr in the face of White House hostility would have left public opinion open to persuasion by the defenders of

Table 7.2 Starr: partisan or impartial? (%)

Do you think ... Starr has mostly conducted an impartial investigation to find out if anything illegal occurred, or has he mostly conducted a partisan investigation to damage Bill Clinton?

	All	Republican	Democrat	Independent
Impartial	27	49	11	25
Partisan	64	40	82	64
Don't know	9	11	7	11

Source: 22–23 September 1998, CBS/*New York Times* poll.

the President. Seeking to influence public opinion, Starr attempted to repeatedly compare Clinton's damage limitation effort with that of Nixon during Watergate, and implicitly suggested, in an open forum, that the Clinton White House was similarly corrupt. He alleged it was impeding a justifiable investigation. Starr's comparisons had little impact, as a poll taken in October 1998, and displayed in Table 7.3, indicates.

Starr attempted to uphold his legal authority and, at the same time, cultivate public sympathy which would not only convince the Congress of his legitimacy but might also encourage the public to question the statements being issued by the White House. He had limited success in achieving his objectives.

(ii) Congress

Congress became a fully-fledged participant in the scandal during late 1998 and early 1999. Before its direct involvement via impeachment proceedings, members of the Congress had good reason to observe the Lewinsky scandal and pay particular heed to public opinion. As cited previously, the 1998 mid-term elections were an important political consideration. Of wider institutional importance was that Starr had as his mandate the task of finding grounds for the possible impeachment of the President and members of Congress might find themselves, in time, deciding the fate of the Clinton presidency. This judgement could theoretically be made without reference to public opinion. However, in practice, the buoyant popularity of the President suggested that to oust him in the early months of 1999 would overturn popular will as expressed in the 1996 presidential election, and conflict with general satisfaction with his performance. Congress, when evaluating Clinton's position, and pinpointing the key election themes of

Table 7.3 Clinton and Nixon: comparable scandals?

Next, comparing the charges against Bill Clinton with the charges against Richard Nixon in the Watergate controversy, which do you think are the more serious: the charges against Richard Nixon, the charges against Bill Clinton, or do you think the charges against both men are about equally serious?

Nixon charges more serious	64%
Clinton charges more serious	10%
Equally serious	23%
No opinion	3%

Source: 6–7 October 1998, Gallup/CNN/*USA Today* poll.

1998, also had to consider whether Starr's investigation had any real credibility and whether his interpretation of Clinton's actions warranted serious consideration. As outlined in Chapter 5, public opinion was generally advanced by Democrats in the Congress as a pivotal consideration in the impeachment hearings, but was cast by Republicans as an inconsequential factor. House Manager Henry Hyde (R-Ill), for example, pleaded with Senators during the trial of the President: 'your judgement, respectfully, should rise above politics, above partisanship, above polling data'.[5] It nevertheless posed an irksome problem for the Congress. To which aspects of public sentiment should it pay heed, if any? As presently demonstrated, although Clinton retained high levels of approval with regard to the job he was doing as President, there existed limited public trust in him as a person, and popular recognition of a credibility gap between his words and his actions.

(iii) President Clinton

Clinton was the primary focus of the media, the Congress, and Starr's investigation, and this forced his conduct, both as an individual and a President, to the forefront of public debate. Of all the participants in the Lewinsky matter, Clinton had most to gain and lose as a consequence of high or low levels of public approval. He found, to his benefit, that as the scandal progressed, in some areas of political approval his ratings steadily rose. What mattered to Clinton was how his own popularity would affect other institutions involved in the scandal, particularly the Congress. If he could sustain a healthy degree of support in the country at large, then additional pressure was placed upon the Congress and upon Starr, both of whom had to consider the long-term ramifications of removing a popular President. Previous scandals had shown the importance of public opinion as a contributory factor in the evolution of impeachment. During Watergate, Richard Nixon had expressed his concern that changes in public opinion might have an adverse effect upon his political destiny: 'As I increasingly saw it . . . the main danger of being impeached would come precisely from the public's being conditioned to the idea that I was going to be impeached'.[6] Clinton had therefore little choice but to address public opinion with the utmost seriousness.

Popular evaluation of the President is normally gauged in two ways:

- personal approval ratings which evaluate the President in terms of his character and personal attributes

- job approval, which evaluates how the President is performing politically in carrying out the policies he was elected to implement

Presidents require a solid base of support in either category during
scandal.[7] Reagan, for example, temporarily lost public support in the
realm of job approval following the exposure of Iran-Contra. He did
however retain support in the realm of personal approval, testament to
a cleavage in the identification of the President as a person, and the
President as a political leader. Nixon, by contrast, found that the
Watergate scandal eroded his job approval ratings steadily across 1973
and 1974 (23 per cent by August 1974), and his personal approval
ratings declined also.[8] Observing a catastrophic fall of support in both
areas, Congressmen, of both parties, readily pressed on with impeachment proceedings in the knowledge that their actions entertained
widespread popular support. In the light of these historical precedents
Clinton had to plan a strategy to ensure his survival. It was imperative
that he worked to sustain long-term support in at least one of the two
key areas of presidential evaluation, and in this particular scandal it
was clear that the easiest to address, by far, was that of job approval, an
area where stability and success had earmarked his second term. The
White House, via its damage limitation strategies, attempted to convince the American people that Clinton's political record was important, and his personal activities were not of legitimate public concern.
As this text has identified, it repeatedly advanced the following
themes:

- That the Starr investigation was an unwarranted and unjustifiable
invasion of the President's private life
- That what mattered were the election issues President Clinton was
elected to implement
- That any move to impeach the President would overturn popular
sovereignty as expressed in the 1996 presidential election
- That the private conduct of the President, although inappropriate,
did not constitute a high crime and misdemeanor

Public opinion and the Lewinsky scandal: the evolution of public sentiment

Upon the release of information which suggested that the President
had had an affair with Lewinsky, poll samples were immediately taken
to ascertain whether the public believed the information to be true,

and whether it had an adverse effect upon his popularity ratings. Clinton was acutely aware that public opinion was a decisive factor in determining his political fate. According to his former political strategist Dick Morris, Clinton concurred with Morris that a poll be taken to evaluate the public's response to the revelations.[9] The results contributed to the formulation of administration policy, allowing it to reflect and, in some respects, exploit prevailing public sentiment. Clinton could play to his strengths and, observing public opinion, avoid rash statements or commitments in areas where he was not assured of a positive reaction. The *Starr Report* explained the results of the internal poll:

> Mr. Morris telephoned the President later that evening with the poll results, which showed that the voters were 'willing to forgive [the President] for adultery, but not for perjury or obstruction of justice[.]' When Mr. Morris explained that the poll results suggested that the President should not go public with a confession or explanation, he replied, 'Well, we just have to win, then.'[10]

The President might be able to admit to an affair and escape condemnation, but legal transgressions would not be forgiven. He decided initially to both deny an affair and deny lying under oath. His decision shaped the damage limitation strategies enacted by the administration in the following twelve months. Clinton played heavily upon the theme of legal consistency, maintaining throughout the scandal, from its exposure to the conclusion of the impeachment proceedings, that while he was personally at fault, he was legally truthful throughout. If Morris's recollections are accepted at face value, public opinion had a contributory role to play in causing the President to adopt this position. Similarly, the President also understood that the public might sympathize with his position if he admitted an affair, and this occurred when Clinton belatedly admitted to an inappropriate relationship in August 1998.

Clinton's forceful denials of an affair with Lewinsky were greeted by a skeptical public. A majority of those sampled on the first day the allegations of an affair were made, believed that Clinton had had an affair.[11] Although no hard evidence had been advanced to substantiate the allegations, many American were predisposed to believe the charges. This was unsurprising given the plethora of sexual allegations made against the President and the ongoing irritant of the Paula Jones sexual harassment case. A CNN/*Time* poll, taken on 22 January 1998, showed the public to be disappointed and disgusted with news of Clinton's activity, but not surprised, as shown in Table 7.4.

Clinton faced particular problems as perceptions of his integrity, and whether he could be trusted, dipped when allegations of an illicit affair were made. In February 1998, only 40 per cent of one sample thought Clinton honest and trustworthy. This figure slumped to 35 per cent by April and then to a lowly 28 per cent by August.[12] While maintenance of job approval could be manipulated through the creation of popular social and economic policy, the resurrection of public trust could not be so readily recouped via policy measures or public statements about presidential honesty.

In a CNN/*USA Today*/Gallup poll taken on 23/24 January 1998, it was clear that Starr's investigation appeared to entertain some broad justification, as 60 per cent of those questioned believed that Clinton had had an affair.[13] At the same time, as displayed in Table 7.5, Clinton's job approval stood at 58 per cent, a drop of only two points since a poll conducted on 16/18 January. This gave the White House encouragement that Clinton's legislative agenda held greater resonance than scandal allegations. Other statistics offered further hope. A feature

Table 7.4 Popular reaction to allegations of a presidential affair (%)

Would you describe yourself as ... ?

	Yes	No
Disappointed	60	37
Disgusted	55	42
Surprised	26	72
Outraged	26	72

Source: 22 January 1998. CNN/*Time* poll.

Table 7.5 Clinton job approval: 16–28 January 1998 (%)

Do you approve or disapprove of the way Bill Clinton is handling his job as President?

	Approve	Disapprove	No opinion
28 January 1998	67	28	5
25–26 January	59	37	4
23–24 January	58	36	6
16–18 January	60	30	10

Source: January 1998. Gallup polls.

of the early poll samples taken in January 1998, and one which would continue through the whole of the scandal, was a disinclination to see Clinton leave office, even if an affair were to have occurred. Seventy-one per cent of those questioned thought it better for the country if Clinton remained in office, while only 23 per cent believed that he should leave office. This too suggested that while many believed the allegation, it was considered neither a subject nor an event which warranted radical political action. If it could be proven that Clinton had obstructed justice or had committed perjury then the matter assumed more serious overtones. In an ABC News/*Washington Post* poll, conducted on 23/25 January, 63 per cent believed that Clinton should resign if he perjured himself under oath.[14] This again stresses the reasons why Clinton argued vehemently that he was legally upstanding, and maintained that all his answers under oath were technically true. If they were not, then he would not only face the threat posed by Kenneth Starr, but might also find public opinion turning against him in a decisive manner.

A lack of public anger over Clinton's actions was a key feature of the early exposure phase. While the allegations leveled against the President consumed an extensive amount of media time, few, it seemed, believed that they were of such note that they warranted severe action against the President. This allowed the scandal to work on two levels. On the one hand it provided entertainment, and replete with unexpected revelations, gave the American public an ongoing daily drama. This helps to explain why the scandal entertained prominence among a broad range of media outlets and on the Internet. However, the superficial level of popular observation went hand-in-hand with the fact that a minority believed, in the absence of irrefutable proof, that the President had committed a serious crime or that an affair really mattered to the running of the country. Politically, the revelations appeared to have little impact upon evaluations of his job performance. Few thought political action should be taken to punish the President for his private transgressions.[15] This enhanced Clinton's position, and caused dismay amongst his opponents, who appeared unable to press home what appeared, at first sight, to be an unexpected boon of political fortune. Ralph Reed, former Executive Director of the Christian Coalition, observed: 'There is a lot of discouragement in Republican conservative circles about the stratospheric approval ratings.'[16] A perceived division between Clinton's public duties and private life also existed. This was exploited by Clinton's damage limitation team in casting Starr's investigation as intrusive and improper. However, it had wider ramifications. Polls highlighted an emergent tolerance of inappropriate behavior in the private life of the President. Democrats were quick to identify this as a factor that assisted in explaining Clinton's ability to accommodate charges of moral turpitude. Democratic media specialist Dane Strother contended, 'We don't necessarily want priests for President', while Democratic consultant Neil Oxman stated, 'Most [Americans] agree they don't want the President to lie or have bad morals, but at the same time, they don't want to be snooping.'[17]

As Chapter 6 made clear, media attention on the scandal was intense, and this was partly translated into public tiredness of this particular story in a short period of time. While the initial exposé might have captured public attention, and some events, such as the 17 August presidential confession, were of pivotal importance, there nevertheless was an impression of overkill. This contributed to public apathy, and provoked visible concern among media interests about how to play the story.[18] Peter Jennings, anchor of ABC News, attempted to explain the strain in the relationship between the media portrayal of the scandal and the American people:

> Some of us have been plumbing people's private lives with such vigor that they are saying, 'enough already!' I don't know how to account for the fact that the public is clearly fed up but continues to watch. Rubbernecking is part of the human condition.[19]

Casual observation was a recurrent feature of this scandal. Sufficient public attention existed so as to allow public opinion to be a player in the scandal, but interest was limited, was remarkably selective in deciding which parts of the scandal warranted political action, and was tolerant, in the main, of the President's private behavior.[20]

Poll samples conducted through the spring of 1998 brought to the fore a consistent message. The public disapproved of the alleged presidential affair, but the political job he was doing as President outweighed reservations about his character. This was in keeping with the patterns observed at the onset of the scandal and was endorsed when further allegations of sexual malpractice were leveled at the President. Former aide Kathleen Willey's accusation that the President had sexually harassed her was broadcast on 15 March. It had little bearing upon the support afforded the President in the realm of job approval, as displayed in Table 7.6.. Again, however, Clinton's credibility was clearly under threat. In a poll taken following Willey's accusations, more

Table 7.6 Clinton's job approval rating: March 1998

	16 March	6–9 March
Approve	67%	63%
Disapprove	29%	31%

Source: 16 March 1998, CNN/*USA Today*/Gallup poll.

tended to believe her version of events than believed the plea of innocence coming from the President.[21] Forty three per cent tended to
believe Willey, as opposed to 40 per cent who tended to believe the
President.[22] Nevertheless, Clinton's job approval ratings remained consistent at this time and continued to highlight popular confidence in
the job he was doing as President.

This episode, encompassing themes broadly similar to others which
had damaged Clinton's credibility, demonstrated that the Lewinsky
scandal was not a unique or isolated incident. On more than one occasion the public were willing to disassociate Clinton the man from
Clinton the President, and overlook his private actions. This undoubtedly worked to his advantage as he struggled to contain the fallout
from scandal in 1998.

August 1998: the speech and the polls

Public opinion was a factor for the Clinton White House to consider
when its initial defense of the President's position became untenable in
August 1998. Starr had acquired a stained Lewinsky dress and a DNA
sample from the President. The immediate concern lay in the legal
realm. Clinton had to ensure that his 17 August 1998 Grand Jury testimony was consistent with his previous statements under oath.
However, the Grand Jury testimony made clear that the President had
engaged in a relationship with Lewinsky, a relationship he had previously denied. In advance of the President's appearance several polls
suggested that the public believed that he had had an affair, even if he
had not yet admitted it publicly. There was also a prevailing impression that Clinton had lied under oath in his January deposition, as
highlighted in Table 7.7. This placed additional pressure upon the
President to resolve any contradictions or shortcomings in his original
testimony.

Even in early August, when Clinton's denials appeared increasingly
untenable, the public continued to oppose his removal from office in

Table 7.7 President Clinton: lying under oath? (%)

	Definitely true	Probably true	Probably not true	Definitely not true	No opinion
7–8 August	22	46	18	8	6
29 July	16	40	27	10	7
17–19 April	21	39	21	10	9

Source: 7–8 August 1998, Gallup poll.

large numbers, even if it were found that he had participated in a relationship and had concealed its existence. In a poll taken on 10–12 August, prior to the Grand Jury appearance, only 20 per cent favored impeaching Clinton, while 76 per cent opposed his removal. Moreover, 45 per cent of respondents pledged their support for Clinton 'even if charges are true'.[23] Clinton could therefore approach the Grand Jury testimony with some confidence that even if he were to admit a relationship with Lewinsky, it would be tolerated by a significant section of the American public. Poll evidence suggested that a confession of an affair by Clinton was by this juncture the most prudent damage limitation exercise to adopt. Asked what would cause a loss of confidence in Clinton, a poll sample provided the following information:

'*Would you lose confidence in Clinton if he . . .?*'
Admitted having affair   26%
Denied having affair   33%
Cancelled testimony   60%
Refused to answer questions   53%
(*Source*: 10–12 August 1998, CNN/*USA Today*/Gallup poll)

Public demand for Clinton to clarify his position appeared to be a factor which contributed to his decision to address the nation on the evening of 17 August 1998. Seventy-three per cent of those sampled in one poll wanted the President to explain the exact nature of his relationship with Lewinsky following his testimony.[24]

Poll evidence highlighted muted public acceptance of Clinton's explanations of his inappropriate behavior, highlighting why senior Republicans resisted attacking Clinton in a forthright manner following his confession. There was clear disapproval of Clinton, but this disapproval lay exactly where Clinton wanted it to lie, in the realm of personal rather than job approval. This was highlighted by polls taken in the aftermath of Clinton's speech. Table 7.8 contrasts the political and personal fortunes of the President in the wake of 17 August. Notably, his personal rating rose by a small amount following his apology to the nation, evidence that it held some influence in convincing the American people that he was sincere in his regret.

Clinton's August speech failed to resolve all the remaining questions as far as many Americans were concerned. Forty-one per cent believed that he had not 'answered all of the important questions', and 47 per cent thought that he needed to say more in the way of an apology to the nation. These statistics however were positive ones for Clinton, as 54 per cent thought all the questions had been answered, and 51 per cent thought his apology sufficient.[25] The speech held enough force to be deemed a success for Clinton. It was by no means a satisfactory episode, but in terms of public relations it contained the damage in the personal realm, and held sufficient sway in the area of job approval to allow Clinton to proceed to the next phase of the scandal.

There were several reasons why the American people felt able to overlook the scandal and consider the political accomplishments of Clinton's second term as a contributory factor in their evaluation of his job performance. Analysis and poll samples taken by the PEW Research Center pinpointed the areas of popular satisfaction with Clinton among those who held a negative view of his personal

Table 7.8 Clinton's job approval and personal approval ratings: 17–18 August 1998 (%)

Do you approve or disapprove of the way Bill Clinton is handling his job as president?

	18 August	*17 August*	*10–12 August*
Approve	66	62	65
Disapprove	29	32	30
No opinion	5	6	5

Thinking about Bill Clinton as a person, do you have a favorable or unfavorable opinion of him?

	18 August	*17 August*
Favorable	44	40
Unfavorable	48	48
No opinion	8	12

Source: 18 August 1998, Gallup poll.

conduct.[26] Thirty-four per cent thought that the state of the economy was a reason for their continued support of Clinton in the realm of job approval, while 18 per cent cited his handling of foreign affairs and 14 per cent identified a need to disassociate Clinton the man from Clinton the politician. This last figure is significant as it suggests that only a small proportion of those polled actively differentiated between the job and personal approval evaluations. What appeared to have greater importance to those questioned was the practical application of policy and how it was implemented across the country, particularly in the economic realm. One poll respondent, interviewed in September 1998 for a *New York Times*–CBS survey, commented: 'The stock market is doing well. There are more jobs for people. Basically, I think the American people are happier than they've been in many years.'[27] There was still a pronounced lack of confidence in the President's integrity, but if he was to retain his office, this was of minor concern as he antic-ipated the release of the *Starr Report* and the prospect of impeachment hearings.

The Starr Report and impeachment: the public reaction

Following the release of the *Starr Report*, the President made reference to the power and influence of public opinion in helping to determine the outcome of the scandal. When questioned by reporters about the possibility of resignation, the President replied, 'They [the American people] want me to go on and do my job, then that's what I intend to do. That is the right thing to do.'[28] The *Starr Report*, conforming to its initial mandate, addressed alleged unlawful activity on the part of the President and recommended grounds for impeachment. The clear statements and charges leveled by Starr held potentially damaging con-sequences. However, familiar patterns of public support and disap-proval for the President were evident. Job approval remained high, personal approval remained low, and condemnation of the President's personal conduct was widespread. Popular support for impeachment had risen slowly as the year had progressed, from a figure of 19 per cent in early June, to 31 per cent on 10 September 1998. When the *Starr Report* was published there was a drop of one per cent in those who thought the President should be impeached.[29] This did not induce a bipartisan rush in the Congress to impeach the President. Indeed, Starr's report was greeted by a public divided over its merits and its interpretations. While 45 per cent thought it a 'fair and accurate account of Clinton's actions', 42 per cent considered it 'an unfair and distorted account'.

This balance only served to reiterate to members of the Congress, and members of the House in particular, that in advance of the congressional mid-term elections, there was no clear strategy which would entertain widespread public approval. Contradictory poll figures made it additionally difficult for those in the Congress to plan a clear strategic attack upon, or defense of, the President.[30] Jonathan Rauch, writing for *National Journal*, noted the conflicting information provided by the polls:

> the people in front of the television sets will not have it. They view elite opinion with the sort of exasperation they usually reserve for animal-rights activists and the French. Solid majorities oppose impeachment and resignation, and want Clinton to finish his term. Will the scandal have a 'serious impact on Clinton's administration in the next two years?' Yes, say 69 per cent to the CBS pollsters. But can Clinton 'still be an effective President?' Yes again, by 62 per cent. As long as the public believes that Clinton can govern, he lives.[31]

What was more, according to the polls the public wanted the Congress to follow its lead and allow Clinton to remain in office, as the data displayed in Table 7.9 indicates.

This was a difficult task to accomplish as elite and popular opinion appeared to be at odds with one another, and adherence to the message supplied by polling data would have brought this scandal to a rapid conclusion, one which would have avoided the rarely used Constitutional procedure of impeachment and trial.

Table 7.9 Public opinion and the Congress

Do you think members of Congress should stick closely to American public opinion when deciding what steps to take next – including the results of polls like this one – or should members of Congress do what they think is best regardless of what the American public thinks?

	11–12 September 1998	*21–23 August 1998*
Stick close to public opinion	63%	61%
Do what they think is best	34%	37%
No opinion	3%	2%

Source: 11–12 September 1998, Gallup poll.

The *Starr Report* was generally greeted with apathy by the American public. Knowledge of the document increased as time progressed, due, in the main, to the media coverage it received, combined with increased circulation following the publication of the report in book form. Poll samples highlighted only moderate attention, as displayed in Table 7.10. The release of the videotape of Clinton's 17 August Grand Jury testimony served to reinforce the conclusions reached by Starr and remind the public of Clinton's seeming inability to give forthright answers. However, even though the video was shown in full on several channels, public interest was again slight. Fifty-nine per cent of those questioned had seen at least some of the video testimony. Of those who had watched the material, 12 per cent had watched the whole four hours, and 38 per cent had watched over an hour.

Moreover, the attention span of the remaining 50 per cent who had watched the video appeared short, with little desire to watch the President. This assisted Clinton. A lack of interest in the detail of the affair helped to obscure the legal issues at the heart of the scandal, and made it all the more difficult for those in the Congress favoring impeachment to advance a compelling case. Following the *Starr Report* and Clinton's admission of an affair, the videotape delivered little in the way of new information. Its content reiterated many of Starr's conclusions, and these had already been released in document form. As Table 7.11 makes clear, this event was far from catastrophic for the President.

During September 1998 the release of information detrimental to Clinton's position did not seriously dent public confidence in the ability of the President to do his job. Concern existed that the scandal might adversely affect the amount of time he could devote to a national agenda, but with a prosperous economy, and with his

Table 7.10 Public interest in the *Starr Report* (%)

How much have you read or heard about the specific details of Starr's Report to Congress?

	14–15 September	*13 September*	*11–12 September*
A great deal	23	21	14
A moderate amount	37	33	32
Only a little	28	34	38
Nothing at all	12	12	16

Source: 14–15 September 1998, Gallup poll.

Table 7.11 The release of the Grand Jury videotape (%)

As you may know, the videotape of Bill Clinton's testimony in the Starr investigation was released to the public today. Thinking about both the release and the contents of the videotape and documents from the Starr investigation, has what you've seen or heard about these matters made you feel less favorably toward Bill Clinton than you did before, or not?

| | All | Watched videotape | |
		Yes	No
Less favorably	41	45	36
Not less favorably	51	51	51
No opinion	8	4	13

Source: 21 September 1998, Gallup/CNN/*USA Today* poll.

confession and apology already in the public domain, the *Starr Report* had far greater impact within the Congress than it had on the American public. Support for impeachment at this time remained low, in spite of Starr's recommendations. This convinced Democrats in the Congress, in particular, that opposition to the President would bring no tangible gain in the mid-term elections nor indeed in the longer term. This was, of course, borne out in the mid-terms when Democrat candidates defied pre-election predictions of losses for the party. The scandal failed to capture public interest, nor did it prove to be, for those who did go to the polls, a defining political issue worthy, on its own, of consideration. Voter turnout in 1998 was the lowest since the mid-term election of 1942.[32] With public apathy over the Clinton scandal an obvious issue to consider, the legislators in the Congress had then to decide whether to impeach the President. Republicans elevated the process, controversially, above and beyond the sentiment held in the country. Bob Inglis (R-SC), for example, stressed a 'constitutional obligation to act . . .'.[33] This was legitimate as the Constitution removed the impeachment process from the control of the people. Although popular sentiment was clearly expressed in opinion polls and at the 1998 mid-term elections, it was plausible to contend that it played second fiddle to the partisan disposition of members of the Congress. A record number of incumbent victories (98.5 per cent) also contributed to a feeling of security on the part of both parties to advance their case and feel justified in doing so.[34]

The House Judiciary Committee's discussion of the articles of impeachment commenced in the winter of 1998. A high proportion of the public opposed impeachment and supported a more moderate route of censure. On 9 December 1998, 34 per cent of those sampled in a CNN/*USA Today*/Gallup poll thought that the House Judiciary Committee should vote to impeach Clinton, while 61 per cent thought that it should not.[35] The fact that the mid-terms were over by this time meant that the members of the Committee could act in the full knowledge that the electorate would next judge them in two years, at a time when the specific action of an individual member might well be forgotten. This gave Republicans hope that action would not prompt electoral reprisals. Public interest in the impeachment proceedings was muted. This contrasted with presidential scandals of previous eras. During Watergate, high audience viewing figures testified to heightened interest in the importance of the scandal to the institution of the American presidency. Even during the Iran-Contra scandal, public attention to the televised testimony of Oliver North was strong, and was reflected in substantial audience figures for his congressional appearance in July 1987. Clinton's fight with the Congress failed to follow suit. In December and January 1998, as shown in Table 7.12, the Gallup organization observed lukewarm interest in the hearings, suggesting that the events taking place in Washington were of minimal interest to the country.

Partly nullifying Democrat anticipation of future voter reprisal, public attention to the actions of the individual representing their district was marginal. More than half of those questioned in a poll following the end of the scandal did not know how their House Representative had voted on the articles of impeachment.[36] Although Clinton's impeachment set an important precedent for the institution of the American presidency, for many Americans it held little significance.

Table 7.12 Public attention to the impeachment proceedings: December/January 1998–9 (%)

How closely have you been following the Congressional impeachment proceedings against Bill Clinton?

	Very closely	*Somewhat closely*	*Not too closely*	*Not at all*
8–10 Jan 1999	23	50	21	6
12–13 Dec 1998	25	52	20	3
11 Dec 1998	18	41	25	16
10 Dec 1998	20	36	31	12
9 Dec 1998	16	38	29	17
8 Dec 1998	19	36	28	17

Source: December 1998–January 1999, Gallup polls.

Impeachment proceedings left many of Clinton's positive approval ratings, particularly in the area of job approval, largely unaltered. The events in Washington, and bitter partisan acrimony on the House Judiciary Committee, failed to alter public opinion statistics in a politically consequential manner. Of note, and reflective of popular frustration with the scandal, was widespread disapproval of how the major players had conducted themselves. Starr's investigation was unpopular, as were the actions of members of Congress. In a poll taken during 9–13 December 1998, 44 per cent of those questioned approved of the Democrats' handling of the Clinton investigation in the House. However, 46 per cent disapproved. The Republican party fared no better. While 33 per cent approved of that party's handling of the investigation, 59 per cent disapproved, emphasizing a popular recognition of partisan disposition and its impact during this scandal. Similarly, the Chairman of the House Judiciary Committee, Illinois Republican Henry Hyde, received more disapproval than approval, 37 per cent approving of his handling of impeachment and 43 per cent disapproving.[37] Dissatisfaction was not restricted to the House. Poll samples in January questioned the motivations of Senate Republicans. Party sympathies lay firmly with the Democrats as the procedure moved to its trial stage. A CNN/*Time* poll conducted on 20–21 January 1999, showed that Republican handling of the trial of Clinton in the Senate was approved by 37 per cent, but 54 per cent disapproved. The Democrats' conduct during the trial, by contrast, was approved by 49 per cent and was disapproved of by 40 per cent.[38] These were important figures. They suggest, at the least, that the public identified the partisan affiliation of the members of the Congress as a contributory factor in the impeachment process. Impeachment however was not intended to be an instrument of punishment wielded by one party to inflict damage upon another. That the public perceived it to be such, and identified partisan affiliation as a consideration when interpreting the impeachment process, highlights the success of the Democrats, and particularly the President, in attempting to cast the investigation as a partisan witchhunt. As Rauch stated in *National Journal*, 'No impeachment proceeding can enjoy public confidence if it is a creature of party politics. Impeachment's legitimacy rests on its standing as a great affair of state rather than as a toll of partisan political torture.'[39]

As the President faced an impending trial in the Senate, his job approval statistics rose to their highest of the scandal period; at one point, in a Gallup survey conducted on 19–20 December 1998, touching 73 per cent.[40] This gave the President confidence that when the future of his presidency was debated, he clearly, entertained public support in the political realm. He was not viewed with such esteem in a personal capacity. Even so, following initial problems when he confessed to an affair, his figures had recovered substantially. For example, on 8–10 January, 58 per cent had a favorable opinion of Clinton as 'a person' and only 41 per cent held an unfavorable opinion.[41] The stability in the figures, despite perceptions of Clinton's evasiveness, suggests that by this time public fatigue was having a bearing upon the statistics. Consequently, the impeachment and trial of President Clinton had little popular impact. In many respects the arguments raised during impeachment were very reflective of those advanced in September 1998 when the *Starr Report* was released, and therefore substantial movement of public opinion was predictably limited.

The issue of how to punish the President was also a focus of inquiry for pollsters. Three main alternatives were advanced as options by which to resolve the scandal. These were: impeachment and removal from office, censure, and presidential resignation. The most popular of these options in the public realm was, by far, censure. From September 1998 through to February 1999 polls consistently showed that upwards of 50 per cent thought this the best method of punishing the President. The forced removal of Clinton was considered excessive, and while he deserved punishment, censure was a preferable option. Support for impeachment and conviction, via a trial in the Senate, never rose above 35 per cent. Likewise, resignation received a lukewarm reception. In September 1998, 40 per cent in one poll thought the President should resign, but, in the main, the figures remained consistently in the 30 to 40 per cent range.[42] Opponents of the President demanded his removal from office, via resignation or conviction, and there existed a core element, mainly Republican party members, who considered Clinton's actions so reprehensible that his removal, by whatever means, would be beneficial for the nation. This 30 per cent however did not hold enough power to persuade undecided members of the Senate to oppose the President, nor did they sufficiently influence the opinions of Senate Democrats whose loyalty was vital to Clinton's continuation in office.

The Senate trial, reflecting Clinton's impeachment in the House, attracted low viewing figures. A PEW poll question, displayed in Table 7.13, highlighted widespread disinterest among all partisan groupings.

The conclusion of the scandal provoked widespread public relief. The *Washington Post* observed: 'Weariness rather than anger or glee seemed

Table 7.13 Viewership of the Senate trial: January 1999 (%)

Verdict on the trial? Watching the trial ...

	All	Republican	Democrat	Independent
All/a lot of it	15	18	16	14
Some of it	34	38	33	32
Hardly any of it	28	32	28	27
None of it	22	12	22	27
Don't know	1	–	1	–

Source: January 1999, PEW Research poll.

to characterize the public mood at the conclusion of the nation's second impeachment trial.'[43] In keeping with the poll statistics cited previously, those approving of the Senate decision not to convict Clinton mirrored those who were against the impeachment of Clinton in the first instance. Few had changed their opinion across time. Following the acquittal, 64 per cent of those questioned approved of the 'not guilty' verdict, while 35 per cent disapproved.[44]

In anticipation of further scandals of a sexual nature, the public were questioned on how they might be avoided. Partisan division was evident, suggesting a difference of opinion about the type of person that, following this scandal, sub-groups desired as President. The data is displayed in Table 7.14. The poll evidence reflected the arguments advanced during the congressional debates on impeachment, and suggested that the response was, in part, shaped by observation of the party positions during that episode. Morality was meaningful to Republican party members, having been accentuated by conservative

Table 7.14 Looking to the future: avoiding scandal politics (%)

How to avoid similar scandals?

	All	Republican	Democrat	Independent
Elect President with high moral character	34	64	14	34
Make sure a President's private life stays private	60	31	83	60
Don't know	6	5	3	6

Source: 9–13 December 1998, Princeton Survey Research Associates poll.

elements in the Congress. As stated in Chapter 3 of this text, Trent Lott (R-Miss), Senate Majority Leader, referred to 'a moral dimension to the American presidency'.[45] Conversely, Democrats were more sympathetic in disassociating private morality from public service, and this too reflected Democrat sentiment within congressional circles and the arguments emanating from the Clinton White House. Those of an independent disposition sided strongly with the President's position and ensured that his argument, as advanced during his 17 August 1998 speech, held sway in the public forum. The focus of the debate had also widened since the onset of the impeachment proceedings. Discussions revolved increasingly around the concept of presidential privacy and whether morality was a sound basis for judging a President. Starr's case was specifically interested in whether the President had lied under oath, encouraged others to do so, and had obstructed justice. It was not intended to be a judgement on the moral shackles of the presidency, but often became that, as the moral debate was easier to comprehend than the intricacies of presidential perjury and its legal ramifications. That is not to say that Starr totally failed in his efforts to push legal concerns to the fore. For instance, one poll showed that the public understood that Starr's investigation was about whether the President lied, as opposed to an investigation about sex, by a margin of 48 per cent to 38 per cent.[46] However, he did not have the depth of support he required to encourage wavering Senators on Capitol Hill to adhere to his interpretations of the scandal, or to dominate the media and popular agenda. Although Clinton was immersed in a legal and political quagmire, the poll statistics nevertheless worked decisively to his political advantage in 1998 and 1999.

Conclusion

The movement and changes in public opinion across the duration of the Lewinsky scandal were small and politically inconsequential to Clinton's standing as President in 1998 and 1999. His job approval ratings remained steady, his personal approval ratings were, although low, far from critical, and few were surprised that the President had strayed from his marriage. Consistency and stability earmarked public opinion, any movements being gradual and having little impact upon the key participants in the scandal.

It is overly simplistic to regard Clinton's high job approval ratings as the dominant reason for his survival. Starr, and those investigating the President, were held in low esteem throughout. Indeed, Starr was seen in a negative light as an individual, his investigation was thought overly intrusive, and his recommendations for impeachment were greeted unenthusiastically. This, in turn, translated into muted support for impeachment in the Congress, and negative ratings for those who wished to see Clinton impeached and convicted. Those prosecuting scandal were viewed more unfavorably than the President, allowing him to exploit the apparent weaknesses in his opponents' arguments.

Thereafter, Clinton used damage limitation strategies to play directly to public opinion, casting Starr's investigation as meddlesome, and portraying Starr as an individual with a personal vendetta. It was also profitable for the White House, in seeking to influence public opinion, to play strategically upon the theme of sex, and to suppress the legal aspects of the argument. A violation of ill-defined public moral standards was not a high crime or misdemeanor, but obstruction of justice and perjury might, if advocated appropriately, fall within the scope of that term. As much as the American public might feel disgusted by a relationship between the President and a woman many years his junior, the modification of the debate from one founded on legal matters, to one concerned with sex and morality, was, ironically, beneficial to the President. Thereafter, a confession and apology by Clinton partly nullified the potential damage the *Starr Report* might inflict. In Clinton's own mind, and as presented to the public in his 17 August speech, the scandal was over when a confession was made. Starr and the Congress were left to pick at the scraps of Clinton's admonitions and try to convince a disinterested public that there was more to the case than an inappropriate affair. Public apathy, however, ensured that this would be an exceptionally difficult task, and Clinton's pledges to continue with the business of the nation appeared to be more appealing than raking over sordid sexual escapades.

The disparity between Clinton's job approval record and perceptions of his integrity at first sight appears to testify to an alert and astute public able to actively differentiate between the political and private spheres occupied by the President. It is, however, only part of the equation. Many Americans were not interested in the private liaisons of the President, but were affected directly by the public policy choices made in Washington. As long as the ramifications of Clinton's political choices, such as his economic stewardship, were beneficial, then there seemed no good reason to pry and probe into his personal life. It was not that one aspect of Clinton's activity could be weighed up alongside another, but rather that the personal activity of the President simply paled into insignificance when more pertinent political matters were involved. The President might be an adulterer, might be a liar, and might be evasive in his answers before a Grand Jury, but he was considered by many an astute politician who delivered on his election pledges to the American people. The latter issue mattered, the former did not, and the vast majority of the American people wished to see a skilled politician stay in office and complete his presidential term.

Apathy was a beneficial byproduct of this scandal for Clinton. In part, this occurred because the public were already well attuned to his involvement in scandal politics and allegations of womanizing. A scandal involving the theme of sex was, consequently, a familiar issue. It lacked shock value, and following hard on the heels of the Jones case, public aversion to further sexual revelations and related charges against the President to this end was understandable. Media overkill in the opening phase of the scandal, and the fact that the episode took a year to complete, ensured that boredom was prevalent by the time impeachment hearings commenced in 1998. As a consequence, the duration, nature, and partisan overtones of the scandal contributed to a feeling of weariness, highlighted by poll statistics which suggested that the public, rather than desiring an extensive investigation of the President, or extended impeachment hearings, just wanted the scandal to be over.

Opinion polls made clear that if the Congress followed Starr's recommendations, and removed the President, then there would exist a gulf between public sentiment and the political action taken on Capitol Hill. The congressional mid-term elections had shown that the Clinton scandal meant little to an uninspired electorate, and the polls suggested that censure would be more preferable than impeachment. Clinton's legal aides played upon this fact at the impeachment trial, constantly reminding the Representatives and Senators that sovereignty was a paramount consideration and that the 1996 election results also held significant weight. Although Clinton could not call on public opinion to assist him directly, he could exploit its presence, place pressure upon Republicans in the Congress and, at the same time, remind them that their decisions held the utmost historical importance for the presidency.

Partisanship ensured that the President received support from Democrat sympathizers in the nation, and in the Congress. Consequently, impeachment was beset by acrimony and grievance. It was not designed as, nor intended to be, a weapon for one party to destroy a particular President. That the public were generally split along partisan lines when evaluating this scandal, and that it perceived partisan bickering to be a factor in the prosecution of Clinton, suggests that the grievances between Democrat and Republican were sufficiently wide and identifiable to make conviction in the Senate unsound. Being opposed by Republicans within the Congress and in the polls, Clinton could cast the matter, with some justification, as a politically inspired scandal, one not as serious or as pervasive as other scandals such as Watergate, where bipartisan condemnation of Nixon had ensured that his position was untenable. As a consequence, Clinton's damage limitation strategies consistently stressed partisan affiliation and exploited its impact on the evolution of this scandal.

The Lewinsky scandal had a limited public impact. The American people were tired of scandal, satisfied with the political performance of President Clinton, and generally dissatisfied with the performance and role of the Independent Counsel. While many believed that Clinton had been less than forthcoming during the Jones deposition, and had acted inappropriately in conducting a relationship with Lewinsky, as the matter was essentially a private one, it was for the President and his wife to resolve. Starr failed to convince the American people that the President's efforts to conceal an affair constituted an impeachable offense, and the members of the Congress outraged by the President's linguistic gymnastics similarly failed to mobilize meaningful opposition to the President. Clinton played purposefully to public opinion to further his chances of survival, stressing throughout the scandal his determination to avoid entrapment in scandal politics and to concentrate upon conventional political issues. A small core element of the American people wanted to see Clinton leave office, but they were outnumbered by those who, while admitting that the President had acted in an untoward manner, wished to see him continue unhindered through his second term.

Conclusion

Clinton's ability to endure allegations of scandal while simultaneously conducting the duties of the presidential office was, in part, testament to his familiarity with, and understanding of, the role and mechanics of scandal in contemporary American politics. Having successfully accommodated several scandal allegations while both Governor and President, he nevertheless found, to his cost, that the unlikely evolution of the Lewinsky scandal was detrimental to his reputation within the elite circles of government. Yet Clinton, for all the problems encountered, conducted two full terms in office, entertained high levels of public approval, particularly in his second term, and gained respect in foreign affairs and in the international community as a consequence of his efforts to promote peace in several troubled nations.

Clinton's immediate reflections on the Lewinsky scandal were apparent within a short time of the conclusion of the trial vote in the Senate. At the end of March 1999 he conducted an interview with Dan Rather of CBS News, during which he considered the development of the Lewinsky episode.[1] Clinton stressed the lessons he had learned from the events, albeit that they were perhaps a little late to accommodate given the short remaining tenure of his presidency. He raised four issues. Firstly, he asserted: 'every person must bear the consequence of his or her conduct, and when you make a mistake, you pay for it, no matter who you are'.[2] Secondly, in a comment reminiscent of post-Watergate statements made by Gerald Ford, he declared: 'the Constitution works'.[3] In this instance, however, it had not facilitated in the removal of a corrupt President, but had aided in the retention of one suspected of several criminal acts. He suggested that partisanship underpinned his impeachment predicament and that the Founding Fathers, when constructing the Constitution, had purposefully, through the requirement of a two-thirds majority in the Senate, prevented partisan disposition from playing a decisive role in the removal of a President. Thirdly, Clinton gave tacit credit to the American people: 'the American people almost always get it right if you give them enough time to think through things and really work on it'.[4] Fourthly, Clinton suggested that it was important that elected officials follow the guidance and will of the people, and not lose sight of the function of a representative democracy. This, in part, was a muted criticism of those in the Congress who ignored the opinion polls, the election results of 1996 and 1998, and had stubbornly pressed on with the prosecution of the President. The four lessons reflected central aspects of the scandal's development: morality, partisanship, public opinion and representative democracy. Clinton tactfully ignored the role of the Independent Counsel and the impact of that institution upon his political fortunes, there being no overt suggestion on this occasion that the OIC was damaging to the Executive branch of government.

Clinton reiterated previous comments that he never considered resignation as a viable option during the scandal, as it would have merely damaged the presidential office he occupied. When questioned on how the scandal might be explained to children, he gave an answer reminiscent of his confessional plea for forgiveness at a prayer breakfast in the fall of 1998:

> That's what I think the lessons of all those Bible stories are, of the great figures of the Bible who did things they shouldn't have done. The reason those stories are in the Bible is to say, everyone sins, but everyone is held accountable and everyone had a chance to go on – and that all three of those points need to be made.[5]

No mention was made of the legal themes which underpinned Clinton's scandal concerns, and great weight was predictably placed upon the perceived moral transgressions which superficially characterized this scandal. Damage limitation strategies, which portrayed this scandal as one of individual moral failure as opposed to legal wrongdoing, were sustained in the scandal aftermath. At the heart of Clinton's comments lay his core interpretation which had caused so much acrimony: that this was a sex scandal and nothing more, and did not constitute a serious violation of law.

Rather's final question to Clinton about the Lewinsky scandal was a meaningful one. He suggested that the first paragraph of Clinton's obituary would be that he was the 'only President in the 20th century to be impeached; one of only two Presidents to be impeached'.[6] In response, Clinton was blunt and dismissive:

> ... if it is, if the history writers are honest, they'll tell it for just exactly what it was. And I am honored that something that was indefensible was pursued and that I had the opportunity to defend the Constitution. That doesn't have anything to do with the fact that I did something I shouldn't have done of which I am ashamed and which I apologize for. But it had nothing to do with the impeachment process. And I think that's what the American people, two-thirds of them, knew all along. And I determined that I would defend the Constitution and the work of my administration. And those that did not agree with what I had done and were furious that it had worked and that the country was doing well, and attempted to use what should have been a constitutional and legal process for political ends, did not prevail. And that's the way I saw it.[7]

Clinton thereafter assured the interviewer that he harbored no bitterness or animosity to those who had attempted to oust him from office, partly, one might assume, because he required bipartisan congressional support for the passage of any meaningful legislation during his remaining time as President.

On the eve of his departure from office, Clinton confessed, on 19 January 2001, that he had knowingly made false statements under oath when questioned in the Jones deposition. This belatedly lent additional credibility to Starr's investigation of the President and his charges of perjury. Clinton stated:

> I tried to walk a fine line between acting lawfully and testifying falsely, but I now recognize that I did not fully accomplish this goal and that certain of my responses to questions about Ms. Lewinsky were false.[8]

In remarks reminiscent of those issued in the admissions phase of the scandal, Clinton repeated the apologies which characterized his public damage limitation strategy in the second half of 1998. He commented:

> I have apologized for my conduct and I have done my best to atone for it with my family, my administration and the American people. I have paid a high price for it, which I accept because it caused so

much pain to so many people. I hope my actions today will help bring closure and finality to the matters.[9]

As part of an agreement, the admission served to prevent charges being laid against Clinton by Independent Counsel Robert Ray when he left office. Clinton, however, was punished via a fine and the suspension of his law license. His last minute acknowledgement of wrongdoing not only highlighted his evasive actions during 1998, but also underlined his poise and political shrewdness at that time, in sustaining a barely credible claim of innocence at a decisive moment in his presidency. His damage limitation strategies had been sufficiently effective to keep him in office during a time of crisis, but were no longer needed when he had but a few hours left as President and had negotiated a deal with the Independent Counsel.

The Lewinsky scandal clearly deviated in several respects from previous scandals endured by American presidents. A key feature, and indeed a pivotal one, was that the American people and the elites in government appeared to hold different interpretations of this scandal and entertained different political agendas. Watergate witnessed a political elite and a public both outraged by Nixon's covert dealings and his attempts to subvert the judicial process. Although a small section of the American public opposed the impeachment and removal of Nixon, the overwhelming weight of popular sentiment, in conjunction with the material evidence in the hands of prosecutors, left Nixon with little option but to resign or brave an impeachment process which would inevitably result in conviction by the Senate. In this case therefore both elite and popular opinion were as one – Nixon must go. Reagan faced no such difficulties during Iran-Contra. For all the questionable acts committed during that scandal, Reagan retained substantial support as a person and avoided the onset of impeachment proceedings. Indeed, they were not seriously considered at any point during that scandal. Even though the whole episode raised doubt about Reagan's managerial competence, the American public and the Congress kept faith with the President. The scandal did impact negatively upon Reagan's presidency in the short term, but nevertheless suggested that popular enthusiasm for scandal was on the wane, and that damage limitation measures enacted to protect the President from liability for the scandal were sufficiently effective so as to make the Iran-Contra scandal a serious irritant, but far from catastrophic, for Reagan. Elite and popular opinion, as during Watergate, appeared to be generally in accordance with one another. During Iran-Contra neither the elites nor the masses wished to see Reagan ousted from office. Clinton's experience during the Lewinsky matter was altogether different. While not losing sight of the fact that it was rooted in individual as opposed to institutional wrongdoing, the popular reaction to the scandal was instrumental in shaping Clinton's defensive posture. The scandal failed to resonate politically among the American people, yet held gravity among elite groups, the OIC and the Congress among them, which perceived Clinton's actions as sufficiently serious to warrant impeachment proceedings. A discernible void between popular sentiment and elite interpretation suggests that scandal themes are losing their popular impact and that, in this episode at least, elite outrage over presidential action proved difficult to convey to the American people in a consequential manner. The Lewinsky scandal produced feelings of disgust and revulsion, but no popular clamor for the President to be removed from office for his transgressions.

Explanations for the disparity between elite and mass opinion are readily identifiable, but weighting them appropriately presents a more challenging task. It is clear that Clinton's damage limitation efforts to portray the Lewinsky affair as a sex scandal to the American people entertained some success. As much as Starr tried to cast Clinton's actions as serious violations of law, a competing interpretation of the scandal was that it was rooted in moral misbehavior, and this was in no small way cultivated by the Clinton White House as it endeavored to protect its client. The frequent discussion of sexual issues in the media, in the *Starr Report*, in the White House 'prebuttal' and rebuttal, and in the Congress, contributed to a widespread perception that this was ultimately about sex. For all the efforts of those investigating Clinton to present it as a legal concern, that argument inevitably led through a maze of sexual intrigue which served to substantiate the sexual arguments to an ever greater degree. This was significant in explaining why Clinton cultivated support within the country and avoided popular recriminations. Moreover, the sexual revelations about members of the Congress which were exposed during the scandal only served to suggest that there was little to choose in this realm between investigators and investigated.

A key explanation for Clinton's survival, and one which will undoubtedly have a bearing upon future presidential scandals, be they individual or institutional, is that of scandal weariness. In *Politics by Other Means*, Ginsberg and Shefter identified an institutionalized scandal process of 'Revelation, Investigation, Prosecution' (RIP).[10] That the scandal machinery of the Independent Counsel, the media, and the Congress is institutionalized and is wheeled into operation at the slightest suggestion of presidential wrongdoing only serves to downplay the true nature and severity of any single scandal allegation. Clinton's frequent encounters with scandal allegations attuned the American people to the fact that this President, like no other, was subject to charges of serious wrongdoing and personal excess on a frequent basis. Starr's pursuit of Clinton across several potentially scandalous episodes suggested that a multitude of charges would be thrown at the President until one stuck. Rather than making Clinton seem particularly aggressive or abusive in his employment of presidential power, it appeared as though he was a besieged President whose private life was subject to unwarranted and unlimited investigation. Moreover, the plethora of scandal allegations turned the American people off this aspect of American political life. Several elite elements, however, identifying the problems posed by the probability that the President had lied under oath, entertained an alternative interpretation. That Clinton violated the law was not a problem created by investigative machinery, but one simply uncovered by that machinery, thereby proving its worth. Furthermore, although several scandal allegations had preceded the Lewinsky affair, they did not minimize its importance. Clinton, it appeared to his opponents, habitually abused the political offices he held. Ultimately two conflicting interpretations shaped this scandal: that Clinton was subject to unwarranted and intrusive investigation and, conversely, that he was a frequent perpetrator of scandalous action in both a political and a private capacity.

The Lewinsky scandal has had an important and potentially long-term impact upon the presidential office and the conduct and evolution of scandal politics. Many allegations of presidential wrongdoing during the scandal were dismissed by Clinton as partisan vindictiveness designed to undermine his credibility and inflict damage upon his political office. Starr's Republican affiliation lent some credence to albeit exaggerated claims that a vast right-wing conspiracy sought to destabilize Clinton's position. The nature and evolution of the impeachment proceedings only fuelled this argument. Partisan voting patterns dominated proceedings, with only a handful of dissenting opinions evident through the entire process. This made the scandal appear as run-of-the-mill politics, with clear and distinct party division apparent over the seriousness of the President's actions. There was, additionally, no realistic prospect of the attainment of a two-thirds majority in the Senate required to ensure conviction. Any future impeachment proceedings will be conducted against the backdrop of the Lewinsky experience, with appropriate scrutiny directed at the partisan disposition of those in a position to decide the fate of the President. This fact was not lost on those debating the articles of impeachment in the House and the Senate, and due recognition was given to the signal any exoneration or conviction might send to future Congresses. For example, Senator James M. Jeffords (R-Vt) argued: 'I am gravely concerned that a vote to convict the President on these articles may establish a threshold that would make every President subject to removal for the slightest indiscretion, or that a vote to convict may impale every President who faces a Congress controlled by the opposing party'. Similarly, House Democrat Martin T. Meehan (D-Mass) anticipated further concerns: 'It is not history's verdict alone that I fear. I also fear how our actions will shape history'.[11] The fact that the major presidential scandals of the modern era have occurred when the Executive has been controlled by one party and the Legislative has been controlled by the other provides tangible evidence that partisan disposition has been a contributory factor in propagating and sustaining scandal politics. Clinton's allegations against the Republicans appeared to hold some weight, and the more he suggested that partisanship was a root cause of the scandal, the greater the attention given to that factor and the greater the pressure on members of both parties to consider their party affiliation when voting in the Congress. Clinton's experience merely complicates the conduct of scandal politics, and makes impeachment a problematic Constitutional measure for both parties to consider when faced by any future suggestion that high crimes and misdemeanors have been committed by a Chief Executive.

While Iran-Contra appeared to suggest that those accused of scandal held a small but distinct advantage over those prosecuting scandal, the Lewinsky affair overtly suggested that the Executive was very much on the defensive and subject to measures which were, in essence, beyond the scope of its direct control. Kenneth Starr conducted his investigation of Clinton with little obvious hindrance, and even on the rare occasions when Clinton challenged him directly, it was ultimately Starr who prevailed in his quest to accumulate incriminating information. While damage limitation strategies might have been somewhat effective in influencing Democratic congressional opinion, and certainly held a pivotal role in addressing public opinion, they proved largely ineffective when directed at Starr and the Republican majority in the Congress. Indeed the White House attempted to attack Starr by seeking to discredit him in the eyes of those who would later evaluate the validity of his report, namely the public and the Congress. Both before and after his confession of inappropriate behavior, Clinton appeared powerless to stem the momentum achieved by the scandal. Beyond the irritant of Starr's investigation lay the fact that the Republicans held the Congress. Clinton could exert little influence over the decision of the House to release documents and evidentiary material, to commence with impeachment proceedings, or to force a trial in the Senate. In many respects this was a scandal where the President, beyond his initial denials, was forced to react to events and the bidding of others. Consequently, Clinton purposefully distanced himself from the scandal as often as was possible in both the denial and admissions phases, and thereby minimized his direct association with the ongoing events. This strategy ultimately proved successful in the court of public opinion, as opinion poll statistics suggested that Clinton's minimal attention on scandal issues, and concentration upon populist concerns, held some resonance across the nation. Reagan and Nixon had both previously held scandal allegations at arm's length with varying degrees of success and, consequently, Clinton's reaction to the Lewinsky matter was neither unique nor surprising.

Clinton's damage limitation exercise, for all its problems and short-comings, was aided throughout the duration of the scandal by strategic blunders and oversight by his opponents. The investigation of the President's private activity by Starr appeared to show an overly lurid concentration on the private dealings of the President and the details of his intimate relationship with Lewinsky. The coverage of material of a sexual nature in the *Starr Report* coincided neatly with Clinton's claims that the whole scandal boiled down to sex and nothing more. Similarly, the media appeared disunited and ineffectual in its attempts to present this scandal, and its inability to translate its outrage about Clinton's misleading claims of innocence into public disapproval high-lighted presentational and structural problems within the fourth estate. In the political forum things were no different. The Republican party appeared to hold a significant advantage over Clinton when the scandal broke, and its numerical supremacy in the Congress ensured that it would dominate in that forum if partisan voting patterns appeared during impeachment proceedings. Yet the structural con-straints of the Constitution nullified this advantage in the Senate, and the determination of many Republican leaders, Henry Hyde (R-Ill) among them, to stop at nothing short of impeachment ensured that this was an all-or-nothing conflict. Censure and other compromise positions were summarily dismissed. Clinton's avoidance of institu-tional punishment during this scandal was unsurprising, and occurred as a consequence of the strategies and tactics of those who demanded his removal, yet ended up reflecting on just how, given the weight of evidence, he had evaded Constitutional punishment.

Clinton's scandal experience cannot be viewed in total isolation. Economic good fortune, an appearance of stability in foreign affairs, and healthy employment figures produced a sense of well-being within America which assisted in offsetting the potentially damaging impact of presidential scandal. Public opinion seemed more concerned with Clinton's public policy performance than with the superficial messages of an illicit presidential affair or the deeper concerns of legal transgression. Whether Clinton would have faced more severe public reproach for his actions if the state of the nation had been less healthy is a matter for speculation, but the existing evidence suggests, particularly with respect to job approval, that for many the scandal was an issue best reserved for the tabloid media outlets and television comedians. This only served to further complicate the efforts of the elite elements within government determined to prosecute Clinton and oust him from office.

The impact of the scandal upon the American political system appears significant. Clinton's presidential legacy has been tarnished by scandal allegations and outcomes. Whether his reputation will be sullied by the Lewinsky matter in the same fashion that Nixon's was tarnished by Watergate is a leading question, but one that is presently unanswerable. That Clinton's presidency is synonymous with scandal is nevertheless in little doubt. His survival of the Lewinsky scandal, alongside several other problematic scandalous episodes, does however embellish his reputation as the Comeback Kid and provides evidence that Clinton, for all his errors and repeated troubles, had an uncanny ability to extricate himself from political crisis.[12]

Notes

Introduction

1. See 'Figure 3-1. 1996 Presidential Election', Michael Nelson, 'The Election: Turbulence and Tranquillity in Contemporary American Politics', in Michael Nelson (ed.), *The Elections of 1996* (Washington D.C.: CQ Press, 1997) p. 61.
2. There are several interpretations of the plight faced by the modern presidency and the problems created and endured by the presidential office; see Burt Solomon, 'Do We Ask Too Much of Presidents?', *National Journal*, 18 June 1994, pp. 1390–92.
3. '19 August 1998. The Ratings: Good News for Networks', *NYTimes.com* [http://www.nytimes.com/library/politics/081998clinton-ratings.html]
4. '1 March 1998. Republicans Abandon Restraint on Clinton', *NYTimes.com* [http://www.nytimes.com/library/politics/030198clinton-repubs.html]
5. '19 August 1998. The Reaction: Prominent Democrats Are Unhappy With Clinton', *NYTimes.com* [http://www.nytimes.com/library/politics/081998 clinton-politics.html]

Chapter 1   The Clinton Scandal Epidemic

1. See, 'Clinton's Latest, Worst Troubles Put His Whole Agenda on Hold', *Congressional Quarterly Weekly*, 24 January 1998, pp. 164–5.
2. '27 January 1998. Hillary Clinton: "This is a battle" ' *CNN.com* [http://www.cnn.com/US/9801/27/hillary.today]
3. Theodore Lowi, 'Foreword', in Andrei S. Markovits and Mark Silverstein, (eds), *The Politics of Scandal: Power and Process in Liberal Democracies* (New York: Holmes & Meier, 1988) p. viii.
4. Cited in 'Watergate's Clearest Lesson: Ten years later, the point remains: Not even a President is above the law', *Time*, 14 June 1982, p. 36.
5. '25 January 1998. Other Presidents Have Been the Talk of the Pillow', *NYTimes.com* [http://www.nytimes.com/library/politics/012598clinton-history.html]
6. Joseph P. Lash, *Eleanor and Franklin* (New York: Signet, 1971) pp. 302–3.
7. Cited in Gayle Worland, 'Scandals Throughout Presidential History', *Washingtonpost.com* [http://www.washingtonpost.com/wp-srv/politics/special/clinton/stories/scandalhistory.htm]
8. Denise M. Bostdorff, 'Clinton's Characteristic Issue Management Style: Caution, Conciliation and Conflict Avoidance in the Case of Gays in the Military', in Robert E. Denton Jr. and Rachel L. Holloway, *The Clinton Presidency: Images, Issues and Communication Strategies* (Westport, Connecticut: Praeger, 1996) p. 189.
9. Elizabeth Drew, *On The Edge: The Clinton Presidency* (New York: Touchstone, 1995) pp. 32–3.

10. Dilys M. Hill, 'The Clinton Presidency: The Man and His Times', in Paul S. Herrnson and Dilys M. Hill, (eds), *The Clinton Presidency: The First Term, 1992–1996* (Basingstoke: Macmillan, 1999) p. 8.

11. Drew, *On the Edge* (1995) p. 41.

12. Ibid., p. 175.

13. For an excellent and concise review of Whitewater, see Robert Williams, *Political Scandals in the USA* (Edinburgh: Keele University Press, 1998) pp. 63–88.

14. 'Timeline: Whitewater Special Report', *Washingtonpost.com* [http://www.washingtonpost.com/wp-srv/politics/special/whitewater/timeline2.htm]

15. Williams, *Political Scandals* (1998) p. 65.

16. James B. Stewart, *Blood Sport: The President and His Adversaries* (New York: Touchstone, 1996) pp. 27–35, 293–5.

17. Ibid., pp. 297–303.

18. 'Foster's Death a Suicide', *Washington Post*, 1 July 1994, p. A1.

19. Cited in ibid., p. A1.

20. 'Starr Probe Reaffirms Foster Killed Himself', *Washington Post*, 11 October 1997, p. A4.

21. Ibid.

22. Ibid.

23. Drew, *On The Edge* (1995) p. 414; Larry J. Sabato and S. Robert Lichter, *When Should the Watchdogs Bark?: Media Coverage of the Clinton Scandals* (Washington D.C.: Center For Media and Public Affairs, 1995) p. 8.

24. '4 March 1998. The Web That Widened From Whitewater', *NYTimes.com* [http://www.nytimes.com/library/politics/030498whitewater-2.html]

25. Cited in Gregory S. Walden, *On Best Behavior: The Clinton Administration and Ethics in Government* (Indianapolis: Hudson Institute Press, 1996) p. 206.

26. '23 July 1994. Exchange With Reporters in Hot Springs, Arkansas', *Weekly Compilation of Presidential Documents*, 30 no.30, 1 August 1994, p. 1545.

27. Hill, 'The Clinton Presidency', in Herrnson and Hill, *The Clinton Presidency* (1999) p. 11.

28. Walden, *On Best Behavior* (1996) p. 237.

29. Ibid., p. 248.

30. 'Hillary Clinton and the Whitewater Controversy: A Close-Up', *Washington Post*, 2 June 1996, p. A1. See also, Stewart, *Blood Sport* (1996) p. 426.

31. 'September 16, 1996. Review and Outlook: Will Anyone Believe?', Robert L. Bartley (ed.), *A Journal Briefing: Whitewater Vol. III* (New York: Dow Jones/Wall Street Journal, 1997) p. 33.

32. Matthew Robert Kerbel, 'The Media: Viewing the Campaign Through a Strategic Haze', in Michael Nelson (ed.), *The Elections of 1996* (Washington D.C.: Congressional Quarterly Press, 1997) p. 95.

33. '9 January 1996. The President's News Conference', *Weekly Compilation of Presidential Documents*, 32, no.2, 15 January 1996, p. 29.

34. *Washington Post*, 2 June 1996, p. A1.

35. Ibid.

36. 'On the griddle again: New evidence and new questions plague the first family', *U.S. News and World Report*, 22 January 1996, p. 26.

37. 'Prosecutors Question First Lady at Length', *Washington Post*, 26 April 1998, p. A1.

38. Fiske was worried that a congressional investigation 'would pose a severe risk to the integrity of our investigation'. Cited in Walden, *On Best Behavior* (1996) pp. 212, 213.
39. Ibid., p. 232.
40. Ibid., pp. 235–6.
41. Ibid., p. 245.
42. 'Editorial: The Real Whitewater Report', *U.S. News and World Report*, 29 January 1996, p. 101.
43. 'The Hearings End Much as They Began', *Washington Post*, 19 June 1996, p. A1.
44. Williams, *Political Scandal* (1998) p. 75.
45. Walden, *On Best Behavior* (1996) p. 255.
46. *Washington Post*, 19 June 1996, p. A1.
47. Walden, *On Best Behavior* (1996) p. 203.
48. Dick Morris, *Behind the Oval Office: Winning the Presidency in the Nineties* (New York: Random House, 1997) pp. 285–6.
49. Walden, *On Best Behavior* (1996) p. 213.
50. '24 March 1994. The President's News Conference', *Weekly Compilation of Presidential Documents*, 30, no.12, 28 March 1994, p. 627.
51. Ibid., p. 634.
52. Ibid., p. 627.
53. Ibid., p. 634.
54. '23 July 1994. Exchange With Reporters in Hot Springs, Arkansas', *Weekly Compilation of Presidential Documents*, 30, no.30, 1 August 1994, p. 1545.
55. '5 April 1994. Remarks in Town Meeting in Charlotte, North Carolina', *Weekly Compilation of Presidential Documents*, 30, no.14, 11 April 1994, p. 684.
56. '3 August 1994. The President's News Conference', *Weekly Compilation of Presidential Documents*, 30, no.31, 5 August 1994, p. 1616.
57. *Weekly Compilation of Presidential Documents*, 30, no.14, 11 April 1994, p. 684.
58. '17 May 1995. Statement of the White House Press Secretary', *The White House: Office of the Press Secretary*.
59. '10 August 1995. The President's News Conference', *Weekly Compilation of Presidential Documents*, 31, no.32, 14 August 1995, p. 1419.
60. '12 January 1996. The President's News Conference', *Weekly Compilation of Presidential Documents*, 32, no.2, 15 January 1996, p. 36.
61. '30 May 1996. More People Think Clinton is Hiding Something in Whitewater', *CNN.com* [http://allpolitics.com/news/9605/30/poll.whitewater]
62. Ibid.
63. 'NBC/Wall Street Journal August 1995 poll', cited in 'A Sampling of Public Perception on Whitewater', *PoliticsUSA.com* [http://www.politicsusa.com. PoliticsUSA/nes/1218if10.html.cgi]
64. Kerbel, 'The Media: Viewing the Campaign Through a Strategic Haze', in *The Elections of 1996* (1997) p. 96.
65. Sabato and Lichter, *When Should the Watchdogs Bark?* (1995) p. 79.
66. Ibid., p. 66.
67. Gene Lyons, *Fools For Scandal: How the Media Invented Whitewater* (New York: Franklin Square Press, 1996) pp. 22–3.

68. Walden, *On Best Behavior* (1996) pp. 310–11.
69. Cited in Sabato and Lichter, *When Should the Watchdogs Bark?* (1995) p. 71.

Chapter 2   The Lewinsky Affair

1. Drew, *On The Edge* (1995) p. 381.
2. Alan M. Dershowitz, *Sexual McCarthyism: Clinton, Starr, and the Emerging Constitutional Crisis* (New York: Basic Books, 1998) p. 102.
3. Cited in ibid., p. 99.
4. Richard A. Posner, *An Affair of State: The Investigation, Impeachment, and Trial of President Clinton* (London: Harvard University Press, 1999) pp. 217–18.
5. 'Review and Outlook: Jones 9, Clinton 0. May 28, 1997', Bartley, *Whitewater Vol. III* (1997) p. 440.
6. 'High Court Set Stage for Crisis', *Washington Post*, 29 January 1998, p. A12.
7. Cited in Howard Kurtz, *Spin Cycle: The Clinton Propaganda Machine* (New York: The Free Press, 1998) p. 209.
8. Ibid., p. 209.
9. Dershowitz, *Sexual McCarthyism* (1998) p. 114.
10. Cited in 'Review and Outlook: Paula's Aftershocks. May 29, 1997', Bartley, *Whitewater Vol. III* (1997) pp. 447–8.
11. See Dershowitz, *Sexual McCarthyism* (1998) pp. 15–16.
12. Cited in 'The Testimony Of Kenneth Starr. November 19, 1998', in Merrill McLoughlin (ed.), *The Impeachment and Trial of President Clinton: The Official Transcripts, from the House Judiciary Committee Hearings to the Senate Trial* (New York: Times Books 1999) p. 9 (hereafter, *The Impeachment and Trial of President Clinton*).
13. Posner, *An Affair of State* (1999) p. 64.
14. 'President Clinton's Videotaped August 17, 1998 Grand Jury Testimony', in Phil Kuntz (ed.), *The Starr Report: The Starr Evidence. Complete Testimony from President Clinton and Monica Lewinsky, and other Documents from the Independent Counsel's Investigation* (New York: Pocket Books, 1998) p. 437 (hereafter *Starr Evidence*).
15. *The Starr Report: The Findings of Independent Counsel Kenneth W. Starr on President Clinton and the Lewinsky Affair* (New York: Public Affairs/ Washington Post, 1998) p. 48 (hereafter *Starr Report*).
16. Ibid., p. 49.
17. 'President Clinton's Videotaped August 17, 1998 Grand Jury Testimony', *Starr Evidence*, p. 372.
18. Ibid., p. 437.
19. See *Starr Report*, p. 63.
20. Ibid., p. 64.
21. Ibid., p. 65.
22. Ibid., p. 67.
23. 'Cast of Characters in the Clinton–Lewinsky Scandal: 29-1-98', *CNN.com* [http://allpolitics.com/1998/resources/lewinsky/cast.characters]
24. Goldberg represented law enforcement officials during Troopergate and had worked for Nixon.

25. See 'Linda Tripp's Handwritten Notes', *Starr Evidence*, pp. 514–41.
26. Posner, *An Affair of State* (1999) pp. 26, 61.
27. *Starr Report*, p. 73.
28. Ibid., p. 80; see also 'The Dress', in *Starr Evidence*, pp. 545–59.
29. 'President Clinton's Videotaped August 17, 1998 Grand Jury Testimony', ibid., p. 417; also cited in the *Starr Report*, p. 82.
30. For example, regarding the failure to resurrect her relationship with the President, Lewinsky e-mailed to her friend Catherine Allday Davis: 'So it's over. I don't know what I will do now but I can't wait any more and I can't go through all of this crap anymore. In some ways I hope I never hear from him [Clinton] again because he'll just lead me on because he doesn't have the balls to tell me the truth.' 'E-mail to Cathering Davis', *Starr Evidence*, pp. 488–9.
31. These people are listed in the *Starr Report*, pp. 33–4.
32. Ibid., p. 82.
33. 'President Clinton's Videotaped August 17, 1998 Grand Jury Testimony', *Starr Evidence*, p. 422.
34. *Starr Report*, p. 87.
35. Ibid., p. 100.
36. 'President Clinton's Videotaped August 17, 1998 Grand Jury Testimony', *Starr Evidence*, p. 401.
37. Ibid., p. 376.
38. *Starr Report*, p. 113.
39. Cited in ibid., p. 115.
40. Ibid., p. 116.
41. Ibid., p. 120.
42. 'President Clinton's Videotaped August 17, 1998 Grand Jury Testimony', *Starr Evidence*, pp. 374–5.
43. '17 January 1998. President Clinton's Deposition', *Washingtonpost.com* [http://www.washingtonpost.com/wp-srv/politics/special/pjones/docs/clintondep031398.htm]
44. 'President Clinton's Videotaped August 17, 1998 Grand Jury Testimony', *Starr Evidence*, p. 379.
45. Ibid., p. 417.
46. *Starr Report*, p. 132.
47. 'Tapes Make Tripp's Role Clearer', *Washington Post*, 3 October 1998, p. A1.
48. Some details of the recorded conversations can be found in the *Starr Report*, p. 135.
49. 'J. January 13–14: Lewinsky–Tripp Conversation and Talking Points', ibid., p. 135; see Jeffrey Toobin, *A Vast Conspiracy: The Real Story of the Sex Scandal That Nearly Brought Down a President* (New York: Random House, 1999) pp. 198–9.
50. '6 February 1998. Text of Linda Tripp's Sworn Statement About Lewinsky, Willey' *Washingtonpost.com* [http://www.washingtonpost.com/wp-srv/politics/special/clinton/stories/tripptext020698.htm]
51. '30 January 1998. Text of Linda Tripp's Statement.', *Associated Press Release* [http://www.washingtonpost.com/wp-srv/politics/special/clinton/stories/tripptext013098.htm]
52. Ibid.
53. Ibid.

54. Posner, *An Affair of State* (1999) p. 70.
55. *Starr Report*, p. 22.
56. 'President Clinton's Videotaped August 17, 1998 Grand Jury Testimony', *Starr Evidence*, pp. 367–9.
57. '17 January 1998. President Clinton's Deposition', *Washingtonpost.com* [http://www.washingtonpost.com/wp-srv/politics/special/pjones/docs/clintondep031398.htm]
58. *Starr Report*, p. 36.
59. Ibid., p. 138.
60. '17 January 1998. President Clinton's Deposition', *Washingtonpost.com* [http://www.washingtonpost.com/wp-srv/politics/special/pjones/docs/clintondep031398.htm]
61. Ibid.
62. 'The Lewinsky Affidavit', *Washingtonpost.com* [http://www.washingtonpost.com/wp-srv/politics/special/clinton/pjones/docs/lewinskyaffidavit.htm]
63. Ibid.
64. 'President Clinton's Videotaped August 17, 1998 Grand Jury Testimony', *Starr Evidence*, p. 368.
65. Extracted from 'Article II', *The Impeachment and Trial of President Clinton*, p. 447.
66. Extracted from 'Article III', ibid., p. 448.
67. Ibid.

Chapter 3   Protecting the President: Damage Limitation and the Lewinsky Scandal

1. Michael Isikoff, *Uncovering Clinton: A Reporter's Story* (New York: Crown Publishers, 1999) pp. 328–38.
2. Cited in *Starr Report*, p. 228.
3. Ibid.
4. Ibid., p. 226.
5. 'Article III – Section (6)', *The Impeachment and Trial of President Clinton*, p. 448.
6. 'Article III – Section (7)', ibid., pp. 448–9.
7. See the Drudge Website at: http://www.drudgereport.com/
8. The content of Drudge's web page scoop are detailed in Toobin, *A Vast Conspiracy*, (1999) pp. 229–33.
9. 'An accuser's troubling tale: Willey's past raises credibility questions', *U.S. News and World Report*, 30 March 1998, pp. 20–1.
10. Gloria Borger, 'The Art of Smearing 101', ibid., p. 28; 'News Analysis: Cornered, White House Brandishes Facts on Willey', *Washington Post*, 18 March 1998, p. A1.
11. See 'The Willey Letters', released 16 March 1998, at *Washingtonpost.com* [http://www.washingtonpost.com/wp-srv/politics/special/clinton/stories/willeyletters.htm]
12. 'Grilling the Secret Service: Starr will get agents' testimony, but what can they tell him?', *U.S. News and World Report*, 27 July 1998, p. 24.

13. 'Independent Counsel Seeks Clinton Testimony', *Washington Post*, 12 March 1998, p. A1.
14. Toobin, *A Vast Conspiracy*, (1999) pp. 300, 305–7.
15. 'FBI to Test Dress', *Washington Post*, 31 July 1998, p. A4.
16. See 'Letter from the OIC to David E. Kendall', *Starr Evidence*, p. 547.
17. 'FBI Transcription', ibid., p. 555.
18. See Posner, *An Affair of State*, (1999) pp. 44–8.
19. *Starr Report*, p. 19.
20. Ibid., pp. 154–5; see also, 'Starr lists all the President's lies', *The Daily Telegraph*, 12 September 1998, p. 1.
21. 'The net closes on Clinton: Starr alleges perjury and abuse of power', *The Times*, 11 September 1998, p. 1.
22. 'For Political Pros, the Moment Was a Dud', *Washington Post*, 22 September 1998, p. A19.
23. 'President Tries to Boost Support on Hill', *Washington Post*, 9 September 1998, p. A1.
24. '21 January 1998. Excerpt of a Telephone Interview with Morton Kondrake and Ed Henry of Roll Call', *Weekly Compilation of Presidential Documents*, 34, no.4, 26 January 1998, pp. 115–16.
25. Ibid., p. 115.
26. '21 January 1998. Interview With Jim Lehrer of the PBS "News Hour" ', *Weekly Compilation of Presidential Documents*, 34, no.4, 26 January 1998, p. 104.
27. Clinton stated: 'We are doing our best to cooperate here, but we don't know much yet. And that's all I can say now. What I'm trying to do is to contain my natural impulses and get back to work. I think it's important that we cooperate. I will cooperate.' ibid., p. 104.
28. Ibid., p. 114.
29. '22 January 1998. Remarks Prior to Discussions With Chairman Yasser Arafat of the Palestinian Authority and an Exchange With Reporters', *Weekly Compilation of Presidential Documents*, 34, no.4, 26 January 1998, p. 124.
30. '26 January 1998. Remarks on the After-School Child Care Initiative', *Weekly Compilation of Presidential Documents*, 34, no.5, 2 February 1998, p. 128.
31. Cited in 'Clinton Forcefully Denies Affair, or Urging Lies', *Washington Post*, 27 January 1998, p. A1.
32. Stephen Gettinger, 'Forget the Eloquence; How Does He Look?', *Congressional Quarterly Weekly*, 24 January 1998, p. 206.
33. 'Presidential Address: Clinton Stresses Accomplishments, Calls State of the Union "Strong" ', *Congressional Quarterly Weekly*, 31 January 1998, pp. 251–5.
34. 'Clinton Succeeds in Slowing Scandal's Momentum', *Congressional Quarterly Weekly*, 31 January 1998, p. 215.
35. 'White House Uneasy About Lack of Long-Term Strategy', *Washington Post*, 11 February 1998, p. A14.
36. '6 February 1998. Reflective Clinton speaks at Annual Prayer Breakfast', *NYTimes.com* [http://www.nytimes.com/library/politics/020698clinton-prayer.html]

37. '6 February 1998. The President's News Conference with Prime Minister Blair', *Weekly Compilation of Presidential Documents*, 34, no.6, 9 February 1998, p. 216.
38. Ibid., p. 219.
39. See, for example, 'Mandela Offers Support to Clinton', *Washington Post*, 23 September 1998, p. A11.
40. '5 March 1998. Remarks Prior to Discussion With Medicare Commission and an Exchange with Reporters', *Weekly Compilation of Presidential Documents*, 34, no.10, 9 March 1998, p. 382.
41. '3 April 1998. Remarks on the Legislative Agenda and an Exchange With Reporters', *Weekly Compilation of Presidential Documents*, 34, no.14, 6 April 1998, p. 565.
42. '30 April 1998. The President's News Conference', *Weekly Compilation of Presidential Documents*, 34, no.18, 4 May 1998, p. 736.
43. Cited in 'Day Could Narrow Credibility Gap', *Washington Post*, 17 August 1998, p. A1.
44. Ibid.
45. Cited in 'President Prepares for Historic Test', *Washington Post*, 17 August 1998, p. A1.
46. See 'President Clinton's Videotaped August 17, 1998, Grand Jury Testimony', *Starr Evidence*, pp. 357–451.
47. 'Clinton's quandary: The President looks for a route around Starr's perjury "trap" ', *U.S. News and World Report*, 17/24 August 1998, pp. 18,20.
48. '3am: Clinton tells America of his regrets', *The Times*, 18 August 1998, p. 1.
49. 'Address to the Nation on Testimony Before the Independent Counsel's Grand Jury', *Weekly Compilation of Presidential Documents*, 34, no.34, 24 August 1998, p. 1638.
50. Ibid.
51. Ibid.
52. Ibid.
53. Ibid.
54. 'Clinton Admits Inappropriate Intimacy, Challenges Starr to End Personal "Prying" ', *Washington Post*, 18 August 1998, p. A1.
55. 'The Legal Gamble: To Say Just Enough', *Washington Post*, 18 August 1998, p. A1.
56. ' "Disappointed" Democrats Let Clinton Face the Fallout Alone', *Congressional Quarterly Weekly*, 22 August 1998, p. 2279; 'Opponents Praise Admission But Say Trouble's Not Over', *Washington Post*, 18 August 1998, p. A4.
57. 'Reactions: Conciliation, Condemnation', *Congressional Quarterly Weekly*, 22 August 1998, p. 2282.
58. 'Edging Back to Limelight, Clinton Silent on Scandal', *Washington Post*, 28 August 1998, p. A1.
59. Ibid.
60. 'Clinton Says "I'm Sorry" for Lewinsky affair', *Washington Post*, 5 September 1998, p. A1; '4 September 1998. Exchange With Reporters Prior to Discussions With Prime Minister Bertie Ahern of Ireland in Dublin', *Weekly Compilation of Presidential Documents*, 34, no.36, 7 September 1998, p. 1720.

61. In Orlando, Florida, Clinton stated: 'And I have no one to blame but myself for my self-inflicted wounds.' In Coral Gables, Florida, he stated: 'I've tried to do a good job taking care of this country even when I haven't taken such good care of myself and my family, my obligations. I hope that you and others I have injured will forgive me for the mistakes I've made, but the most important thing is you must not let it deter you from meeting your responsibilities as citizens.' Cited in 'Excerpt From Clinton's Comments', *Washington Post/Associated Press*, 9 September 1998; see also, 'Clinton says sorry again as Starr files report', *The Times*, 10 September 1998, p. 1.

62. '11 September 1998. Remarks at a Breakfast with Religious Leaders', *Weekly Compilation of Presidential Documents*, 34, no.37, 14 September 1998, p. 1762.

63. Ibid.

64. Ibid., pp. 1762–3; see also, 'Forgive me Monica, I have sinned', *The Daily Telegraph*, 12 September 1998, p. 3.

65. '16 September 1998. The President's News Conference with President Havel', *Weekly Compilation of Presidential Documents*, 34, no.38, 21 September 1998, p. 1805.

66. Ibid., p. 1806.

67. 'Millions to witness lies and anger: Salacious film will humiliate the President', *The Times*, 19 September 1998, p. 1.

68. 'For Political Pros, the Moment was a Dud', *Washington Post*, 22 September 1998, p. A19.

69. 'Analysis: Clinton Plays Many Roles, Assuredly', *Washington Post*, 22 September 1998, p. A1.

70. See 'Shades of Nixon: America relives the dark days of Watergate lies', *The Times*, 11 September 1998, p. 2.

71. Ibid., p. 3; 'Reaping the Whirlwind', *Congressional Quarterly Weekly*, 12 September 1998, p. 2380.

72. '24 August 1998. Torn Between Lawyers and Aides, Clinton Chose Strategy of Denial', *NYTimes.com* [http://www.nytimes.com/library/politics/082498clinton-strategy.html]

73. '24 January 1998. The Clinton Camp: Clinton Is Handling This Crisis Alone', *NYTimes.com* [http://www.nytimes.com/library/politics/012498clinton crisis.html]

74. 'Hillary Clinton goes into battle for her husband', *The Times*, 26 January 1998, p. 1.

75. *NYTimes.com* [http://www.nytimes.com/library/politics/012498clinton-crisis.html]

76. '24 January 1998. The Defenders: Many Longtime Supporters Not Rushing to Clinton's Defense', *NYTimes.com* [http://www.nytimes.com/library/politics/012498clinton-politics.html]

77. 'A Confidant for Every Crisis', *Washington Post*, 29 January 1998, p. B1.

78. '27 January 1998. Clinton Reaches Out to Veteran Trouble-Shooter', *NYTimes.com* [http://www.nytimes.com/library/politics/012798clinton-kantor.html]

79. 'White House's Damage Control: The President's lawyers have become the new palace guard', *U.S. News and World Report*, 23 February 1998, p. 31; see also, 'Office of Damage Control', *Washington Post*, 31 July 1998, p. A1.

80. 'When the First Lady took her gloves off', *The Times* (weekend), 31 January 1998, pp. 1, 3.
81. '27 January 1998.Excerpts of Mrs.Clinton Interview', *Associated Press/ Washingtonpost.com* [http://www.washingtonpost.com/wp-srv/politics/ special/clinton/stories/excerpts012798.htm]
82. Ibid. For an analysis of Hillary Clinton's accusations, see 'Persecuted or Paranoid? A look at the motley characters behind Hillary Clinton's "vast right wing conspiracy" ', *Time*, 2 February 1998, pp. 38–41; see also, Norman Mailer, 'Clinton for Pres. No, not you, Bill', *The Observer* (Review), 8 February 1998, p. 1.
83. 'First Lady Launches Counterattack', *Washington Post*, 28 January 1998, p. A1.
84. '30 January 1998. White House Has 3-Pronged Strategy for Dealing With Crisis', *NYTimes.com* [http://www.nytimes.com/library/politics/013098 clinton-strategy.html]
85. 'Clinton's "Captain of the Defense" ', *Washington Post*, 5 February 1998, p. A12.
86. '2 March 1998. Analysis: White House Continues to Attack Starr', *NYTimes.com* [http://www.nytimes.com/library/politics/030298clinton-starr.html]
87. 'Clinton Advisers Agree to Attack Starr', *Washington Post*, 7 February 1998, p. A1; Mortimer B. Zuckerman, 'Starr has hit a new low: It's tough to do, but the prosecutor has beaten his previous indiscretions', *U.S. News and World Report*, 29 June 1998, p. 94.
88. 'White House Uneasy About Lack of Long-Term Strategy', *Washington Post*, 11 February 1998, p. A14.
89. Cited in 'White House Strategy Evolving Day by Day', *Washington Post*, 17 September 1998, p. A15.
90. 'Turning Up the Heat: By grilling Monica's mom, Ken Starr lays the ground-work for his very reluctant star witness', *Time*, 23 February 1998, pp. 32, 34.
91. For information on the subpoena served to Blumenthal, see 'Prosecutor Lobs a Grenade', *Washington Post*, 25 February 1998, p. A7; also, for Podesta testimony, see 'Clinton Aide Appears at Grand Jury 3rd Time', *Washington Post*, 24 June 1998, p. A2.
92. See 'The Master Fixer in a Fix', *Time*, 2 February 1998, pp. 40–2.
93. David Gergen, 'Stepping up to the truth: Why Clinton will give a full expla-nation to Starr – and the public', *U.S. News and World Report*, 10 August 1998, p. 67.
94. 'Advisers Lean Against Clinton Testifying', *Washington Post*, 5 July 1998, p. A4; see also, 'White House Counsel Irks Political Aides', *Washington Post*, 28 July 1998, p. A1.
95. 'Business-as-Usual Fails to Hide White House Uncertainty', *Washington Post*, 30 July 1998, p. A8.
96. '18 August 1998. Next on agenda: Restoring credibility', *USAToday.com* [http://www.usatoday.com/news/index/clinton/clin551.htm]
97. Cited in 'Shalala's Remarks Irk President', *Washington Post*, 11 September 1998, p A1.
98. For example, one unnamed cabinet aide stated: 'The thing that dominated over here more than anything else is a sense of sadness, especially among

what's left of the old guard. They're having a wake for someone who's not dead yet.' Cited in '21 September 1998. The White House: Deep Sense of Gloom Among Clinton Aides', *NYTimes.com* [http://www.nytimes.com/library/politics/092198clinton-scene.html]

99. Ibid.
100. '31 August 1998. Clinton Advisers Map Out Defense in Lewinsky Matter', *NYTimes.com* [http://www.nytimes.com/library/politics/083198 clinton-starr.html]
101. 'Kendall Wants to Preview Starr's Report', *Washington Post*, 8 September 1998, p. A4.
102. See 'Long List of Its Own Trespasses Tempers Congress' Judgment', *Congressional Quarterly Weekly*, 31 January 1998, pp. 223–4; Carroll J. Doherty, 'Will Congress' Hand Be Stayed By Fear of "Glass Houses"?', *Congressional Quarterly Weekly*, 12 September 1998, p. 2395.
103. *Congressional Quarterly Weekly*, 24 January 1998, p. 164.
104. Ibid., p. 165.
105. *NYTimes.com* [http://www.nytimes.com/library/politics/012498 clinton-politics.html]
106. *Congressional Quarterly Weekly* stated: 'But members of Congress had a different agenda than the media. Like good card players, Democrats displayed no anxiety that Clinton's problems would sink him, or them. And Republicans stuck to their political advisers' instructions that they say nothing might risk converting the president's problems into a partisan brawl.' In 'Both Parties Focus on Speech . . . not Scandal, to Chagrin of Some', *Congressional Quarterly Weekly*, 31 January 1998, p. 216.
107. 'The Burden Of Proof: Ken Starr may be able to get the goods on Clinton and Lewinsky, but it won't be easy', *Time*, 2 February 1998, p. 46.
108. 'Impeachment Inquiry Discussed in House', *Washington Post*, 10 February 1998, p. A9.
109. 'The Man Who Would Be Judge', *Time*, 23 February 1998, p. 37.
110. 'Hatch Warns Clinton on Testimony', *Washington Post*, 13 July 1998, p. A4.
111. '3 August 1998. Hatch Urges Clinton to "Pour His Heart Out" ', *NYTimes.com* [http://www.nytimes.com/library/politics/080398clinton-starr.html]
112. Ibid.
113. 'A Cautious Reunion Awaits Clinton on Hill', *Washington Post*, 5 August 1998, p. A12.
114. 'They Didn't Ask, He Didn't Tell', *Washington Post*, 6 August 1998, p. A13.
115. '18 August 1998. Analysis: Clinton's Calculated Gamble', *NYTimes.com* [http://www.nytimes.com/library/politics/081898clinton-assess.html]; see also, ' "Disappointed" Democrats Let Clinton Face the Fallout Alone', *Congressional Quarterly Weekly*, 22 August 1998, pp. 2279–80.
116. 'Opponents Praise Admission But Say Trouble's Not Over', *Washington Post*, 18 August 1998, p. A4.
117. Ibid.
118. Ibid.

119. 'Hill Democrats See Speech as a Failure', *Washington Post*, 20 August 1998, p. A1; 'Reactions: Conciliation, Condemnation', *Congressional Quarterly Weekly*, 22 August 1998, p. 2282.
120. 'White House Crisis: Next on agenda: Restoring credibility', *USAToday.com* [http://www.usatoday.com/news/index/clinton/clin551.htm]
121. '23 August 1998. The Legacy: Clinton Haunted by the Impact of His Choices', *NYTimes.com* [http://www.nytimes.com/library/politics/082398 clinton-legacy.html]
122. 'Gingrich Raises the Bar for Impeachment', *Washington Post*, 24 August 1998, p. A1.
123. 'Democrats Echo Gingrich on Impeachment Outlook', *Washington Post*, 25 August 1998, p. A4.
124. 'White House to Court Democrats on Hill', *Washington Post*, 23 August 1998, p. A1.
125. See Ronald Brownstein, 'Along for the ride', *U.S. News and World Report*, 10 August 1998, p. 27.
126. 'Lott: Clinton Has Lost "Moral Dimension" of the Presidency', *Washington Post*, 1 September 1998, p. A4.
127. 'Sen. Lieberman's Castigation of Clinton Could Be a Turning Point', *Congressional Quarterly Weekly*, 5 September 1998, p. 2327; 'Clinton Critic's Words Hold Weight', *Washington Post*, 4 September 1998, p. A10.
128. 'President Tries to Boost Support on Hill', *Washington Post*, 9 September 1998, p. A1.
129. Cited in 'Clinton Team Says Hill May See Backlash', *Washington Post*, 21 September 1998, p. A1.
130. '12 September 1998. Party Battle Lines Begin to Emerge', *NYTimes.com* [http://www.nytimes.com/library/politics/091298clinton-pols.html]
131. 'Clinton Allies Seek Compromise on Hill', *Washington Post*, 23 September 1998, p. A1.
132. Ibid.
133. 'Defenders Optimistic as Battle Moves to Political Realm', *Washington Post*, 25 September 1998, p. A18.

Chapter 4   The Starr Investigation

1. John Anderson, 'The Clock is Running Out on the Independent Counsel Law', *The American Lawyer*, April 1998.
2. Benjamin Ginsberg and Martin Shefter, *Politics by Other Means: Politicians, Prosecutors, and the Press from Watergate to Whitewater* (New York: W.W. Norton & Company, 1999) p. 30.
3. Harold Hongju Koh, *The National Security Constitution: Sharing Power After the Iran-Contra Affair* (London: Yale University Press, 1990) pp. 22–37.
4. Robert N. Roberts and Marion T. Doss Jr., *From Watergate to Whitewater: The Public Integrity War* (Westport, Connecticut: Praeger, 1997) p. 93.
5. Stuart Taylor Jr., 'The Clock is Running Out on Kenneth Starr', *National Journal*, 7 March 1998, pp. 498–9.
6. Cited in Lawrence E. Walsh, 'Kenneth Starr and the Independent Counsel Act', *The New York Review of Books*, 5 March 1999, p. 4.

7. 'Starr's Inquiry Prompts Questions on Independent Counsel Law', *Congressional Quarterly Weekly*, 31 January 1998, p. 219.

8. Kermit L. Hall *et al.* (ed.), *The Oxford Companion to the Supreme Court of the United States* (New York: Oxford University Press, 1992) p. 563.

9. *Congressional Quarterly Weekly*, 31 January 1998, p. 221; for discussion on the Supreme Court viewpoint on the Independent Counsel law, see 'Morrison v. Olsen', in Posner, *An Affair of State* (1999) pp. 220–5.

10. *Starr Report*, p. 27.

11. See Posner, *An Affair of State* (1999) pp. 76–7.

12. Andrew Morton, *Monica's Story* (London: Michael O'Mara Books, 1999) pp. 171–2; 'Some in the Law Uneasy with Starr's Tactics', *Washington Post*, 13 February 1998, p. A1.

13. Ibid., p. 28; also quoted in 'Is the Prosecutor Running a Starr Chamber?', *Time*, 2 February 1998, p. 46.

14. Cited in 'Starr struck', *U.S. News and World Report*, 2 February 1998, p. 28; Toobin, *A Vast Conspiracy* (1999) p. 204.

15. Daniel Klaidman, 'Starr on the Stand', *Newsweek*, 23 November 1998.

16. William Schneider, 'Clinton's Improbable Life Raft', *National Journal*, 7 March 1998, p. 546.

17. Stuart Taylor Jr., 'Leaks Sometimes Spring from Unlikely Sources', *National Journal*, 23 May 1998, pp. 1162–3.

18. 'Clinton Advisers Agree to Attack Starr', *Washington Post*, 7 February 1998, p. A1.

19. Ibid.

20. '6 February 1998. Pointing to Leaked Articles, White House Strikes Back', *NYTimes.com* [http://www.nytimes.com/library/politics/020698clinton-leaks.html]

21. Ibid.

22. 'Clinton Vows to "Never" Step Down', *Washington Post*, 7 February 1998, p. 1.

23. Ibid.

24. See also, 'Who's obstructing whom? As Starr pursues Clinton, the President pursues Starr – and a public-relations war continues', *U.S. News and World Report*, 16 February 1998, p. 25.

25. '2 March 1998. Analysis: White House Continues to Attack Starr', *NYTimes.com* [http://www.nytimes.com/library/politics/030298clinton-starr.html]

26. '5 March 1998. Clinton Deposition in Jones Case Leaked', *Reuters press release* [http://www.yahoo.com/headlines/980305/news/stories/lewisky_11.html]

27. 'Clinton Denounces Leak of Deposition as "Illegal" ', *Washington Post*, 6 March 1998, p. A18.

28. Chief Justice Burger wrote, in a unanimous opinion for the Court, that the President's 'generalized interest in confidentiality' is outweighed by 'the demonstrated, specific need for evidence' in a criminal proceeding. See 'Legal Guide: Untangling the Issues', *Washington Post*, 23 February 1998.

29. 'For Bill Clinton, a man for all scandals: Bruce Lindsey and executive privilege claims', *U.S. News and World Report*, 6 April 1998, p. 24; see also,

'3 March 1998. Clinton Invokes Executive Privilege in Lewinsky Probe', *CNN – Allpolitics* [http://allpolitics.com/1998/03/21/clinton.lewinsky]

30. Ibid.
31. 'Starr Compares Battles of Clinton and Nixon', *Washington Post*, 2 May 1998, p. A8. The media also picked up on the comparisons: see 'Presidents and Privilege', *The Christian Science Monitor*, 26 March 1998; William Schneider, 'Starr's Case Comes Into Focus', *National Journal*, 9 May 1998, p. 1082.
32. 'Privilege Claim Covers Some Talks With First Lady', *Washington Post*, 24 March 1998, p. A6.
33. '24 March 1998. Exchange With Reporters Prior to Discussion With President Yoweri Kaguta Museveni of Uganda in Kampala', *Weekly Compilation of Presidential Documents*, 34, no.13, 30 March 1998, p. 490.
34. 'President Is Denied Executive Privilege', *Washington Post*, 6 May 1998, p. A1.
35. Starr's Evidence Swayed Judge', *Washington Post*, 28 May 1998, p. A1.
36. 'Clinton Says Nixon Analogy Is Inaccurate', *Washington Post*, 7 May 1998, p. A10.
37. '*Washington Post*, 28 May 1998, p. A1.
38. Starr wrote in his petition to the Supreme Court: 'This case is of high moment. It is strongly in the nation's interest that the case be resolved quickly so that the grand jury's investigation can move forward at the earliest practicable date'. Cited in 'Starr Asks for Expedited Ruling on Privilege', *Washington Post*, 29 May 1998, p. A1.
39. 'Clinton given Deadline On Response to Starr', *Washington Post*, 30 May 1998, p. A7.
40. Michael Kelly, 'Starr Whiffs, But New Scandals Loom', *National Journal*, 9 May 1998, pp. 1036–7.
41. Stuart Taylor Jr., 'The Secrets of the Secret Service', *National Journal*, 2 May 1998, pp. 977–8.
42. Cited in '23 August 1998. The Law: Losers in Clinton–Starr Bouts May Be Future U.S. Presidents', *NYTimes.com* [http://www.nytimes.com/library/politics/082398clinton-privilege.html]
43. *Starr Report*, p. 250.
44. Ibid.
45. Cited in 'Advisers Lean Against Clinton Testifying', *Washington Post*, 5 July 1998, p. A4.
46. Ibid.
47. 'Starr's Endgame: As the prosecutor presses Clinton to testify, the President's lawyers target a key Starr deputy', *U.S. News and World Report*, 3 August 1998, p. 16.
48. *Starr Report*, p. 250; Toobin, *A Vast Conspiracy* (1999) p. 300.
49. Toobin, *A Vast Conspiracy* (1999) p. 302.
50. Stuart Taylor Jr., 'Clinton's Dilemma: The Risk Of More "Lying About Sex" ', *National Journal*, 1 August 1998, p. 1794; also, 'Truth', *U.S. News and World Report*, 10 August 1998, p. 17.
51. *Starr Report*, p. 251.
52. '31 July 1998. Letter from OIC to David E. Kendall', *Starr Evidence*, p. 547.
53. '31 July 1998. Letter from David E. Kendall to OIC', ibid., p. 548.

54. '31 July 1998. Letter (second of the day) from OIC to David E. Kendall', ibid., p. 550.
55. '3 August 1998. Letter from David E. Kendall to OIC', ibid., pp. 552–3.
56. 'Starr Report Hits Capitol Hill, Drawing Outrage and Trepidation', *Congressional Quarterly Weekly*, 12 September 1998, p. 2387.
57. Ibid., p. 2388.
58. 'Richard E. Cohen and Kirk Victor, 'At Last, the Starr Report: The Independent Counsel Makes a Constitutional Confrontation Inevitable', *National Journal*, 12 September 1998, p. 2080; 'The Weighty Why and How of Punishing a President', *Congressional Quarterly Weekly*, 12 September 1998, p. 2378.
59. 'Vote Sets Capitol Process in Motion', *Washington Post*, 11 September 1998, p. A1.
60. Jeffrey Toobin, *A Vast Conspiracy* (1999) pp. 330–1; *Congressional Quarterly Weekly*, 12 September 1998, p. 2388.
61. See 'Preliminary Memorandum Concerning Referral of Office of Independent Counsel', *Starr Report*, pp. 357–451.
62. Ibid., p. 359.
63. Ibid., p. 362.
64. Ibid., pp. 364–5.
65. Ibid., p. 363.
66. Ibid., p. 364.
67. See 'Initial Response to Referral of Independent Counsel', *CNN.com* [http://www.cnn.com/SPECIALS/multimedia/timeline/9809/starr.report/cnn.content/clinton.rebuttal2/index2.html]
68. Carl M. Cannon, 'The Survival Strategy', *National Journal*, 14 September 1998, p. 8.
69. 'Initial Response to Referral of Independent Counsel', *CNN.com* [http://www.cnn.com/SPECIALS/multimedia/timeline/9809/starr.report/cnn.content/clinton.rebuttal2/index2.html]
70. Ibid.
71. Ibid.
72. Cited in 'Scandal Chronology', *Congressional Quarterly Weekly*, 26 September 1998, p. 2571.
73. *Congressional Quarterly Weekly*, 12 September 1998, p. 2378.
74. *National Journal*, 12 September 1998, p. 2080.
75. 'Starr Power: What the Probe Means for the Presidency', *Congressional Quarterly Weekly*, 15 August 1998, p. 2224.
76. '23 August 1998. The Law: Losers in Clinton–Starr Bouts May Be Future U.S. Presidents', *NYTimes.com* [http://www.nytimes.com/library/politics/082398clinton-privilege.html]
77. Charles L. Black Jr., *Impeachment: A Handbook* (London: Yale University Press, 1974) p. 1.

Chapter 5   Impeachment and Trial

1. Richard M. Nixon, *RN: The Memoirs of Richard Nixon* (London: Arrow Books, 1978) p. 1072.

2. See 'Impeachment: How It Would Work', *Congressional Quarterly Weekly*, 31 January 1998, p. 929; also, Posner, *An Affair of State* (1999) pp. 95–105; 'How a President is Impeached and Tried', in United Press International (ed.), *The Impeachment Report: A Guide to Congressional Proceedings in the Case of Richard M. Nixon* (New York: Signet, 1974) pp. 300–2.

3. Black Jr., *Impeachment: A Handbook* (1974) p. 5.

4. Ibid., pp. 10–11.

5. 'The Judiciary Panel: A Mix of Extremes', *Washington Post*, 27 September 1998, p. A1; see also, 'On the Fringes', *National Journal*, 10 October 1998, p. 2366.

6. Cited in 'House's Challenge: Define "Impeachable" ', *Washington Post*, 8 September 1998, p. A1.

7. 'The House Resolution: Text of H. Res. 581, adopted 258–176 by the House on Oct. 8', *Congressional Quarterly Weekly*, 10 October 1998, p. 2708.

8. 'Impeachment Inquiry Approved; 31 House Democrats Back GOP', *Washington Post*, 9 October 1998, p. A1.

9. Ibid., p. A1.

10. 'On the Floor, History in the Making, and Remaking', *Washington Post*, 9 October 1998, p. A1.

11. '8 October 1998. Remarks Prior to a Meeting With the Economic Team and an Exchange With Reporters', *Weekly Compilation of Presidential Documents*, 34, no.41, 12 October 1998, p. 2010.

12. Ibid., p. 2011.

13. Jack W. Germond and Jules Witcover, 'The Impeachment Implosions', *National Journal*, 7 November 1998, p. 2682.

14. William Schneider, 'It's the Economy Stupid', ibid., p. 2686.

15. Karen Foerstel, 'Elections Expected to Produce Modest Gains for Republicans', *Congressional Quarterly Weekly*, 24 October 1998, pp. 2866–7.

16. 'GOP Scales Back Hyde Hearings', *Washington Post*, 5 November 1998, p. A1.

17. Ibid.

18. '8 November 1998. At the White House, a Sudden Sense of Relief and Elation', *NYTimes.com* [http://www.nytimes.com/library.politics/110898 clinton-agenda.html]

19. '5 November 1998. Judiciary Committee's Requests for Admission', *Washingtonpost.com* [http://www.washingtonpost.com/wp-srv/politics/special/clinton/stories/questions110598.htm]

20. '6 November 1998. Judiciary Chairman Asks Clinton to Admit or Deny 81 Findings', *NYTimes.com* [http://www.nytimes.com/library/politics/110698 clinton-impeach.html]

21. '27 November 1998. White House Answers to Judiciary Committee Requests for Admission', *Washingtonpost.com* [http://www.washingtonpost.com/wp-srv/politics/special/clinton/stories/answertext112798.htm]

22. '30 November 1998. Henry Hyde Responds to President Clinton's 81 Answers', *United States House of Representatives: Committee on the Judiciary*, 30/11/98 Press Release [http://www.house.gov/judiciary/113098a.htm]

23. Kirk Victor and Alexis Simendinger, 'And Now, The Denouement', *National Journal*, 14 November 1998, p. 2717.

24. '10 November 1998. It's Impeachment or Nothing, Scholars Warn Lawmakers at Hearings', *NYTimes.com* [http://www.nytimes.com/library/politics/111098clinton-impeach.html]

25. Ibid.
26. '10 November 1998. Democrats Full of Glee at Hearing', *NYTimes.com* [http://www.nytimes.com/library.politics/111098clinton-scene.html]
27. Dan Carney, 'GOP Looks for Impeachment Course By the Lights of a Single Starr', *Congressional Quarterly Weekly*, 14 November 1998, p. 3069; 'Hyde Leads Impeachment Drive In Growing Isolation', *Congressional Quarterly Weekly*, 5 December 1998, pp. 3247–9.
28. '18 November 1998. Shifting Strategies Play Out on a Capitol Hill Stage', *NYTimes.com* [http://www.nytimes.com/library/politics/111898impeach-assess.html]
29. For detail on Starr's objectives, see Daniel Klaidman, 'Starr on the Stand', *Newsweek*, 23 November 1998
30. 'The Testimony of Kenneth Starr', *The Impeachment and Trial of President Clinton*, p. 5.
31. Carl M. Cannon and Kirk Victor, 'Starr's Last Chance', *National Journal*, 21 November 1998, p. 2763.
32. *The Impeachment and Trial of President Clinton*, p. 30.
33. Dan Carey, 'An Aggressive Defense', *Congressional Quarterly Weekly*, 12 December 1998, pp. 3287–9.
34. *The Impeachment and Trial of President Clinton*, p. 59.
35. 'GOP Pushes Toward a Vote on Articles of Impeachment', *Congressional Quarterly Weekly*, 28 November 1998, p. 3214.
36. *The Impeachment and Trial of President Clinton*, p. 147.
37. Ibid., p. 158.
38. For discussion on the censure alternative, see Dan Carey, 'GOP Pushes Toward a Vote on Articles of Impeachment', *Congressional Quarterly Weekly*, 28 November 1998, pp. 3213–14.
39. '9 December 1998. Proposed House Censure Resolution', *The Impeachment and Trial of President Clinton*, pp. 451–2; 'Democrats Offer Censure Resolution', *Congressional Quarterly Weekly*, 12 December 1998, p. 3294.
40. '10 December 1998. Impeachment Counts are Unveiled as Democrats Draft a Censure', *NYTimes.com* [http://www.nytimes.com/library/politics/121098impeach.html]
41. Alexis Simendinger, 'A Remarkable Week', *National Journal*, 19/26 December 1998, p. 2985.
42. '13 December 1998. The President's News Conference With Prime Minister Binyamin Netanyahu in Jerusalem, Israel', *Weekly Compilation of Presidential Documents*, 34, no. 51, 21 December 1998, p. 2476.
43. *National Journal*, 19/26 December 1998, p. 2986.
44. Evan Thomas and Debra Rosenberg, 'How Clinton Lost the Capital', *Newsweek*, 28 December/4 January 1998–9
45. 'End Games: Clinton is impeached, Iraq attack winds down – and Livingston abruptly resigns', *U.S. News and World Report*, 28 December 1998, p. 19.
46. Cited in 'We're all Hillary now', *U.S. News and World Report*, 28 December/4 January 1998–9, p. 30.
47. 'Impeachment Debate Set; Livingston Admits Marital Indiscretions', *Washington Post*, 18 December 1998, p. A1.
48. Ibid.

49. *U.S. News and World Report*, 28 December 1998, p. 21.
50. *Washington Post*, 18 December 1998, p. A1.
51. 'The House: Floor Debate and Impeachment', *The Impeachment and Trial of President Clinton*, p. 173.
52. Ibid., p. 178.
53. Ibid., p. 183.
54. Ibid., p. 203.
55. Ibid., p. 181.
56. Ibid., p. 206.
57. Ibid., p. 177.
58. Ibid., p. 170.
59. Ibid., p. 177.
60. Ibid., p. 184.
61. Ibid., p. 207.
62. '19 December 1998. Remarks Following the House of Representatives Vote on Impeachment', *Weekly Compilation of Presidential Documents*, 34, no.52, 28 December 1998, p. 2516.
63. Ibid.
64. Ibid.
65. Howard Fineman and Debra Rosenberg, 'Washington at War', *Newsweek*, 28 December/4 January 1998–9.
66. 'Conviction's unlikely – not impossible', *U.S. News and World Report*, 21 December 1998, p. 29.
67. Stuart Taylor Jr., 'Why The Senate Might Remove Him', *National Journal*, 19/26 December 1998, p. 2976.
68. 'Senate's Quandary: Does a Trial Have to Look Like "Perry Mason"?', *Washington Post*, 7 January 1999, p. A12.
69. Howard Fineman, 'A Time of Trial', *Newsweek*, 18 January 1999.
70. Mark Hosenball and Evan Thomas, 'Trial and Tribulation', *Newsweek*, 11 January 1999.
71. *Washington Post*, 7 January 1999, p. A12.
72. '5 January 1999. President's Lawyers Preparing New Attack on Articles of Impeachment', *NYTimes.com* [http://www.nytimes.com/library/politics/010599impeach-clinton.html]
73. 'Lewinsky on House List for Live Testimony', *Washington Post*, 7 January 1999, p. A1.
74. 'Clinton Team Studies Options', *Washington Post*, 28 January 1999, p. A17.
75. 'From White House, Strategic Silence', *Washington Post*, 15 January 1999, p. A1.
76. '13 January 1999. Remarks Prior to a Meeting With Labor Leaders and an Exchange With Reporters', *Weekly Compilation of Presidential Documents*, 35, no.2, 18 January 1999, p. 46.
77. 'Making Case Fresh Is a Huge Hurdle', *Washington Post*, 15 January 1999, p. A15.
78. '11 January 1999. White House Response to Trial Summons', *Washingtonpost.com* [http://www.washingtonpost.com/wp-srv/politics/special/clinton/stories/whtext011199.html]; '13 January 1999. White House Trial Memorandum' *Washingtonpost.com* [http://wwww.washingtonpost. com/wp-srv/politics/special/clinton/stories/shtext011399.html]

79. 'Clinton's Defense to Stress Conflicts', *Washington Post*, 18 January 1999, p. A1.
80. Ibid.
81. Evan Thomas and Mark Hosenball, 'The Endgame', *Newsweek*, 8 February 1999.
82. 'Senators Look for Ways to Halt Proceedings', *Washington Post*, 22 January 1999, p. A1.
83. On the issue of witnesses, see Posner, *An Affair of State* (1999) pp. 126–7.
84. 'Senate Votes to Subpoena Three Witnesses', *Washington Post*, 28 January 1999, p. A1.
85. '4–6 February 1999: The Depositions', *The Impeachment and Trial of President Clinton*, p. 369.
86. Closed sessions caused some disagreement within the Senate: see 'Debate To Decide Clinton's Fate Still Likely To Be Held in Secret', *Congressional Quarterly Weekly*, 16 January 1999, p, 142.
87. '9–12 February 1999: The Debate and the Vote', *The Impeachment and Trial of President Clinton*, p. 433; see also, 'GOP Defections Could Presage Majority Acquittal', *Washington Post*, 11 February 1999, p. A1.
88. 'Feinstein: A Last-Minute Push for Censure', *Washington Post*, 12 February 1999, p. A23.
89. 'Senate Blocks Censure, Ending Trial Without a "Unifying Statement" ', *Congressional Quarterly Weekly*, 13 February 1999, p. 367.
90. 'Clinton's Public Reaction: Humility, Regret', *Congressional Quarterly Weekly*, 13 February 1999, p. 365.
91. '12 February 1999. Remarks on the Conclusion of the Senate Impeachment Trial and an Exchange With Reporters', *Weekly Compilation of Presidential Documents*, 35, no.6, 15 February 1999, p. 225.
92. Ibid.
93. 'Schippers Calls Clinton Trial a "Sham" ', *Washington Post*, 12 February 1999, p. A22.
94. Carroll J. Doherty, 'Senate Acquits Clinton', *Congressional Quarterly Weekly*, 13 February 1999, p. 361.
95. Lars-Erik Nelson, 'The Republicans' War', *The New York Book Review*, 4 February 1999, p. 8.
96. 'Activist President Presses on in Hope of Tempering History's Judgment', *Congressional Quarterly Weekly*, 30 January 1999, p. 238.

Chapter 6   The Media: Intrigue and Revulsion

1. See Suzanne Garment, *Scandal: The Culture of Mistrust in American Politics* (New York: Times Books, 1991) pp. 57–8.
2. 'Will There Be a Backlash?: The media play it carefully but love the chase', *Newsweek*, 15 December 1986, p. 40; 'Comment: So Why Not Play It Like Watergate?', *Columbia Journalism Review*, January/February 1987, p. 15.
3. Sabato and Lichter, *When Should the Watchdogs Bark?* (1995) pp. 27–8.
4. Ibid., pp. 29–37; William Powers, 'Yuck! What a Great Story!', *National Journal*, 22 August 1998, p. 1989.
5. Cited in 'Public Disgusted With a Frenzy Fed by Its Interest', *Washington Post*, 12 February 1998, p. A1.
6. Sam Smith, *Shadows of Hope: A Freethinker's Guide to Politics in the Time of Clinton* (Bloomington, Indiana: Indiana University Press, 1994) p. 178.
7. For discussion on tabloid presentation of the scandal, see William Powers, 'All This and Leonardo, Too', *National Journal*, 5 September 1998,

pp. 2042–3; Mortimer B. Zuckerman, 'Malevolent obsessions: Salacious reporters and a zealous, partisan prosecutor have run amok', *U.S. News and World Report*, 9 February 1998, p. 72.

8. Cited in Howard Kurtz, *Spin Cycle: Inside The Clinton Propaganda Machine* (New York: The Free Press, 1998), p. 295.

9. Isikoff, *Uncovering Clinton: A Reporter's Story* (1999) pp. 335–6; see also, 'Newsweek's Melted Scoop', *Washington Post*, 22 January 1998, p. C1.

10. Joan Konner, 'Of Clinton, the Constitution and the Press', *Columbia Journalism Review*, March/April 1999.

11. '23 January 1998. A Whiff of Sexual Scandal Has Everybody Talking', *NYTimes.com* [http://www.nytimes.com/library/politics/012398clinton-media.html]; for a discussion on the debate over the long-term coverage and the prominence of the Lewinsky matter, see William Powers, 'Monica Madness? Not Really', *National Journal*, 17 October 1998, pp. 2452–3.

12. See William Schneider, 'What? Washington Has Bounced Back', *National Journal*, 14 February 1998, p. 374.

13. 'Allegation Inundation', *Washington Post*, 27 January 1998, p. E1.

14. Ibid.

15. '27 January 1998. Media Struggling With Pressures to Report Unproven Allegations', *NYTimes.com* [http://www.nytimes.com/library/politics/012798clinton-media.html]

16. For a discussion on news source material and the Clinton crisis, see 'The Clinton Crisis and the Press: A New Standard of American Journalism', *Committee of Concerned Journalists* [http://www.journalism.org/Clinton report.html]

17. '19 February 1998. Report Shows Shifting Content in Journalism', *NYTimes.com* [http://www.nytimes.com/library/politics/021998clinton-coverage.html]

18. Cited in 'Clinton Denounces Leak as "Illegal" ', *Washington Post*, 6 March 1998, p. A18.

19. *Washington Post*, 12 February 1998, p. A1.

20. Ibid.

21. See 'Will Today Bring Vindication for Media?', *Washington Post*, 17 August 1998, p. B1.

22. '20 August 1998. A Vast Audience for an Admission', *NYTimes.com* [http://www.nytimes.com/library/politics/082098clinton-ratings.1.gif.html]; '19 August 1998. The Ratings: Good News for Networks', *NYTimes.com* [http://www.nytimes.com/library/politics/08199clinton-ratings.html]

23. Cited in 'After the Speech, Instant Media Spin', *Washington Post*, 18 August 1998, p. E1.

24. Tom Shales, 'Unfortunately Not the Last Word on the Subject', *Washington Post*, 18 August 1998, p. E1.

25. 'Reactions: Conciliation, Condemnation', *Congressional Quarterly Weekly*, 22 August 1998, p. 2282.

26. '19 August 1998. The Editorials: Excerpts From Newspaper Judgments on Clinton', *NYTimes.com* [http://www.nytimes.com/library/politics/081998 clinton-pundits.html]

27. 'What Newspapers Are Saying', *National Journal*, 14 September 1998, p. 5; also 'What Newspapers Are Saying', *National Journal*, 19 September 1998, sp. 2189.

28. 'Media Chorus of "Resign" Grows Louder', *Washington Post*, 26 August 1998, p. D1.
29. 'Public Declines to Share Media's Sense of Betrayal', *Washington Post*, 15 September 1998, p. A10; see also James A. Barnes, 'Defying Nixon-Like Gravity', *National Journal*, 23 January 1999, pp. 220–1.
30. 'Newspapers Weigh In', *Washington Post*, 13 September 1998, p. A31.
31. Ibid.
32. 'TV Viewers to Witness Milestone', *Washington Post*, 19 September 1998, p. A10.
33. 'Clinton and the Kenneth Inquisition', *Washington Post*, 22 September 1998, p. E1.
34. Stuart Taylor Jr., 'Decadence: The President and the Press', *National Journal*, 26 September 1998, pp. 2215–16.
35. 'Gingrich Blames the Media', *Washington Post*, 5 November 1998, p. E1.
36. Ibid.
37. 'After Monica, What Next?', *Columbia Journalism Review*, November/December 1998.
38. 'How Impeachment's Playing', *National Journal*, 19–26 December 1998, p. 3034.
39. Ibid., p. 3035.
40. 'Debate To Decide Clinton's Fate Still Likely To Be Held in Secret', *Congressional Quarterly Weekly*, 16 January 1999, p. 142.
41. '8 January 1999. Network Opposes a Provision to Hold Private Deliberations', *NYTimes.com* [http://www.nytimes.com/library/poltics/010899impeach-broadcast.html]
42. Ibid.
43. 'The Day the Impeachment Trial Went Dark', *Washington Post*, 27 January 1999, p. C1.
44. See 'Clinton Trial Not Made for TV', *Washington Post*, 15 January 1999, p. C1; '8 January 1999. Television Highlights Discordance Between History and Emotional Force', *NYTimes.com* [http://www.nytimes.com/library/poltics/010899impeach-tv.html]; '15 January 1999. No, Dozing Is Not Impeachable', *NYTimes.com* [http://www.nytimes.com/library/politics/011599impeach-media.html]
45. '13 February 1999. At Long Last, Trial Gains Sense of Gravity and Historical Import', *NYTimes.com* [http://www.nytimes.com/library/politics/021399impeach-media.html]
46. Cited in Michael J. Gerson, 'America's "Puritan" press: Journalists wonder why the public isn't outraged too', *U.S. News and World Report*, 5 October 1998.

Chapter 7   Public Opinion: Reluctant Observers

1. Carl M. Cannon, 'Downfall and Defiance', *National Journal*, 19/26 December 1998, p. 2979.
2. See '23 February 1998. The Pollsters' Greatest Enemy: Themselves', *Washingtonpost.com* [http://www.washingtonpost.com/wp-srv/politics/polls/wat/wat.htm]
3. Dick Morris, *Behind The Oval Office: Winning the Presidency in the Nineties* (New York: Random House, 1997) p. 11.

4. Burt Solomon, 'Democracy's Dilemma', *National Journal*, 19/26 December 1998, pp. 2996–8.
5. *The Impeachment and Trial of President Clinton*, p. 272.
6. Cited in Gladys Engel Lang and Kurt Lang, *The Battle for Public Opinion: The President, the Press, and the Polls During Watergate* (New York: Columbia University Press, 1983) p. 94.
7. Frank Newport and Alec Gallup, '27 January 1998. Presidential Crisis: Job Approval Is What Matters', *Gallup.com* [http://www.gallup.com/PresCrisis/980127pc.htm]
8. Ronald D. Elving, 'Opinion Polls' Lag Time May Benefit Clinton', *Congressional Quarterly Weekly*, 7 February 1998, p. 342; 'Table 5–3. Aggregate Public Approval, Truman to Clinton (per cent)', in Lyn Ragsdale, *Vital Statistics on the Presidency: Washington to Clinton* (Washington DC: CQ Press, 1996) p. 201.
9. *Starr Report*, p. 149.
10. Ibid.
11. A CNN/*USA Today*/Gallup Poll found that 54 per cent thought allegations that Clinton had an affair were true, while only 37 per cent thought them to be untrue. See '21 January 1998. Poll: Public Believes Alleged Affair Is True', *CNN.com* [http://allpolitics.com/1998/01/21/clinton.poll]
12. '23 August 1998. Post-ABC News August 1998 Poll Results', *Washingtonpost.com* [http://www.washingtonpost.com/wp-polls/vault/ stories/ data 082398.htm]
13. '25 January 1998. Poll: Clinton Should Not Leave Office: President's ratings rebound; Gore seen as qualified for presidency', *CNN.com* [http://allpolitics.com/1998/01/25/poll]
14. '26 January 1998. Post-ABC News Poll Highlights', *Washingtonpost.com* [http://www.washingtonpost.com/wp-srv/politics/special/clinton/stories/pollchart012698.htm]
15. '3 February 1998. Public Reaction to Scandal Reflects Changes in Nation's Mores', *NYTimes.com* [http://www.nytimes.com/library/politics/020398 clinton-publicmood.html]
16. 'Clinton's Poll Numbers Surprised Political Pros', *Washington Post*, 9 February 1998, p. A6.
17. Ibid.
18. William Schneider, 'Clinton's Improbable Life Raft', *National Journal*, 7 March 1998, p. 546.
19. Cited in 'Public Disgusted With a Frenzy Fed by Its Interest', *Washington Post*, 12 February 1998, p. A1.
20. William Schneider, 'Why Clinton Hasn't Been Singed', *National Journal*, 14 March 1998, p. 606.
21. See Stuart Taylor Jr., 'Tolerance of Lying Cheapens Our Politics', *National Journal*, 21 March 1998, p. 618.
22. '16 March 1998. Poll: Clinton Approval Rating Up Despite Allegations', *CNN.com* [http://allpolitics.com/1998/03/16/clinton.poll]; see also, Jack W. Germond and Jules Witcover, 'And Suddenly, Bill's Memory Cleared', *National Journal*, 21 March 1998, p. 654.
23. '13 August 1998. Poll: Public Wants Clinton to Testify: Public wishes they knew less about Clinton–Lewinsky story', *CNN.com* [http://allpolitics.com/1998/08/13/poll]

24. '16 August 1998. Americans Demand Truth: ABC Poll: Talk or Walk', *ABC News.com* [http://www.abcnews.com/sections/us/DailyNews/polnation_intro.html]
25. 'American Voters See Two Very Different Bill Clintons', *Washington Post*, 23 August 1998, p. A1.
26. 'Late August 1998: It's Still The Economy They Say', *PEW Research Center For The People & The Press* [http://www.people-press.org/lateaugrpt.htm]
27. Cited in '16 September 1998. The Public: Keep Clinton in Office, Most Say in Poll, but His Image is Eroding', *NYTimes.com* [http://www.nytimes.com/library/politics/091698clinton-poll.html]
28. Cited in Carl M. Cannon and Richard E. Cohen, 'No East Way Out', *National Journal*, 19 September 1998, p. 2157.
29. 'Friday–Saturday Poll: Reaction to the release of the *Starr Report*, September 11–12, 1998', *Gallup.com* [http://www.gallup.com/poll_archives/980912.htm]
30. See 'Voter Group Typifies Conflicts on Clinton', *Washington Post*, 2 September 1998, p. A4.
31. Jonathan Rauch, 'The People Are Right: Keep Him', *National Journal*, 26 September 1998, p. 2213.
32. 'For Voters, It's Back Toward the Middle', *Washington Post*, 5 November 1998, p. A33.
33. *The Impeachment and Trial of President Clinton*, p. 145.
34. *National Journal*, 19/26 December 1998, pp. 2996–8
35. '9 December 1998. Poll: Public says censure Clinton, don't impeach him', *CNN.com* [http://www.cnn.com/allpolitics/stories/1998/12/09/poll]
36. 'Public Gives Clinton Blame, Record Support', *Washington Post*, 15 February 1999, p. A1.
37. 'Poll Taken 9–13 December 1998. Public's Good Mood and Optimism Undeterred by Latest Developments: Support for Clinton Unchanged by Judiciary Vote', *The PEW Research Center For The People & The Press* [http://www.people-press.org/dec98rpt.html]
38. '23 January 1999. Poll: Public skeptical about Senate Republicans', *CNN.com* [http://www.cnn.com/Allpolitics/stories/1999/01/23/poll]
39. Jonathan Rauch, 'It's All Over But the Whining', *National Journal*, 7 November 1998, p. 2596.
40. '8–10 January 1999. The Gallup Poll', *Gallup.com* [http://www.gallup.com/poll_archives/990110.htm]
41. Ibid.
42. Ibid.; see also, 'Senate Trial: Little Viewership, Little Impact', *The PEW Research Center For The People & The Press* [http://www.people-press.org/jan99rpt.htm]
43. *Washington Post*, 15 February 1999, p. A1.
44. Ibid.
45. 'Lott: Clinton Has Lost "Moral Dimension" of the Presidency', *Washington Post*, 1 September 1998, p. A4.
46. 'Late August 1998: It's Still the Economy They Say', *The PEW Research Center For The People & The Press* [http://www.people-press.org/lateaumor.htm]

Conclusion

1. '31 March 1999. Interview With Dan Rather of CBS News', *Weekly Compilation of Presidential Documents*, 35, no.13, 5 April 1999, pp. 550–61.
2. Ibid., p. 556.
3. Ibid.
4. Ibid.
5. Ibid., p. 557.
6. Ibid.
7. Ibid., pp. 557–8
8. '19 January 2001. Text: Clinton's Statement on Lewinsky Investigation', *Washingtonpost.com* [http://www.washingtonpost.com/wp-srv/onpolitics/elections/clintonstatement011901.htm]
9. Ibid.
10. Ginsberg and Shefter, *Politics by Other Means* (1999) pp. 39–46.
11. Cited in 'Impeachment's Future: Just Another Political Weapon?', *Congressional Quarterly Weekly*, 13 February 1999, pp. 368–9.
12. 'Activist President Presses On in Hope of Tempering History's Judgment', *Congressional Quarterly Weekly*, 30 January 1999, p. 238.

Index

Connect